Bob Wildman was born in 1946 and educated in York, Edinburgh, Cambridge and London. He has taught in schools, colleges, for the Open University and for the closed university of the prison. He lives with his wife in London and studies everything and anything.

LIVING ON GOLD TIME

Vol 3

Autumn: Evil Be To Him Who Evil Thinks
(Honi Soit Qui Mal Y Pense)

BOB WILDMAN

ComePress

Published in Great Britain by Come Press 2011
This edition first published by Come Press, 27 Old Gloucester
Street London WC1N 3AX
www.comepress.com

ISBN 978-0-9555110-2-8

Printed and bound in Great Britain by Lightning Source UK Ltd.
Cover design by William Russell

To all those generations of men and women of courage, genius and enterprise, who, having reached what they thought was the high ground, discover that it is private property, and therefore held by others in perpetuity.

Author's Note

Much of what you are about to read is not on the record, and, everything you are about to read has an obvious ring of truth about it. Of course, any resemblance of the actors, other than myself, to persons living or dead, is purely coincidental.

Contents

Part 1 **The Way**

The motto *Honi soit qui mal y pense* owes as much to legend and folklore, as to historical fact. Its literal translation from the Old French is *Shame be to him who thinks evil of it.* It is sometimes re-interpreted as *Evil be to him who evil thinks.* The statement supposedly originated when King Edward III, at a grand ball, was dancing with Joan of Kent, Countess of Salisbury. The Countess's garter slipped down her ankle. In an act of chivalry Edward picked up the blue garter and placed it around his own leg, and admonished his courtiers by saying: 'Honi soit qui mal y pense.' The phrase later became the motto of the English chivalric Order of the Garter, apparently founded by the Black Prince around 1348. The Round Table of Arthurian legend suggests the foundation of the Order. Being Knights without reproach; bearers of the motto are assumed to be pure in thought and intent. According to another legend, the motto refers to Edward's claim to the French throne, and the Order of the Garter was created to help pursue this claim.

As with all legends, I am inclined to think this is more of a mythical narrative, than historical fact.

A connection exists between the Order of the Garter and the Middle English romantic poem, and chivalrous fairytale, dating back to the twelfth century, *Sir Gawain and the Green Knight*. The romance outlines the adventures of Sir Gawain, a Knight of King Arthur's Round Table. In *Sir Gawain*, a girdle, a sexual trophy with similar overtones to the garter, plays a prominent role. It highlights the importance of honour and chivalry in the face of danger. At the heart of the manuscript is the test of Gawain's adherence to the code of chivalry, and tests that prove his moral virtue. At the end of the manuscript *honi soit qui mal y pense* is written, but it appears to have been a later addition, probably by a copyist rather than the original author. Feminist interpretations of this manuscript point to women's ultimate power over men, whilst homosexual interpretations point to the incidents of male kissing as blurring the lines between homosociality and homosexuality.

Clearly, the associations with the Masonic Order of the Garter, gives the motto a respectable edge. But as popular folklore and imagery, it has had a chequered history, and has been given an entirely different meaning, none more so than in its widening association with overt sexual motives.

Harriette Wilson, a Regency courtesan and consort of the King and high society, published her memoirs in 1825, after support from the first Duke of Wellington, who said 'publish and be damned,' when informed of her plans. In 1830, her novel, incorporating the motto *Honi soit qui mal y pense* was published. But through her life Harriette Wilson had violated the courtesan's code of silence, and employed blackmail and libel against her clients; actions for which she was vilified.

The cross bars in the centre of the Order of the Garter have been re-read for their occult, or hidden, meaning. As a compound astronomical symbol of equinoctial and solsticial colures, they have solar, and therefore, phallic, significance, and are connected with the last mystery divulged to initiates in the ancient mysteries.

The motto has even been published as a song.

However, none of this has stopped the motto appearing on the shield which is displayed in all Courts in England and Wales.

**Truth becomes fiction, when the fiction's true
Real becomes not-real when the unreal's real.**

Cao Xueqin

Cast of Actors in Order of Appearance

Jack Goodman	Prisoner
Young Benny	Prisoner
Ian Bradley	Prisoner
Paul Nerrity	Prisoner
Mr. Dodge	Civilian Instructor
Mr. Hodges	Civilian Instructor
Mr Badger	Civilian Instructor
Ralph Brown	Deputy Wing Governor
Wing Governor	Wing Governor
Chief Officer	Chief Officer
Clive	Prison Chaplain
Wendy	Senior Probation Officer
Patrick Molloy	Prisoner
Kenny Bruce	Prisoner
Ron Gifford	Prisoner
Pat	Bar Hostess
Michelle	Prostitute
Sebastian	Punter/Photographer
Anon	Female Punter
Mr Jones	Security Officer
Graham	MI5 Service staff officer
Charles	MI5 Service staff officer
Bob Wildman	Narrator

1

'Where the fuck have those matchsticks gone?' Jack said, looking around, distressed, and addressing no one in particular.

Young Benny, a kindly young man, with peace in the pools of his eyes, ambled into my prison cell with an oil painting under his arm.

'Benny, where are the matchsticks?'

'In the Swan Vestas box, next to the book. Look.' Benny pointed to a corner of my desk with its piles of bric-a-brac. In fact, my little Education Office cell was by now a sanctuary. Unlike the other cells it had declared UDI. The floor was unswept, the walls were covered in paintings, and piles of books lazily heaped themselves in every available space. Yards of ancient religious tomes, rescued from a skip somewhere, propped up a rickety shelf.

Jack triumphantly picked up a copy of the *I Ching* which I had only recently brought into the prison. He cleared a large space on the desk and tipped out the matchsticks.

'What are you doing? Benny asked.

At that point Ian, the rapist and wife killer, sloped in and quietly propped one arm up on the wooden cell door

'It's divination. I'll find out what fate has in store. I'll find out if birth and destiny are closely linked,' Jack said.

'Silence,' I said sarcastically, 'for Jack's first lesson.'

He ignored me and pressed on: 'We start with eight trigrams from the Chinese Book of Changes.' Jack spoke with the authority of a man in the know. He split some matchsticks into half, and some he left whole. He built one trigram. It had three tiers made up of some full and some broken lines of matchsticks. 'That's the first trigram.' Meticulously, and in a line across the desk, he constructed the possible combinations of three-tier trigrams to make eight in all.

'These are the eight trigrams that can form sixty four further combinations of upper and lower-tier trigrams which are called hexagrams.'

Ian the wife killer had had enough. He yawned, rolled his eyes behind Jack's back, and sloped out.

Jack had lost me too. It all reminded me of Joss Sticks, the loony language of the hippy movement, and kaftans.

Nevertheless, the sagely advice went on: 'If we adopt the words of the hexagrams as a guide, this is like receiving divine help for us to be successful, and a guide for us in our actions. It gives us the ability to influence the outcome of events.'

Just then the tannoy rasped: '36486 Goodman. A visit.'

'Fuck. I've gotta go. I haven't had a visit for ages.'

Jack gathered together his matchsticks and his book, put then on the corner of the desk near the wall, and rushed off.

*   *   *

Jack approached me unseen one morning, and announced loudly: 'Cop an eyeful of this.'

I moved back startled.

His arm came up momentarily in a phantom embrace around my shoulder. I paled perceptibly. 'Grief. When did you do that?' I said, taking the oil painting from him and looking at it carefully.

'Last night, in my cell, with the oil paints you nicked from the stock cupboard.'

I reddened slightly with embarrassment. Jack smiled gently through the mass of black hair which enveloped his upper lip: a real Nietzschian moustache. He had a theatrical mouth which wilted only slightly at the corners. Today he had his hair on the back of his head in a small plait, making him look like a pint-sized, Chinese coolie. In many ways he looked every bit a throwback to the Sixties. Neither time, punishment, nor fashion could break him from old habits. Neither had it poisoned his confidence in himself. He liked to live in and off the past.

I felt slightly uneasy. I remembered my own baptism into the excesses of that permissive decade. I gazed for a moment into his eyes, and through to those haunted pleasures that I had once known.

Jack's painting stood propped against the wall, resting on the table. The oil was still wet and a line of ultramarine appeared along the brickwork. I rubbed some of it between my forefinger and thumb, before putting my finger to my nose. It had a pungent, linseed odour; just a hint of new life.

'Oil enables me to mix the colours. Gives it action and power,' Jack explained. 'I've never worked with oil like this before. It's a new medium. I'm just beginning to get used to it. I don't use brushes, just a palette-knife.'

Miraculously, Jack could switch with apparent ease from his London working-class expressions to the language and vocabulary of the better educated. He was unwilling to be 'placed.' Often, he spoke in an intense confessional way without knowing it, and dropped in the odd jewelled phrase here and there. It was a response everyone recognized in prison as civilized amiability.

He stood back looking at the painting and moved his head to one side. 'Can you see what it is?' he scoffed, half expecting the wrong answer.

'It's a young couple making love in a field of corn with three trees reflected in a lake.' I replied, matter-of-factly, knowing for once I was not going to be sidelined with respect to a prisoner's art.

'You've got it.' Jack's voice rose a pitch as if his cover had been broken. 'Obviously, I've educated you to read my work now,' came his put-down.

I had observed the way his paintings developed before, the hide-and-seek images maturing into life forms.

LIVING ON GOLD TIME

'The subjects are already there,' he had said. 'I just bring them out.'

Like a sculptor whose subject is already in the stone. I found this intriguing and somewhat mysterious.
However, this time I was slightly flattered to know I could be right on some arty things at least. So much of what I was doing in that prison occasioned more questions than answers.

A knock came at the wooden door of my prison cell which acted as my improvised education office. It didn't blow wide open as it usually did, but opened just three centimetres and a pink piece of paper slid though the gap.

'Application to see the education officer,' a meek voice from behind the door wailed, with none of the usual bumptiousness I was accustomed to.

Jack retreated smartly and a small, insignificant figure, with a short over-neat haircut and regulation blue denim slid by, and sat at the chair next to the desk.

I opened the door fully to the cathedral of sound outside. I placed a ragged bible at the bottom of the door to prevent it closing and had a brief look outside.

A chatter of keys sounded in the distance. The workshops were disgorging their human cargo and small knots of men trooped along a cavernous prison Wing. The eyes had come. They were streaming in, watching. Very soon a few men stood at the door of their cells, alone, upright, with hands behind backs, protecting or guarding something important within; a private meeting perhaps.

A wooden handcart with a human horse at the front pulled up by the education office door. The soft pneumatic tyres shuddered slightly on the highly polished floor as the brake was applied. Some trays of vegetarian food heaved themselves to one side and collapsed. Special diet they called it. A tea urn splashed its contents from within. A bellow of command came from a screw. An inmate's name

4

was repeated from the rasping tannoy imploring him to report to the Movements' Desk.

After returning to my seat I stared out through the opening of the doorway to the greater light outside. The small man in the chair by the desk fidgeted.

He said: 'I've just come in.'

He broke my sad gaze into the light outside.

'I want to go on education,' he murmured.

'You'll have to submit to an education test first. Not now. This afternoon. I'll call you then.' I was curt, off-putting. 'I've got to go now. Sorry.'

The man in his ill-fitting denims and bland features rose from his seat and obediently shuffled off through the opening.

'Fuck you for a start.' He said, barely audible below his breath, then he scuttled out of the little office with its lingering residue of tobacco smoke, for the desert of male sweat and cabbage water outside.

A small fart hung in the air.

After I had gathered together my folder, my hand moved across to my belt, to the pouch and the keys on their obscenely long chain, ready for my next appointment.

Jack re-appeared, humming. He stood at the door rocking on his heels. For a few seconds the low noise of the Wing went on. Jack's hand seemed to gesture to something behind him. I flashed a brilliant smile, shrugged my shoulders but made no comment.

Jack advanced and took my arm in a comradely fashion.

'Look at this.' His eyes swivelled my way. 'What do you think?'

In front of me was another painting, more elaborate, softer, seemingly more meaningful than the one I had seen earlier. I looked at him assessingly. 'It's okay.'

'Okay?' With the beginnings of exasperation, Jack gasped. He sounded almost affronted. 'Why! it's a masterpiece.

Damning me with faint praise eh!? It's as good as Balthus eh!?'

I daren't ask him who the hell Balthus was for fear of appearing too unknowing. Such confidence was unnerving and inwardly I withered. I preferred to reserve judgement until I felt less threatened by another man's ego. But I knew there was some indescribable genius at work here, to create such visual power and variety.

No one was allowed the fulsomeness of praise in an embattled environment which stifled natural human warmth. Proper appreciation of another could take years, like a sentence in itself.

Jack was nothing if not productive. That is why I had gone out of my way to get him extra oil paint beyond the usual quota allowed to inmates.

'It's yours then.' Jack added smartly: 'Worth 20K after my exhibition at the Tate.'

He obviously believed his star was in the ascendant. As an act of self-belief it was a handsome pose for a prisoner. I could see that it had been signed in the corner with an artist's flourish. I laughed to myself then grinned at Jack. 'You reckon you'll get an exhibition one day?'

'No doubt about it. But the art establishment is corrupt like everything else.'

I was rather taken aback by this point, for I hung on to that British post-war notion that talent, rather than preferment, could overcome all obstacles.

'How come?'

'Well, how can a pile of bricks win the Turner prize? It's an insult to Turner.'

I gave the man a brief but searching inspection.

'Turner is concerned with painting, with ideas and technique being inseparable, not with political statements. Real painting is a mysterious struggle with chance. An interlocking of image and paint; the image is the paint and vice versa. It means going from the accidental to find the subject, by bringing out the spirit or life force.' Jack paused and said laconically: 'Geddit?'

'Where on earth did you get these ideas on art?'

He stood straighter. 'I may be a prisoner, but I've been in the company of some well known artists in my time.'

'Perhaps you're right.'

*   *   *

Early next day a knock at the door was followed indecently by a rush of air as it swung open. Outside, a landing cleaner, a black inmate with a deferential stoop, slapped his mop noisily on the plastic flooring.

A figure stood framed indignantly in the doorway. Paul Nerrity's voice exploded in the air with a crack.

'I want to come off the fuckin biology class and come on to your current affairs.'

My question was small and flat: 'But why?' I was questioning because Nerrity was a pathological liar and a class nuisance. His antics were those of an overgrown Borstal Boy, sulphurous and unstaunchable.

'The screw who's teaching the class is giving me a hard time. He's well out of order. I fink …' He floundered, then regained composure. 'Get me on yours tonight if you can,' he demanded, firmer than ever.

I watched his face, unblinking. My whole consciousness attuned itself to the new state of affairs. 'It's full. It's not possible to …' My moment of indecision. I broke off. I knew, that he knew, that it was untrue, as inmates are worldly wise as to the comings and goings in classrooms.

An unbearable silence followed and I fixed my gaze at a class register on the chair. I swallowed hard, then said, slowly reflecting: 'Perhaps I can squeeze you in if you don't come for just one session then disappear like last time.' His glance upwards met mine. 'Promise?'

He nodded. Paul Nerrity was subdued. 'See you later then.' He laughed aloud in one of his mercurial changes of mood. I made a face. He disappeared before the healed wound opened again.

It was Thursday, the day set apart from general teaching duties for participation in prison meetings. The Education Department was responsible for maintaining a presence and pestering everyone about encroachments on their hard-earned territorial gains; for everyone hated educationalists as much as they despised psychologists. Then there were obligations to fulfil towards prison Wing Management. The views of the Probation Department and the Psychological Services were begrudgingly sought after, to process and induct new trainees. Trainees were those about to undertake a life sentence. Prison officers were forced to defer to civilians whom they felt were unworthy of doing a job which, they believed, they could do better themselves.

The formality of the induction meeting was a convicted prisoner's first port of call, before embarking upon what the Prison Department euphemistically called his "long term training." No one was in any doubt that training was far from the minds of the originators.

'Training for what?' Men asked, '…incarceration?'

But who needed training? Since many new prisoners had previous convictions, it was little more than a farce for them. More like bending their will, since there were few options for rehabilitation. Nevertheless, everyone went through the motions and put a brave face on it at least.

Ironically, the Education Department was particularly vulnerable because it became a repository for everyone's expectations. Years and years of idleness could at least be justified, if they were spent reading books or learning to read and write. Undertaking self-reform, the authorities liked to call it. Seeing that no one had the slightest idea whatsoever how rehabilitation and reform were to be brought about, the unwilling prisoner was expected to participate in what little in the way of personal enrichment was on offer.

My heart was filled with foreboding. The Wing Labour Board and Induction Board were to be crammed into one morning. The niceties of a prison security meeting that afternoon had precluded any possibility of a separate afternoon session.

Three cells had been knocked through and painted white to accommodate the Boardroom. High up in one wall were the barred windows which failed to eclipse its identity as a former group of cells. A comfortable chair was perched midway down the long side of a rectangular table. Above the chair, on the wall, hung a photograph of the Queen. Opposite this dignified chair cowered a lone seat. It too was overlooked, by an imposing matchstick model of a galleon, tirelessly, but lovingly, fashioned by a former old boy, with all the time bestowed upon him by some indeterminate sentence or other.

Mr Dodge, Mr Hodges and Mr Badger, managers of the prison workshops were already sitting in their places as I came through the door.

'Well, we're here,' Mr Dodge lamented. 'Such lateness wouldn't have been tolerated in Slater's day. Dodge, brushed the smooth mineral blue of his chin and looked up at the ceiling. Slater was a deceased governor who had been notorious for punctuality: before my time of course. Folklore had it that what he lacked in creativity and imagination he made up for in speed and attendance to formality: a man who took sides, burnished grudges and got his retaliation in first for causes he wanted championed. 'The quicker it's done the better,' had been Slater's motto. I had been regaled on numerous occasions with this, from the mouth of the trusted servant Dodge. Mr Dodge would have felt more at home in the reign of Good Queen Bess. He was a man without rebellion, never questioning an order, (if it was an order, that is), and never questioning the order of things. Of late he was prone to defend his corner, for some mysterious reason.

'Many labour changes today?' I asked meekly, conscious of Dodge's general indifference to the Education Department in such weighty matters.

'Two. Bradshaw and McLintock. And they're not coming to the machine shop, I can tell you that for nothing.' His bald patch gleamed in the subdued sunlight.

Mr Dodge was proud of running the flagship of the prison workshops. His shop carried more prisoners than any other and therefore took precedence in allocations. Getting the men to work was a Wing priority. Only the sick, unemployed, unemployables or politically motivated like the IRA refused. Whether they shirked, or played cards at work, indifferent to the meagre wages, was no concern of Wing Management. Allocation to plum jobs on the hotplate, where scarce food was to be had, or in the laundry where wages were higher and overtime plentiful, remained the prerogative of senior officers. Strange Masonic rituals of selection, necessarily, (or should it be unnecessarily?), shrouded in mystery, kept this work for the chosen few. The general consensus was that you had to be in with the right people, or the right inmates.

Deputy Wing Governor Brown breezed through the door with the Principal Officer and Senior Officer in tow. He plonked himself into the dignified seat. I shuffled my papers in sham subservience.

'Right. How many job changes today?'

'Two,' said a voice.

'Ralph Brown placed the yellow forms on the desk in front of him, one above the other.

'Ahhh! ... my friend Bradshaw. Birdman Bradshaw, the man who can hold a canary in his mouth for twenty seconds.

'Poor canary,' said a voice.

Brown tried falteringly to read Bradshaw's semi-literate scrawl – I wanna go, if pos, go machine shop. My nerves tailor's shop bad.'

Brown raised his eyebrows looking to me for approval. 'Be better off on education, if you ask me.'

Heads turned towards me. We've had him. Spent two years on the remedial education class then left for no reason at all. He'd be better off at work,' I said.

'You have a moral obligation to teach illiterates have you not – prison rule 29? Piped up some impatient, clever dick.

'Errh!' I hesitated, plumbing the depths, searching for an excuse.

'Brown saved the day for me and said with an airy tone: 'Keep him at work I say.' Brown had a knack of getting to the nub of any situation. 'Well, Mr Dodge, it's the machine shop for Bradshaw.'

Dodge shook his head. 'He's not coming to me.'

'But you've got two vacancies.'

'He's too disruptive,' Dodge told him briskly. I've had him there before.' He was adamant.

I know why he wants to leave the tailors,' the Principal Officer spoke out of inside knowledge. 'He and his boyfriend have fallen out of love. He's been threatening all kinds of things.' I never knew whether to believe any of these stories; whether fiction was reality, or whether it was all theatre, contrived and rehearsed beforehand.

Governor Brown looked contrite.

The Senior Officer cut in sharply: 'Put him down as unemployed. We'll hold him there for a while. Let him cool off. He'll apply again soon for a labour change no doubt.'

Brown concurred.

Dodge was visibly moved by the concession. 'Thank you,' he clipped, his beetroot-red face beaming with satisfaction.

'Now for the other man, McLintock. He says he's been underemployed on the garden party too long and he knows that there is a vacancy as a wing cleaner.' Brown eyed the Principal Officer quizzically. 'Over to you, Sir.'

'McLintock won't fit in. The man's a shit. The others won't have him,' the Principle Officer said with a sharpness he immediately regretted. He sounded unconvincing. He hesitated, grasping for a better excuse. 'Besides, he's been in debt before and had to go down the Block at his own request.'

'All agreed. We'll leave him where he is then?'

I nodded, unable to disentangle a right motive from a wrong one, amid the speculation and paranoia which were ever commonplace. Just then more suits and uniforms came through the door. The Governor got up and left.

The Board Room was crowded now. Although not required to do so, uniformed staff sat at one end of the table and civilian staff at the other. The Wing Governor was flanked by the Wing Chief Officer and the Chaplain. Two officers who dealt with reception cases entered. The Psychology Department and the Probation service had one representative each.

Mumbling ebbed to a silence. With grave solemnity the Governor undid a red ribbon which tied securely a flat manila folder of documents; someone's inerasable record. He said with the crisp assurance of a natural commander: 'One reception this morning.' He leafed through the first two pages of the huge tome; a biography of a man's inhumanity to fellow man; an unpublished epitaph to the life of a nobody. 'The name is Molloy, X324683 Molloy. Date of birth – twenty sixth of the eleventh nineteen fifty six. Height five feet ten inches. Distinguishing marks – none. No fixed abode, although he gives the address of his sister in Gravesend. Previous convictions – four – going equipped, burglary, theft, grievous bodily harm. Dover borstal, Pentonville Prison.' The Governor paused then said: 'Has been on report three times at Pentonville for possession of an offensive weapon, possession of a quantity of alcohol brewed in his cell, and assaulting a prison officer.

The Governor looked around him over the top of his bifocals at this memorable cast of the disappointed and oppressed.

'Anymore?'

Someone added: 'Religion?'

Turning to the Chaplain he said: 'One of yours Clive, C of E. God help you.'

Wendy held her pen above the Probation Office note-book and said primly: 'Any reports from his probation officer?'

The Governor turned some pages: 'He's had correspondence with a Mr Flaherty from the Southwark Office.'

Appeased, Wendy scribbled down a few sentences while I stared knowingly at her.

Wendy was unlike the many social workers I had met in the nineteen seventies. She wore twin-sets and pearls. Educated in the nineteen sixties the ones I met were dressed in recidivist chic and had roughed-up accents. They wanted their clients to like them. They believed they should not label clients, so they treated them as if they were cats and dogs, not responsible for their actions.

'Education?' I said briskly, before I lost out to the next part of the proceedings.

'He left school at fifteen with no qualifications, although he purports to have gone on a bricklaying course at Dover Borstal.'

Anymore?'

A few heads shook. The audience lapsed again into contented silence.

'Some cuttings here from the national press.' The Governor picked one of them up and it unfolded itself as it was released from the dungeon of the file. Eager heads craned forward. 'Local Man Butchered in Frenzied Knife

Attack.' it proclaimed. This succulent piece of headline drama was placed to one side.

The Governor rested his arms on the table and began: 'Patrick Molloy was sentenced at the Central Criminal Court for murder, with a judge's recommendation that he serve a minimum of twenty years. The facts of the case are that on the night of the sixth of November last, Patrick Molloy, after an evening of excessive drinking, entered by force the premises of the victim, aged forty two years, who lived the life of a recluse, with intent to burgle the premises. The victim was woken from his bed and upon discovery that an intruder was in the house, picked up an ornamental lamp stand with which to defend himself. The victim came face to face with the intruder in the dining room of the house. Molloy, alarmed by the man rushing at him, pulled a butcher's knife from his jacket and pierced the victim in the chest. The Coroner's report says that the victim died instantly from a stab wound to the heart. Molloy confesses that he was shocked by what he had done and for some unknown reason hacked away at the dead man's neck, with intent to decapitate the victim. The room was, quote, 'awash with blood,' the police reported. Molloy admits to taking amphetamines as well as excessive quantities of drink on the night of the murder. He pleaded not guilty, at his trial.'

Although the meeting was accustomed to weekly tales of gore and inhumanity, the sickening description of the crime heaped more depression on the assembled throng.

Wendy protested: 'When will we have some bank robbers for a change?'

There was no reply.

The processing of inmates like Molloy was part of the Governor's responsibility. He was empowered to see that inmates were sufficiently aware of the induction process and that they undertook the first part of their life sentence while abiding by the rules of good order and discipline. The initial four or so years of training were for assessments to be made of their character and conduct, with a view to their placement in another establishment. Essentially the task was one of man-management, and that is what everyone called it. Governorship and staff skills were deployed to spot trouble in a man before it happened. In the main, however, they were not in sympathy with their charges.

Of course, matters could be left at that, with little room for manoeuvre, and no ideas whatsoever from the Prison Department concerning rehabilitation. The Governor still felt a moral obligation to see that an inmate made the best use of his time available by attending workshops, being assessed by psychologists and probation staff, and if needs be, attending classes as a token gesture towards self-reform. While the Governor did not frame the rules, the question of a man's dangerousness hung heavy on his shoulders. When could a man be released without posing a danger to the public? He was never sure. Who would carry the can for an ill-timed decision? The civilian staff in the prison may not have been liked by anyone, but they were necessary. Perhaps they knew?

'Any remarks on this man, Chief?' the Governor sighed impatiently. The Chief had his hands placed across his huge stomach. He shook his head negatively. He thought for a moment, weighing possibilities before answering with: 'As long as he doesn't fall in with bad company he might be okay.' The Chief then smiled knowingly and continued: 'I can see though that we will have trouble with this man. He's got a history of indiscipline against prison staff.'

'Chaplain' The Governor turned to the man on his left, giving him a full blast from his blue eyes. 'Anything?'

The Chaplain gave his benign judgement. 'I've seen Molloy already. He's a shy young man. He's a devoted Catholic so I'll pass him over to Sister Mary.'

'Probation'

Wendy looked up from her doodles. 'Geoffrey, my colleague, will deal with him.'

'Education'

I paused and nodded judiciously. 'I'll test him to see whether he's the right material for an education class.'

"Okay, let's have him in.' The Governor's voice was flat, with less conviction than previously.

A screw at the door jumped up, catching his chain on the arm of the chair. He opened the door falteringly and bellowed down the wing: 'Molloy.'

The Board Room was hushed in expectation. I had seen many Molloys come through that door. Each time I had been misguidedly filled with some kind of expectation. There was an irrational fear, iced over with uncertainty, as to whether the man and his crime were real. I had seen a television play where all the news was invented by a group of journalists who sat in one room. The public had never been led to suspect its authenticity.

Had Molloy really hacked away at the man's neck? My mind rehearsed the incident. The blood and the anguish. What if it never happened? What if the case, the publicity, even my being here was just a figment of an imagination? I pictured what Molloy would look like, what the victim was like in his death agony; Molloy's murderous and distorted face. Would it be calm now? Would it have the lines of remorse on it or be cold and calculating?

Molloy entered the room and sat alone in the chair with arms stretched out on the table. On three sides of the table were the first of the many sea of faces he would be answerable to while in prison.

'Mr. Molloy, this is your Reception Board and around you are some of the people who will become familiar to you during your stay with us,' the Governor said starkly.

He droned on about rules and good behaviour, appeals and applications. I stared at the subdued face, the blond unruly hair, the apathetic frown. The skin of the face, in profile, was smooth, the nose flattened. The eyes looked hollowed and smudged in black. A hint of strain vibrated in his manner.

Each member of his audience recited in turn a much-rehearsed monologue to outline their function, and how useful they could be to him. Slowly, the face turned to me. The droning of the voices stopped. The silence was awkward. Suddenly, unexpectedly, I realised it was time for me to do my bit.

'My name is ...' And so it went on. I had done it so many times before. I could stand beside myself and listen now.

Molloy had no questions. He left.

However, a question nagged me. How was it that in time the reception officer's reports on new inmates, the newspaper cuttings and the details of the crime, seemed to be washed clean of all brutality? A man became a different person in prison, as if no crime had taken place. What was a crime, after all? Were those initial details indeed true? Supposing the victim had made previous threats on Molloy's life prior to the offence? I brushed the reservations aside.

Each entry in Molloy's file would carry forward the judgements of previous entries. A balanced record is one that coheres, that confirms itself in all its parts. It is considered objective, the truth of the matter in hand, further compounded by continual rewriting. The writers have similar viewpoints, having read previous reports. They have shared perspectives. The record would be a lengthening shadow, the record of the way a guilty man does not win, written by potential pensioners of the prison system; hopers for promotion, not risk takers.

*   *   *

Jack Goodman's grinning countenance appeared artfully around the Education Office door.

'Beating your head against the wall again?' he said.

I smiled a tired half-smile in reply. How could he be so right I thought to myself, disheartened.

Goodman tried to buoy my sagging spirits. 'Cheer up. Don't you know meetings are fruitless ways of channelling energy?'

I bleated: 'These things have to be attended, if only for the inmate's sake.'

'They can find all they need to know for themselves. Most of them have been inside before anyway. They've had rules up to here.' Jack placed his hand in line with the bridge of his nose. 'The rules are favourable only to them, so they can always be on the side of right. Rules were only invented by the authorities to act as hurdles. The more hurdles, the more the punters are incapacitated. You don't need balls and chains. Just rules. I learned a lot about rules while doing National Service. Psychological warfare you see. Think of this: if you put a black man in that meeting all he sees is white faces. How do you think he feels then?'

I wasn't prepared to answer at that point in time, but was beginning visibly to cheer up at the news. 'P'raps you're right,' I said.

'I've got something to tell you, Jack said, edging towards me.

'What?'

He told me, deadpan: 'Someone tried to kill me last night.'
'I regarded him levelly with clear brown eyes.

'This is not one of your jokes again?' Judging by Jack's expression I thought it wasn't. 'How? With what?' I stopped for a moment.

'No. I'm deadly serious.'

'How then?'

'With pure heroin.'

'C'mon, there's no drugs on the Wing.'

'There is. The place is awash with them. The screws don't mind. It keeps everyone comatose.'

'Go on.' I said, impatient now.

'Well. This certain person knows that I like a smoke now and again, and I guess he figured I was a dope-head and on the hard stuff. Anyhow, after association he comes up to me with this bag of white powder and says: 'Do you want some of this? It's a present for you.'

'Then?'

'Well, I took it back to my cell and realised I had got a bag of the best.'

'And then?'

'If I'd have taken it I would have been spark out. Overdosed. Don't you see?'

'But why would he want to kill you, were you in debt or something?'

'No. Of course not. He wanted to kill me because of what I know.'

'What's that?

'I can't tell you. I'll tell you someday. Then you'll tell everyone for me.'

'What do you mean?' It was one of Jack's enigmas again. He often came out with partial answers.

'Just wait and see.' He looked guilty as much as flustered. 'This morning he comes to my cell and looks in. His face collapsed. It blew his mind that I was still there.'

I raised an eyebrow, sceptically. 'I find this hard to believe.'

'You'd better believe it, cos it's true. If they'd have found me dead this morning, they'd have put it down to an overdose. Suicide. Topped myself.'

I was silent now, considering. 'You're not telling me that all suicides in here are really murders?'

'We don't know. Do we? But you must remember things are not quite what you think.' Jack went on: 'When no civilians are around the place, particularly at night, all sorts of things happen.' He paused. 'There's blood all over the place.'

I looked sideways at him, eyes wide, and thought about the Wing cleaners with their mops cleaning it up.

'Take the other night for instance. A guy on the three's landing has his wrists slashed.'

'Not a murder?'

'No, a genuine attempted suicide, I think. Anyhow, he's in his cell above me. I hear the screws scampering around and a lot of muffled voices. The Wing door opens and closes. I stood up on the pipe, and could just see the pathway outside bathed in the light of the perimeter fence. They were wheeling him out to the hospital.' Jack drew closer still and squeezed my shoulder. 'He's just slashed his wrists. He's dying. There's blood all over the place and they're wheeling him out in a, you know what?'

'What?' I said, indignant at not knowing the answer.

'That fucking, filthy, old, wooden wheelbarrow which the gardens' party use.

'No,' I said in mock half-belief, thinking of night soil being carted off in medieval times, like in a Breugal print.

'And another thing. They've put me in cell thirteen. My lucky number.'

'So what?'

'It's above the gate and you can't get a decent night's sleep. What's more, the pipes are banging again.'

'Banging?'

'Yes. They bang every night. All night.'

'Water hammer I expect,' I said.

'Fuck it. It's not water hammer. It's a deliberate attempt at psychological torture. They're doing it so the inmates will crack up.'

I stared at Jack, aware of another imponderable entering my increasingly complex little world. I couldn't help laughing though at his answers, whether true or untrue, as they were nothing like I expected. Jack beamed too. He was a reservoir of news and exciting knowledge; a welcome change from the other characters on the Wing. He was someone who could shift the scenery of life. The Wing specialized in those fatally out of step; misfits, struggling with self-pity and deceit, and those caught in an undertow of violence and sexual menace. They made it a prison, with their claustrophobia and their saturated, airless style.

I remember when I first met Jack Goodman. That October morning was particularly well deserved. For two weeks the weather had been remarkably dull. The gloom was given a particular edge by forecasts of high interest rates, balance of payments deficits, and general economic collapse. The country seemed to be falling apart. A gift from God came in the form of a bright blue sky and the forecast of a warm afternoon. Even the footsteps of people going to work were crisper and starchier than usual.

Wadham Prison had changed not one iota, though, in the year I had been away. The immense yellow and brown walls of the Wing, like a perpetual headache, looked grimmer than ever, as if the silence made them longer. Impassive buildings possess a moral authority, far more intimidating than the tired psychiatrists who work within their walls. Prison inures, and minds atrophy. It's boring; it's meant to be. The passage of time and the great human and scientific achievements of the present age, meant little to the imprisoned imaginations of all who worked and were incarcerated here.

I passed through the prison gate and into the lobby with no regrets, however. I collected my keys and waited while a prison van shunted itself into the cavern of the gatehouse, ready to transport its human cargo to the courts. It loomed as large as a bus, but in place of windows upright, rectangular slits of opaque glass stretched its whole length. From another vantage point the observer could see the exit points on the roof. Located above each internal cell, they were like the caps on a nuclear silo where rockets could be released in the event of a nuclear war.

LIVING ON GOLD TIME

The van slipped easily away from the gate and I was allowed in to the compound of the forbidden place. Walking through the Wings was like weaving through an abyss. The shafted sunlight of that October day was paled by the overarching dominance of the windowed palace. Beneath each window of the hive grew a mossy stain from the liquid refuse tipped from the cells.

I heaved a Wing door shut behind me. My hand deftly manoeuvred itself through a gap in the reinforced glass of the Movements Desk, as if were doing an indecent thing. 'A lockdown's about to take place - you'd better be quick,' said a voice. I escaped quickly with my Yale key. My office was uneasily stabled on the ground floor. This was called the ones landing. On either side were the honeycomb of inmate cells, and opposite was the hotplate where meals were served. The stout, metal door of my one-time cell had been replaced by a wooden one.

As I strode towards my office and put the key in the lock a voice came from somewhere near my shoulder: 'I'm Jack Goodman. I'm one of the UK's most prolific pornographers.' I laughed to myself. I thought I'd heard it all before, but not this one. I turned round to see a chiselled face with a look of slightly shop-soiled elegance, and cold, blue eyes. His prison denim had now faded to a melancholy shade of grey-blue. Mystifyingly, the trousers bore a sharp crease so they managed to avoid stifling the body's architecture.

Since a lock-down was about to take place, the frantic mêlée of the day had ended. A couple of wraith-like figures near a dispensary hatch, and some disembodied voices on the upper landings, were all that remained of the morning.

'Okay,' I said with a long, drawn-out emphasis on the 'kay,' ' You've got to go. Tell me later.' Before he left, Jack Goodman pressed a sketch pad into my hand.

Once inside my office I opened the sketch pad. There were about ten sketches, or line drawings, in the pad, all exquisitely drawn. The artist was a craftsman in drawing the human form in subtle, artful and desiring poses. In fact, the fewer the lines, the more precision and character the subjects showed. The female bodies were like those I'd seen produced by dress designers and fashion illustrators to emphasise the ethereal nature of the subject matter. Half were what I'd call ordinary scenes of sexual congress, involving two or three participants; the rest were of groups, mostly females, dressed in plastic or patent leather bodices with whips, canes or chains in hand and other accoutrements. One appeared to be a young woman giving another what can only be described as an enema.

I remember the first time I had seen pornographic photos when I was teaching at a secondary school. The PE master took me into the staff toilets one lunch hour and produced a wad of photos from his inside jacket pocket, much in the way I imagined a spiv would present contraband watches for sale. But at that time I showed a level of disgust, for reasons I could no longer fathom. Jack's sketches, however, were different; different from anything I had ever seen before. The subject matter was unique to me, and provoked a number of questions. For instance, the penises of the men were inordinately large and out of proportion, totally filling the mouths of the women who sucked avidly at them. I'd seen some big dicks in my career, but these were too large for comfort. Men and women appeared in consensual poses with smiles on their faces. From the rear view, the backsides of the females who were bent over with buttocks in the air, rose like ripe plums. It confirmed the idea that ripe fruit had a parallel in the female form.

The subject matter of the S.M. scenes was new to me too: mostly females; one partially clothed in patent leather, one with a phallus strapped below her waist; and naked men on all fours, in bondage, like chained dogs, wearing plastic hoods and being flagellated; a satire on decaying capitalism, perhaps. An older woman had oral sex with a younger woman, and both women and men practised cunnilingus on other women. Mysteriously, in one sketch, what I took to be a plastic phallus was strapped upright on the saddle of a rocking horse.

There was much I needed to learn from the world of pornography.

*   *   *

I rattled off a list of surnames, then said:' We're all here then?'

'Yeah …' came a chorus of approval. There was little in the way of style with this audience.

I read the register and glanced up at each man in turn, putting a tick in a box after his name: 'Kenny Bruce, Paul Nerrity, Jack Goodman, Ian Bradley.' Bradley was the category 'A' prisoner. I made a feeble attempt at a passable joke: 'Where's the dog Ian?'

'Do you know, that screw loves his dog more than his wife,' Bradley explained. 'I've been on the fucking book three years now, and I still have that fucking dog walking beside me wherever I go.'

'Never mind,' said Goodman, 'you'll have it walking to the gate with you on the day you leave. Then you'll be out of the gate, a free man. One day a danger to society, the next, free to sleep on the embankment.'

'I fink you should get a job at Battersea Dog's Home,' Nerrity said sarcastically.

Ian Bradley grimaced and sunk back in the chair, passing his hand over his head. He was unusually old looking for his thirty five years, prison pallored, with long streaks of matted hair.

I squinted down at the register again: 'Where's uncle Ron?'

'On a downer, I suppose,' Nerrity said, 'no seriously, he ain't. He's doin a bit of business. He'll be along soon.' His

24

voice, all the same, was larded with veiled criticism. Nerrity was conscripted as a messenger doing odd jobs for Ron, collecting anything that was due to his 'guvnor'.

Nerrity pushed his snout tin across the table with his huge tattooed hand: 'Snout, anyone?'

The others looked at the matchstick-thin smokes. Only Ian Bradley took one. He lit it and sucked hard. It had nearly all gone in one brief flame. 'Bloody 'ell. I prefer to build my own,' he said, disgusted.

Bradley had one eye closed as the smoke plumed around his face. With one hand he wrestled the wet stub from his lips, and with the other he removed a six inch wooden object, which he had made himself, from the pocket of his denim jacket. 'Here. Have a butcher's at this.' There was pride on Bradley's face from his accomplishment: job satisfaction at its most pure.

'A gift of the Gods?' Goodman was prompted to ask.

'Christ!' Nerrity spluttered, 'It's a coffin.' Nerrity grasped the object quickly. 'Givus a look at that.' He turned it, over and over, inspecting it, before beckoning to the others. 'Ere, put your mincers on this.'

'Careful. I haven't finished it yet,' Bradley stormed, and placed it on the table

On the table, in front of the assembled throng, was a beautifully created miniature coffin, accurate down to the name plate and handles.

'Now. Here's the magic.' Bradley opened the lid.

Inside was an occupant, in dark blue, with a wooden head and peaked hat.

Kenny Bruce strained his neck over towards the coffin. 'It's a dead screw,' he said without conviction.

'It's the Principal Officer,' Bradley informed him. 'And look at this.'

Bradley pressed the little man in the stomach and he sat up.

'Oh my God,' I said, recoiling but laughing at the macabre spectacle. 'Put it away now,' I said, firm but appeasing. Being evening, my mental energy was at its lowest ebb.

The class laughed.

'You see what creative talent we've got in here,' said Goodman, picking up the coffin and admiring the ingenuity of the one who had produced such a thing. 'The mind can create such works of art. Something to ward off evil spirits.'

'I don't care.' I regaled the class. 'Let's get on with this lesson for heaven's sake.'

Bradley pocketed his token and everyone sat down in their chairs. Uncle Ron, a balding man in his sixties with a well-lived-in face, had crept in during the show and was seated nearest the radiator. Kenny offered him his seat.

'Right. Now we're going to discuss the British government and how power is shared between the Executive, the Legislature and the Judiciary.'

I lectured for a few minutes to absolute silence from my class. It made me feel slightly ill at ease. 'I will outline the function of each of the power-sharing bodies and will discuss the relative importance of each, and any checks and balances in the system, 'I said pedantically.

I took some chalk from the desk and put the word Cabinet, Parliament and Courts on the board, before continuing with: 'The elected Cabinet is the Executive, Parliament is the law maker, or Legislature, and the courts form the Judiciary, whose responsibility is to see that the laws are properly obeyed.'

'Why do they break their own laws?' Kenny broke in, more confident than usual, galvanised, most likely, by Bradley's totem into breaking his own taboo on uttering no more than a few words at any one time. Kenny was a young lifer of twenty two serving a recommended fifteen year sentence for the murder of a man in a public house. Not surprisingly, everyone at his Reception Board had agreed that he had been more sinned against than sinning, being pulled from pillar to post as an adolescent. But rather than protect him, they had let him loose to survive as best he could among the most difficult of the prisoners.

'What precisely do you mean, Kenny?' I asked sincerely.

'Well, they ...?'

I cut him short. 'Who's they?'

'Those in power. Your politicians,' he said unsure.

'Okay. Carry on.'

'They break rules for themselves...' Kenny looked at me, the effort of concentration showing. His face mutely said that he was confused.

I was forcing the issue. 'I still don't quite understand.'

Goodman sought to correct Kenny's ill-phrased statement.

'What he means is that the lawmakers are able to do as they like. When they are caught breaking the law they are more frequently than not forgiven for their sins.'

'Fuck all that,' declared Nerrity, folding his mouth into a grim and almost spiteful line. 'But it sounds right to me.'

His thick neck bulged over his collar.

The class was buzzing now and Nerrity stood up defiantly. Bradley lit another one of Nerrity's flame throwers while he was otherwise engaged.

Nerrity went on: 'I read in the Sunday papers that a judge's son got let off when he was caught for importing cocaine. And he drove off from the court in a Roller afterwards. He even got legal aid. The cunt.'

Bradley coughed through a cloud of smoke, and said: 'These rich people should be studied carefully, cos they move in peculiar ways. Those vicars are always caught with their trousers down pumping some schoolboy, prossy, or the like.'

Ron Gifford, declaring no affinity with the church, was eaten up by savage indignation. He said bitterly: 'An Old Bill swore on the bible that he saw me forcibly enter a house. It's fucking diabolical. It's a lie. He perjured himself in court.'

LIVING ON GOLD TIME

I entered the squabble to restore order. 'Hang on a minute. We're going off the point. I'm trying to look objectively at the role of law-making bodies to see how laws are made and administered, not deal with particular cases that might, or might not, be infringements of the code of practice.'

'But the whole authoritarian practice of the state machine is brought into disrepute by these incidents, isn't it?' queried Goodman, who further said that practice was the acid test of theory.

Nerrity banged the table and the cigarette tin hit the floor with a crash. Bradley assembled its contents and put it back in its place.

'Yeah. There's one law for the rich, and another for the poor,' Nerrity bellowed, jabbing the air with a fist, more school-boyish than ever

I conceded defeat in trying to outline abstract concepts of checks and balances, and thought I would follow the drift by approaching the topic from another route. 'Okay. Okay. Let's look at it from the point of view of rules and who should or should not obey them, 'I said passively.

The hubbub subsided.

'Now Jack.' I gazed at the man putting him on the spot. 'Rules are for the guidance of wise men and the obedience of fools. Are they not?'

Jack Goodman was the foil to beat the others into submission, as I knew he wouldn't come out with a limp answer.

'I think rules keep people in their place and nothing else, he said. 'Obeying, or not obeying them is only the choice of those with privileges and power. Isn't that right?' Goodman had a strong, amused face on him and he nudged Kenny Bruce who had been sullen throughout.

Kenny came to life: 'We need rules for good order and discipline.'

'That's right.' I intervened prematurely. 'Otherwise, we'd have anarchy and chaos.'

'Yeah. I want more chaos,' shouted Nerrity, panting a little, but triumphant.

Ron Gifford admonished him. 'Be serious.'

'Absence of rules could mean order too, 'Jack Goodman said with flippancy in his voice.

The sheer paradox of this statement was pregnant with life.

Everyone looked up at me expecting an explanation for the conundrum. Even I was a little puzzled, but anticipated a good answer.

'What on earth do you mean by that?'

'If the state did not interfere so much in everyone's life, free enterprise would not be crushed.'

'So you're a libertarian then?' I asked.

'If you say so. I believe in the classical economist's Laissez-Faire state.'

'Oooh! Get a load of him. What's that for fuck's sake? You trying to stitch us up with nonsense?' Nerrity demanded.

Myself, I was beginning to wonder where he had got these concepts from, and thought that the education must have been better at some other prison.

Jack Goodman turned to Nerrity. 'It means that the less government and the authoritarians intervene, the more able we would be to get on with our lives in the way that we want. Rolling back the frontiers of the state, the government call it.'

'Goodman's a Tory,' declared Bradley, woken from his slumber.

'Perhaps I do believe in the Conservative philosophy of free enterprise. There weren't any rules in the Garden of Eden, were there?' Jack had a well developed view on these matters. It was a powerful challenge he made to the class and I thought I could use that to make further points.

'He's not altogether wrong you know,' I conceded, 'even if we were all on a desert island, with no government, we

would only invent rules necessary for our survival. We
would all get on with doing what we wanted to.'

'Would there be any crime? Kenny wanted to know. I
could see we were drifting on to their favourite topic.

'Like murder and theft, you mean,' said Nerrity. 'I'd nick
your things perhaps.'

The class ignored this comment, for he was bang out of
order. They treated it with the contempt it deserved. Nerrity
looked round at the blank faces and laughed to himself,
without making even a fleeting apology. He was not
intentionally rude, but thoughtless. He was uncouth, and
appeared not to be aware of the effect he had on others, and
would perhaps have been astonished to know I avoided him
whenever I could.

'Crime only comes when there's rich and poor then. When
some have, and some haven't?' said Kenny pertinently.
Kenny Bruce not often said much, but this statement raised
his class score for me.

Uncowed, Nerrity approached seriousness, indirectly
apologising for his former mistake with: 'But we'd all have
what we fucking wanted on this desert island, wouldn't we?'

Goodman assured everyone: 'Of course, and we'd all be
happy doing our own thing. We'd all live in our own houses.
I'd design them, Paul would build them.'

'And me?' said Kenny enthusiastically.

Goodman continued: 'Ian would paint then and Ron could
organise the building work.'

'What'll we do for money. Get fuckall I s'pose. Know
what I mean?' Nerrity whined, back to his former ebullient
self.

'Wouldn't need it really, would we?' someone said.

Everybody nodded appreciatively.

'Heaven on earth. No?' Goodman looked around at
everyone. 'No rules, no prison, no state, no anarchy. All of
us living in harmony.'

Ian Bradley frowned. 'Since we're all together in this prison, against our will I grant you that, why can't we have our own free enterprise economy that Goodman so admires?'

'Why not?' Goodman replied.

Ron Gifford said stridently: 'Cos the screws won't allow it. That's why.'

'The cunts only want to cuff you, bang you up and slop you out. Its all they're good for,' Nerrity said.

'Maybe,' I replied thinking of the possibilities that this line of argument was taking, 'but we could have our own free enterprise economy.'

'How d'ya mean?' asked Kenny Bruce.

'I know,' said Goodman, inspired. 'Privatise the prison.'

'God help us,' moaned Nerrity blithely. His etched eyebrows jumped and arched like skipping-ropes, with genuine surprise.

'Go on,' I implored bristling, 'explain.'

'Well, that's what I think.' Everyone gazed at Goodman in wonderment. 'Let's face it, the rules are there not only because they immobilise prisoners, but because they destroy individual initiative.'

'Fucking too right, the cunts always have it their own way,' Nerrity shouted. The other tried to quieten him with mock blows to the head.

'Shut up a minute, Paul. Will you?' Goodman shook a hand stiffly. 'Believe it or not, those who obey orders are treated with contempt by those who frame them.'

"Contempt,' asked Kenny, 'what do you mean by that?'

'Despise...dislike someone,' Ron chimed in.

Nerrity sulked, then brightened almost to bursting point again. 'Right on. Do you know when I was helping the tea boy the other day, I took a tray of tea into the Governor's office. He had three geezers from the Home Office in there. Two judges and a civil servant someone told me. Anyhow. Fuck me, do you know what the cunts were saying?'

'Come on Nerrity, tell us.' Bradley chided him.

Nerrity stood up compulsively, as if delivering an oration and folded his arms. 'No, be serious,' he said to those about him, trying to disguise some latent nervousness. He laughed at himself, then said: 'I closed the door and did a bit of earwigging, know what I mean? They said prisoners were no better than fucking peasants with nothing between their ears. Eyeup, I said to myself. Fuck this for a bunch of bananas.' He unfolded his arms and corrected himself. 'They didn't use exactly those words, but the meaning was there, you know what I mean.'

'There's a first hand example for you.' Jack Goodman sprang to Nerrity's defence. 'Obviously, I don't mean getting rid of the prison completely.'

I jumped with didacticism on my mind. 'Decarceration that's called.'

'Okay, decarceration. But I wouldn't advocate getting rid of the screws.'

'Fucking why not?' said Nerrity, indignant again.

'Because they're needed for minor organisational matters. But instead of this useless labour we are made to do, we would work for ourselves. Those who can't work on their own account, can work for others.'

Ron Gifford, who had been listening intently to all that was being said, rolled a cigarette, leaned over the radiator, and remarked to his now silent audience. 'Believe me, the only privatisation the authorities would have in mind in this poxy place, would be to turn this dump into a labour camp by selling it off to someone who would then use us as cheap labour, working twenty four hours a day. Alternatively we'd be banged up all the time.'

The little band of revolutionaries looked deflated.

Nerrity said aghast: 'Fuck that.'

Jack Goodman rescued their flagging morale with: 'That's just what I'm trying to avoid. That's why we must work for ourselves. I'll give you an example.' He turned to Ian

Bradley. 'As Ian's a good decorator he could set up his own firm in here with telephones, faxes and an inmate secretary, and tender for contracts with the outside. Even employ labour outside to fulfil them.'

'Fuck...ing, he...ll. This guy's had a brain transplant, or he's a fucking wind-up merchant. 'e's doin' my fuckin' 'ead in.' Nerrity broke into a minor pirouette round the room.

'But I'm serious. Ian, he's a decorator, so he could employ other prisoners to paint the prison, and the Home Office would pay him.'

A soft smile played around Ian's face.

'C'mon, this one's gone too far,' declared Nerrity, thumping a table.

Goodman disarmed him. 'And you Paul, would be a security guard. Looking after everyone's business for them.'

'Too right,' Nerrity shouted. His mood changed. He marched up and down the room apeing the actions of some foreseeable security service.

'And what would you do, Jack?' asked Gifford, half expecting him to be a self-appointed leader of men.

'I'd paint pictures all day and sell them to the public. I could paint one a day at great speed. They could then be sold in a gallery, or in a prison shop. The money we'd get from our work could be sent to our wives. It would cut the social security bill. For those prisoners left without work, they would work in the bakers or in the laundry. Those shops could work twenty four hours a day, in shifts, with men paid trade union rates. They could win contracts with hospitals and the like. Bread would be sold directly to the public in the prison bread van.'

Nerrity joked casually: 'Right. I don't wanna be a security guard. I wanna be a van driver.'

I was enthralled by all this, my euphoria seemingly unprickable. But there was one question: 'What about food? How would it be distributed?'

'We would have our own prison farmyard and allotment growing the vegetables. And by the way, petty theft would disappear, and barony too, because everyone would buy what they want with real money. The prison shop would be like a supermarket selling everything.' At that point Jack stopped. No one spoke. I glanced around at the faces.

'Pie in the sky,' Ron Gifford burst out contemptuously. 'The screws would smash everything before you got it off the ground.'

'Possibly,' Jack replied. He thought long and hard, then said: 'But we'd make a start in some small way. Couldn't we?'

'Small! How big's small?'

'Something us five could do.'

'I've got it,' said Nerrity, enthused once more. 'Let's have some sort of exhibition.'

For once Ron Gifford was coming round to the idea, as the suggestions seemed to him to be more realistic. 'Right,' he said, 'that's a possibility. I've been inside eight years and some of the art and modelling work I've seen is terrific. As good as anything they have on that Prison Department-sponsored Koestler award scheme. If we follow Jack's plans we could collect all the hobbies and art work on the Wing, have an exhibition, sell it, and let the money go back into each man's private cash.'

Jack eyed me. 'Here you are, it's all up to you. Could we arrange an exhibition as a money-raising event?'

'It's a good idea,' I admitted. 'It means first I'll have to get the go-ahead from the Wing managers. Then the sky's the limit. But is everyone up for it? I questioned the gathered throng.

Goodman, Ron Gifford and the irrepressible Nerrity, were enthusiastic. But with Nerrity enthusiasm could be easily dissipated. Kenny Bruce and Ian Bradley were less interested.

'Okay,' said Bradley, reluctantly, after some coaxing from the others. 'I'll give it a go.'

Kenny followed, and said: 'Yes. If that's what everyone wants.'

I envisaged a challenge and a possible management confrontation. Before we could make a final decision I had to see whether it was on first.

Jack remonstrated: 'Remember. Always front up the rules.'

At that precise moment a screw with a slashed peaked hat that imitated an SS officer's cap, entered the classroom. 'Bruce, Nerrity, Bradley, Gifford,' he entreated, 'showers for you. You're wanted on the Wing.'

The room emptied, as if by magic. I sat alone with Jack Goodman.

I spoke first: 'Well. That's that. Not much achieved on British Parliamentary practice tonight. Some of what you had to say was interesting though.' I looked harder at him and asked: 'What's your academic background?'

'I got 'O' levels and 'A' levels while inside.'

'I thought so, because of your vocabulary. But tell me, do you think the men get anything out of these lessons?'

Jack laughed aloud, and nodded. 'Of course they do. But not in the way you think.'

'What do you mean then?'

'Not in terms of an academic course, or working towards some goal like passing examinations. But in their own particular way they do.' He went on: 'Take Kenny for instance. He comes because it builds up his confidence. Do you realise the man's nearly illiterate. No formal education. But this improves his vocabulary and gives him self respect.'

'Nerrity?'

'He's your tearaway. He's in his early twenties but still like a boy. He's only tolerated because he's a gopher for Ron. Says what comes into his head. Out front he's direct; but inwardly cunning. A personality undulled by rough usage. On the class because he's proving to everybody that he's up to it. Gets him out of his cell as well. He'd only be creating some argy-bargy in the Wing otherwise.'

'A man with an attention span that would make a fruit fly look geriatric if you asked me,' I said. Jack was silent.

'Bradley?'

'The man's got talent, and you're one of the only ones who recognises it. He's excluded because of his crime. You give him sanctuary.'

'What crime is that?' I had already read his records but I still asked.

'Jack thought before answering. 'Ask him yourself.'

He remained utterly tight-lipped. It wasn't a question he would have asked himself, except obliquely.

Goodman took me off the subject.

'Ron Gifford. Respected old timer. Bluff, no nonsense northerner. Fitted up by the Old Bill. Inside for a crime he didn't commit. I'm the only recall on this class.'

'Recalled for what?'

'Assault on the police they said. It goes back to the Sixties when I worked Soho. I had an unofficial licence from the Old Bill for a few things I was doing on the side.'

'Unofficial licence?' I exclaimed mystified.

'I paid them.'

I was more confused.

'You know. Brown envelope job.'

I must have looked as though I still didn't understand. 'Is that enough for a recall?' I gingerly posed the question: 'Is that all?'

'No.'

*   *   *

EMPIRE OF SCREAMS

Jack Goodman was sitting on the bed with his legs drawn up under his chin. Kenny Bruce walked up to the half-opened cell door and put his head round.

'Can I ask you something?'

'Sure. Come in. Fire away.'

Do you think Wally Wildman goes for all that stuff you said tonight?'

'I think so. It's not all impossible you know. Getting him to put an exhibition on can be good for us.'

'He's not joking then, cos Bradley and Uncle Ron are getting enthusiastic now.'

'No. He's sincere enough. But if he thinks it's going to be easy, he's got another thing coming, cos he's pissing against the wind'

'What do you mean?'

'The prison rules are unbendable. You know that. The screws are cunts. He's going to get a knockback, of sorts. But he's got plenty of bottle. I must admit. First rule is that prisoners are always in the wrong. They'll give a bit to him, then bosh, bosh, the end.' Jack pushed his fist into his hand. 'Their catchphrase is: 'Give 'em enough rope and they'll hang themselves.

'I hope not.'

'We'll see.'

2

Jack and Young Benny were already at it when I arrived back in my cell. You would be forgiven for thinking Benny danced attendance at his master's side – Jack, the priest, and Benny the willing acolyte.

Jack had the *I Ching* in one hand and was instructing Benny on where to put the matchsticks.

'Benny, based on the *I Ching* numerology, fifty five matchsticks are used in divination. This will answer any divination question we put before them. Let's say, for instance, our question is: what should I do in the future?'

He was partly reading the book and partly giving instructions now. Benny hung on his every word.

'Put aside six matchsticks which represent the six lines of a hexagram. Take the remaining forty nine sticks and divide them into two heaps.'

Benny then chose a heap, removed a stick and put it aside. From the same heap he removed four sticks at a time until one to four sticks remained. From the other heaps he repeated the process.

'Put the matchsticks which are in groups of four, together, then divide it randomly into heaps,' Jack said as he stared bewilderingly down at Benny's heaps. 'The above steps are repeated until six to nine groups of four sticks remain, the book says. Repeat the entire process to build up the lines of a hexagram. The first three lines form the lower trigram, the rest, the next three, the upper trigram.'

By now the situation was becoming unmanageable, but Jack, frustrated, pressed on regardless.

'The hexagram in the matter related to your question, is obtained when you put the six lines together, and the two hexagrams together is the answer to your divination. That's what the book says, anyhow.'

He slapped the book closed. 'Fucking hell,' he said, 'I'll use the coins method from now on.'

'Don't involve me,' I said, after quietly observing the confusion among the group of matchsticks on the table.

Both men sloped off, discussing earnestly what had gone wrong.

*   *   *

The prison classrooms had closed down for a couple of weeks for renovation. The Works Department had promised a first rate job. I couldn't imagine them cutting through the bars though. Some of the men had offered their services, saying they'd paint clouds on the ceiling. Naturally, the offer was rejected. I was to be consigned to my office cell in the Wing for the duration.

'Have no fear,' Jack Goodman barked, as he ambled in, sat in the interviewee's chair and put his feet up on the open drawer of the filing cabinet.

'If you want to know about the porn business in the Sixties, then I'll tell you.' He said this with mischief dancing in his eyes.

It was a tempting offer.

'Okay,' I said, placing a fat bible against the office door to act as a door stop, ready for our tête-à-tête.

'Of course you know about Bent Old Bill and the corruption trials of the Seventies.'

I nodded, not quite knowing how much I was supposed to know.

'I thought Robert Mark, as Met Commissioner, was supposed to have cleaned out the stables,' I said.

'He was,' Jack replied. 'His ambition was to clean out everything: the Drug Squad, Vice Squad and the OPS and get the Met arresting more criminals than they employed. But those who departed the force, or were tried, were only the small fry. The whole shebang was as bent as arseholes, from the DPP upwards. All because of what they called blue films'

Jack's head moved towards mine.

'Did you know the DPP used to get, not a wedge, but a big, brown bag full of used readies, delivered to him at regular intervals by the Bagman?'

Even at this stage, I was starting to get lost.

'Who's the DPP and who's the Bagman?' I exclaimed.

Jack, noting my confusion, said:

'Okay. Let's start at the beginning.'

'Hang on a minute.' I needed some sort of historical continuity. 'How did you manage to get into this business in the first place? That's what I'd like to know?' I was thinking back to the wad of pornographic drawings Jack had given to me.

'First I supplied the shops in the West End. A friend took me to one of the shops one day, a shop with a Books and Magazines sign outside the door. I showed the shop owner my drawings. He said he wanted sequences. You know, pictures which told a story for which he offered me a pound a drawing. He pointed to a wooden box filled with small packets of photographs of drawings of erotic images. One artist produced work that was really first class. There was one guy in Soho at the time who produced the best.

'What was his name?' I butted in with a view to building up a dossier of Soho characters, to give life to a study I now had in mind.

'Michael Muldoon was his name,' Jack said.

'Where is he now?'

'Fuck knows. Probably a millionaire, or doing bird like everyone else.'

'After visiting the shop what did you do then?'

'I needed to be self-employed. I didn't fancy the cunts in the shops making a fortune out of me forever. I was desperate to get money for photographic equipment so I borrowed some dosh, bought a Rolleiflex and flash, and

from Exchange and Mart purchased the second-hand
contents of a darkroom.'

'Then what?'

'I packed the postage-card sized prints into plastic bags
and sealed them with sellotape.'

'How many in a packet?'

'Ten. Then I went back down to Soho, to the shop owner I
told you about. He wanted sale or return. I wanted cash. He
had to give in.'

'Why?'

'Because if he didn't have some, the other shops would, as
it was new stuff. The small porno shops in the West End
always bought 'new stuff' as they called it. I quickly learned
that the punters shopped around until they found what they
wanted. A shop which consistently offered a less varied
selection than its rivals, rapidly lost its regular clientele.
They would always buy more if you agreed to sale or return.
But I never did. I offered them at cheaper prices in return for
cash.'

'So you found that the bigger shops bought larger
quantities, at cheaper prices, offering cash as an incentive?'

'Right. And in Soho they were fucking everywhere; shops
with signs outside saying 'Books and Magazines,' or 'Books
and Films.' They wanted new stuff all the time. It was just a
matter of producing it. I was well pleased.'

Jack got to the end of the sentence when the tannoy
blurted out its message:

'Goodman. A visit.'

'That's me off. See you later,' he said, disappearing
through the open door.

*   *   *

The day was young. The sun was out. Again, Jack sat with
his feet up on the open drawer of the filing cabinet, after
making me a tea, and began:

'The sale of erotic photographs provided a regular income for me. The market trend in the early Sixties was exclusively for pornographic black and white photographs, or smudges, as they were called in the trade. The majority of the punters were toffs; middle class or upper class businessmen, who visited the shops during their lunch hour dressed in pin-stripped suits and bowler hats. This group was discriminating in its tastes and selected only the best quality smudges; that meant a good presentation of poses, good camera angles and lighting, and work artistically produced. New material met a brisk demand as the shops were already flooded with inferior quality work. Erotic imagery was visually stimulating. Quality work got you a good income. But the law of illegal business activity pitted one pornographer against another.

'In what way?'

'To operate I needed a 'licence,'

'Explain that to me again.'

'A payment to the Obscene Publications Squad, or Dirty Squad. Usually a brown envelope job. The Squad was set up to enforce the Obscene Publications Act of 1959. The Act strengthened the law concerning pornography by vesting a broad discretion in policemen to search premises and seize stock without issuing receipts. Obviously, they operated a law which hinged upon personal assessment, and the temptation to share in the spoils from a commodity of dubious danger proved very great indeed. In 1959, pornography published for gain was assumed to deprave and corrupt. Its only proven casualties, however, were dishonest policemen. The police were able to operate because they controlled key individuals, and thereby the West End scene. In exchange for immunity from prosecution, members of the OPS regularly collected their share of the profits in brown paper envelopes from the shops. Pornographers buckled under the threat of prosecution for non payment. So incestuous was the relationship between policemen, shopkeepers and pornographers that in Soho pubs no one could tell who was a member of the OPS and who was a shop owner. I'm sure if they hadn't been thrown together by occupation they'd have sought each other out.'

'Why?'

'Because they were so alike. Don't you see?'

I suppose I did.

'Being so close the usual squabbles would arise and these could break out into open warfare at any time.'

'Let's go back to the nature of the business for a moment before I get too confused.' I said. 'So the pornographers were the sex shop owners, and the likes of you?'

'No. The shops' owners were managers themselves or managers for business men. Producing good porn is an artistic skill. Shopkeepers can't do it.'

Jack was getting frustrated with my little confusions.

'Look,' he said. 'The drive to make a business out of porn, and the illegal nature of the work, created a situation whereby the businessmen were permanently on the lookout for talented artists. Once new artists were discovered they had to be controlled as employees, in case they set up in business and cornered the market for themselves, as I told you yesterday. Pressure was exerted from the licence holders and police to eliminate anyone who threatened profits.

'What type of pressure?'

'From the police, or from the gangsters and their protection rackets. They all behaved like the state, exerting what you'd call social control.'

I took a swig of my tea.

'There was one bloke, I remember, who figured quite prominently in my early dealings in Soho. I first met him in the El Morocco night club in Gerrard Street. We'd also go to the Regency Rooms where other London criminals hung out. A West End gangster and casual acquaintance of mine said to me one day: We don't know the full SP on this geezer, son, so don't let him know your business.'

'SP – starting prices.' I tried out my knowledge.

'Yeah. I'd always took seriously tip-offs from the shop owners. There was one time I was searching for new models and found three young girls whiling away a hot summer afternoon in Trafalgar Square. Even before we met them they had been selling themselves as prostitutes to the punters for a pound a session. We offered them five pounds an hour to pose. From a department store we equipped the girls with school uniforms, pleated skirts, virgin socks and navy knickers. We rented a studio that provided camera and lighting facilities for a day's shooting. We got some great shots. The next time I took them to a luxury flat in Notting Hill and went to a lot of trouble finding a pop musician who occasionally dabbled in glamour shots. He had the reputation of having the biggest cock in the trade. He lay fully clothed on the bed while the girls peeled off his garments to reveal, to their amazement, the man's enormous organ. Within a few days the photos were on sale in the West End. They sold like hot cakes over the next few months. A good selling angle was that they were new girls. See, pornography addicts love new faces. That summer was the highpoint of my early career. But I didn't have a licence to operate and it was restricting the expansion of my business.

'You hadn't paid the police in other words,' I added.

'Correct. Without a licence the OPS were keeping my haunts in the Piccadilly area under surveillance. One morning I received tip-off at a shop we called the Long Shop. Dixie Deans, the manager of the shop said: You're earning a lot of money Jack. You've got to pay The Office. You've got to put something in the kitty. I pay. Everyone pays. It's a message from the OPS. He put an envelope on the counter, then said: It'll stir up a shemozzle if you don't. Come on Jack, be a mensch.'

I broke in: 'Tell me more about the shops.'

'Well. There was the Long Shop run by Dixie Deans, as I've just mentioned, Leo's in Moor Court, Fat Bill's shop in Walker's Court, one in Greek Court run by Chalkie White, Big Dave at Newport Place, Gerrard Street, Old Compton Street and Broadwick Place.'

'A lot then,' I said limply.

Jack moved his head closer to mine. 'Chalkie White from the Greek Street bookshop had a reputation for attending big lunches at the Hilton Hotel with the Director of Public Prosecutions and other high ranking police officers.'

'What were the shops like?' I needed to get a visual picture of the Soho scenery.

'Take Walker's Court run by Fat Bill for instance. There was the main part of the shop as you went in the door, always fluorescently lit, and an inner sanctum at the back. There'd be a doorman around to control the punters. Usually he sat on a chair at the door of the back room of the pornshop. Often it had a box-office like structure with a door release. Its advantage was that it gave off-the-pavement punters who came into the outer shop a chance to catch a glimpse of the forbidden treasures inside the back. Exciting clients to the point of no return, you could say. Every customer was required to make a purchase; a precautionary measure to cover themselves, as the Old Bill was not allowed to buy pornography under the law as it existed'

'What sort of stock did the shops carry?'

'Boxes of photos, soft porn mags, books, rollers showing fladge, rubber bondage, pissing and now and again animal films. But these appealed only to a minority. Lolitas dressed as schoolgirls, or in nurses uniforms, were especially popular; scans or Scandinavian mags, especially after Denmark legalised porn in 1967.'

'But who owned the freehold on the shops?'

'Like most properties in Soho, especially flats rented by brasses, no one ever knew who their real landlords were, as each place had been let, sublet, and underlet again and again.

LIVING ON GOLD TIME

I believe Paul Raymond of Raymond's Review Bar held a
lot of freeholds by the end of the Sixties. A Pole named Jack
Isow owned a swathe of Soho property in the Fifties. Funny
enough, property values were eroded by the downfall of the
OPS in the Seventies, which had done such a lot to reduce
the risks inherent in the porn business and hence the demand
for shop premises. So trying to get to the bottom of who
owned what retail outlet was as difficult as lobster catching
with a tin bucket. Front men were always used in the shops.
A front man who was untrustworthy spelt disaster. An owner
couldn't just put anyone in a shop. A shop in a prime site
might take three or four thousand in a day, and trustworthy
management was essential, especially when they purchased
stock themselves. To prevent dishonesty, managers weren't
just employees, they were made shareholders and part of the
business. Loyalty had to be bought. One shop owner I recall
did find his front man robbing him. To catch the thief he
sent in someone with a wad of dollars to spend. When the
owner went in and found the dollars weren't there the
manager was nicked within the hour. The owner just phoned
Scotland Yard. The owner's name was displayed in the
shops, but whenever a proprietor was nicked the name was
changed. I'll tell you what, Dixie Deans told me that the
Church really owned a lot of properties, and they put in front
men to do the business side of property ownership. They
musn't have in their hearts thought porn was so terribly bad.
So they let it go on.'

'Tell us about the raids Jack,' I said.

'Indian shops were raided all the time. The Old Bill are
racists and they took a dislike to them and vowed never to
give them a licence. It was possible for an Indian-owned
shop to be raided, and yet a licensed shop across the road to
be left entirely alone. If shops had to be raided to satisfy
public opinion, managers were told what to leave in the
shops and what to remove. Raids were notified either by
password, or by a contact man who went round with

information to all and sundry giving the date of the raid. When Denmark legalised porn, books flooded into the West End. The Danish consul complained to the Home Office about the bad image Denmark had in England. Naturally, the Home Office got on to the Porn Squad. They informed the shops of a forthcoming raid and told them what books to leave out. After the so called clean-up, the books were returned to the shelves. Old stock often had to be purchased back from the Porn Squad. Some shops realised that they would lose regular customers over the period of a week or so, even though they could stay open and sell soft core.'

'Surely they had a strong enough regular customer base to carry on?'

'Maybe. But I don't know. I've never owned a bookshop. Things could go wrong. The Broadwick Place bookshop was directly opposite the police station. It had a neon sign outside inviting the world into a paradise of books and flesh. From the police station it was possible to observe the comings and goings of that world. The whole game, Bob, was as bent as arseholes. I was shooting a film once when we were busted by a sergeant from the OPS and a CID man from the local nick. I paid them off as by then I had a licence.'

'But how comes the other CID officer from the local station was in it too. I thought it only worked from Scotland Yard?'

'All matters of obscenity are dealt with at the Yard. Any local forces wishing to make an arrest under the Obscenity Act had to have a member of the OPS with them, even if it's on their own territory. No one gets picked. The OPS gets on to the head of the local station. Can you understand now?'

'I think so,' I said, hiding my confusion.

'The CID is a corrupt network. Someone from the OPS rings up and says: 'I'm investigating an obscenity charge. It's a bit iffy. Who's a reliable man to take with me? I don't want any straights.' So you see, it's no coincidence the CID

47

officer who came on the raid was also bent. Under these arrangements I came to understand that, with my licence, they could be very real protectors in the West End situation. It was either the likes of the Old Bill or the gangsters who bayoneted or shot their enemies. So I didn't have to worry whether I was being watched, followed, or was having my phone tapped. Semi-legal status was part of the way to full legal status.'

'Surely there was more to it than just paying the OPS, even with a licence?'

'What you've got to understand, Bob, is that it was not possible for a rights owner to enforce copyright because pornography was illegal. Making a blue film was not illegal in itself. They can't arrest you for making a porn film. It only becomes an offence if you publish it for gain. And not to put to fine a point on it, there was no chance of enforcing copyright on one's work except by violence. Every independent pornographer had to be a one-man army – lawyer, enforcer and law creator. Even a corrupt situation could work perfectly well until some greedy bastard tried to eliminate the competition; which they often did.'

*   *   *

It was day three of Jack Goodman's tales from the West End

'But there's something missed out in what you say.' I addressed him immediately.

'What's that?'

'How did you get a licence?'

'I cultivated my sources.'

'What does that mean?'

'At first I got pally with Sam Jaffe. He ran a syndicate dominating the vice scene. He virtually controlled West End Central police station and was the official middle man between headquarters and vice in the West End. He was not a producer of porn, but a seller. I met him and the governor of West End Central in their regular nightspot in Carnaby Street. Here Maltese, Greek and Cypriot brothel owners paid off their debts to the police in the familiar brown paper envelopes. But Jaffe's business was vice and it proved to be a dead end. So I went where others went.'

'Where's that.'

'To Fat Bill at Walker's Court.'

'In his shop I met Chris, a sergeant in the OPS. A right smooth bastard he was. Flash suit and executive suitcase. I asked Bill how much I should straighten him. A cockle'll do, he's only a sergeant, Bill said. When I went to the pub with Chris he told me the new man at the OPS had got the right needle with me as I wasn't putting anything into The Office. When we were in the pub Chris never once lowered his voice when he talked to me, which showed the extent to which men like him controlled the West End. Still, I paid him and he promised to put a word in for me with the Head of the OPS. He told me it would cost two grand. Five hundred down, and two fifty a month from then on.'

'What was Chris like?'

'A reckless bastard. On one occasion he took me to a warehouse to stock up on Christmas booze. It was a long-firm operation that he had given a licence to, and the bastards didn't know he was no longer on the Fraud Squad. One day I gets an urgent request from him for some porn. I had stopped paying him by then as he had gone to the Provincial Crime Squad. I didn't know whether he was setting me up, now he was with the rubber-heel mob. I had to drop the consignment in the car park of a police station. This I did, but not before I was nearly nabbed by a police officer. Chris paid me. He pulled out of his pocket a wedge of crisp new banknotes. I asked him whether they were counterfeit, for with Chris anything was possible. He said they were genuine, as he'd taken a little firm five-handed with shooters to get them out. 'Is that bent as well?' I asked him, as I thought about the robbers I had known who said

the Robbery Squad was bent. Of course it's all bent he said.
The whole fucking lot is. But don't spend this in one hit, he
advised me. Split it up in bits.'

'Let's get back to the licence.'

'Where was I?'

'You were going to meet the Guvnor.'

'Yes, I met the Head of the Dirty Squad at a later date.
We met in a Soho pub and I gave him the envelope. He was
a shrewd bastard. He twisted our conversation around in
such a way that he made me want to give him the money.
Nevertheless, it was the first bit of security I had ever had in
my life.'

'I'm still confused about the practicalities of film-making.'

'Ask me anything you want,' Jack said.

'You said that you sold drawings to the shops. Then you
got a dark-room and started producing photos. So where did
the film-making come in?'

'It's a natural progression to the realism of films. Initially I
had shot in eight millimetres. Later they were made in
sixteen mill and reduced down to make a master. First I had
a manually loaded processing tank to make negs for the
printing machine. The final product was a twenty minute
silent film with a simple story line. Then I got a guy with his
own darkroom, light trap and continuous processing
machine to process for me from a dupe neg. I bought a film
camera with a four hundred foot magazine, shot a film and
handed it to my new processing agent. On completion I
boxed it and put a photograph on the front.

'What about colour?

'Right. The master plan was to take the market with colour
films. At the time the Monopolies Commission had broken
the monopoly of the film processing formulas, and I went to
Eastman Kodak to get them. They had by law to release their
formula to any laboratory on application. Since I had a
laboratory I was given the formula. My processing agent
purchased a continuous colour processing machine. It was

capable of producing forty foot of sixteen millimetre colour film a minute, and capable of working twenty four hours a day. A major advantage was that the machine could load in daylight because it had a daylight-proof magazine. Its two hundred gallons of processing fluid were held in five, forty gallon tanks.'

Jack broke off his conversation here and went out to collect the tea. On his return he slumped into the chair beside my cell table and put his feet up on the filing cabinet once again.

'Tell me, in general, about the routines of making films,' I asked.

'Well, I was learning a lot about women and sex, but it took me some time to realise that it was impossible for one man to satisfy, sexually, the type of actresses or models who became porn stars. I did learn that exciting many women was merely a matter of creating erotic images in their minds.'

'What do you mean by that?'

'Take Christina, for instance. She was a great blue film actress, a godsend to the blue film world, because she loved sex. She was a walking testimony to the fact that women are active initiators of sex, not passive receptors of men's desires.'

'Tell us about her.'

'She was a beauty of seventeen with a touch of class thrown in. She had a wide mouth and her eyes were large and brown. In her bare feet she was no more than five feet four inches tall. Her physical dimensions, and the fact that she'd do anything, made her my most popular model. She was employed on and off for a long period. Over the years she must have posed for thousands of photos, not for the money surprisingly enough, but because she liked sex. The reason why Christina was so good as a model was because of her absolute enjoyment of what she was doing.'

'So there's no truth in the suggestion that the girls were prostitutes?'

'Certainly not. Just ordinary girls. People often ask that question. I couldn't afford to pay prostitutes. The models are just housewives or young girls.'

'They do it for the money?' I tried to press the question because there was a big issue over whether poverty was the instigating factor.

'I told you they do it because they like it.' Jack paused then said: 'I've had one or two mercenary models. Sometimes they'd do it for the bread, but those rollers always turn out rubbish. After I met a girl I'd get a model release form filled in.' Jack anticipated my question. 'Before you ask, that's so she agrees that the copyright on the images, and the right of reproduction, either wholly or in part, is mine. The rest is a business transaction. They were paid, not for sex, as often this did not take place, but for their work as an actress, for their ability to weave an erotic spell. The girls knew exactly what they are doing. I act as the seducer and the camera records the seduction. The sequence develops by merging the girl's own erotic fantasies explored and captured on negative. The feeding back of their desires comes into the world as sexual imagery.'

Finally, I wanted to know what consequences, if any, the legality of the sex enterprise had upon social relations in the West End.

'Listen,' Jack said, 'Legalise porn and see what happens. The connection with crime would go. What harm does it do to others? My criterion is, does it harm another person. All the violence in the West End. It's all unnecessary. It's the shop owners. They didn't want it legalised cos they fear their monopoly would go if superior work from other sources flooded in. Banning porn creates corruption. The West End's awash with money. I guarantee that if the law was swept away Britain would be the world leader in erotica.'

I wasn't convinced of that.

'I see the shop owners as parasites. In a free market they'd be obliterated. That's why I set up a mail order business to deal directly with the customers. The corruption here's mind blowing. The way I was brought up I had no conception of the extent of corruption.'

'What, then, did you see as your contribution to the Soho sex industry in the Sixties?'

'I supplied the shops with porn, who in turn supplied the fantasies and needs of the whole country. Soho was, in the Sixties, and still is, the major source of the distribution of porn in this country, and for a while I was an important player. I was catering for the sexual fantasies of a nation. My mail order clients were cultured, educated people who had expectations which were not fulfilled when they went into the shops. The shopkeepers didn't understand their customers and that's where the likes of me came in. The people I came in contact with on my rounds did not object to what I did. In Soho I met authors, artists, film-makers and I was accepted by them all.'

*   *   *

'Did I tell you the one about the hand grenade?'
Jack appeared with a luminous grin. I thought he was practising one of his strange, incomprehensible quirks that would frequently lie in wait for my assumptions, ready to trip them up. I feigned nonchalance, but I was eaten up with curiosity.

'What hand grenade?' I said.

'Sit down. Have another swig of tea and I'll tell you.' He put the warm cup up to my mouth.

'The other day I told you about Micky Muldoon the pornographer.'

I nodded, while Jack pushed the chair back and sat down.

'Well. He used to tell us this one. One day he goes into Fat
Bill's shop.'

'Oh yes. Fat Bill from Walker's Court.' I rehearsed my
new-found knowledge for once.

'Micky was having a bit of trouble with Frankie who
owned a basement shop. When Fat Bill heard about it
everyone coaxed Fat Bill to retell a story about a hand
grenade. And it went something like this.'

Jack retells to me the story he had heard from Muldoon:

'Fat Bill was in his shop when a firm four-handed comes
in. Whoosh, this geezer pulls out a bayonet. We'll be in here
every week and we want a monkey a week. Got it. That's for
fucking starters, the geezer yells. Crrrash … he takes a big
lump out of the table with the bayonet. They tried to move in
to protection on the shop but they didn't know Old Bill had
protection on it. So Fat Bill says to 'im, where can I get you?
He says phone me at the club later. So Fat Bill phones 'im
and says, okay I've got the monkey. I'm going to deliver. No
trouble, you come over the villain says. I've got this fucking
hand grenade, Bill says, and I wires it to a thread round my
finger, and it's in the briefcase. I walks into the fucking
club. The chaps were standing behind with bayonets. I opens
the case to show the geezer Frank and he looks inside and
sees the Mills 36 hand grenade. When he peers in there, cos
his face went white, the colour of paper. I said this is the
only payment you're getting from me, Frank. We can't give
you anythink at all. How about a twoer a week Frank says.
Nothing at all I says, as we're already paying the biggest
firm in the West End. Who's the biggest firm for fuck sake
Frank yells. Cos he thought he was the biggest firm. The Old
Bill I says. We're only the front people, they take the big
end out of the shop. I thought the Italian ponce owned the
shop, the mug says. Well, he owns half and some inspector
at the Yard owns the rest. Fuck that game Big Frank yells,
get out. So as I was leaving I says to 'im not to come to the

shop again or I'll blast him to kingdom come. That's what you have to do with these geezers.'

We both fell about laughing. Jack finished the story by mimicking Big Frank without fluffing a line.

'Tell us what he said again Jack. Do it again.' I implored, ready for another crowd pleaser.

Jack stood up ready to ham it up, more brazen than ever.

'Who's the biggest firm? Frank yelled – cos he thought he was the biggest firm. The Old Bill, that's who, Fat Bill says. Fuck that game, Frank yells, even louder.'

More laughter, then Jack came to.

'By the way, do you want to meet one of the Chaps? He's up on the two's landing?'

'What chap?'

'From the Sixties nightclub the El Morocco that I was telling you about. He used to be a gopher for the Chaps.' Before I could reply Jack said: 'I'll get him.'

With that he disappeared out of the door.

Very soon a large man with a jaunty sense of well-being appeared, nearly filling the doorway of my cell. He must have been going to the gym a lot, for his shoulders looked as though his coat had the coat-hanger still in. He stood with his legs apart. When we shook hands he thrust his stiffened arm forwards to meet mine.

'This is Angelo, Bob,' Jack said.

I shook his hand. A chair appeared for him to sit down and his runner brought in his tea; obviously it was a royal visit.

'Bob's interested in Soho in the Sixties, Angelo.' Jack said.

'Tell him about the Chaps and the scene.'

I fielded several questions and we all had a belly laugh.

Angelo was like a B movie caricature of a villain, playing at being a man; someone who could vary his appeal without losing his image. It was a bish, bash, bosh moment, full of stock nineteen sixties villains and diamond geezers, but instructive all the same.

*   *   *

All in all, what Jack had to say in those few days of discussion made a good story, but I had no corroborative evidence for anything he said. I had to take everything on trust. Moreover, Jack had a habit of turning crime into nothing but counterculture. For the moment I was not sure how to get any evidence either. If I wanted to take it further I had to have first-hand experience of the game myself. Evidently, he saw himself among the uncrowned royalty of the nineteen sixties porn world, before his flag had dropped and he found himself inside, away from his usual fan base and off camera. It was a life recounted and in some sense invented, constantly revised to improve its structural clarity and mythic force. While his statements at times had incendiary power, I had no intention of being held in thrall.

3

Ian Bradley hated Training Boards. If he had known in
advance what would happen that day he would never have
attended. It was not as if he had a galaxy of inmate talent to
compete with. He was on his own and he felt betrayed. A
bitter-sweet celebration turned out to be a fiasco.

I had done my best to give him a good reference. I had
spent more time on it than I usually did with inmates'
paperwork. I had delved deeply into his previous
convictions. Everything was in the file in black and white.
There had been some doubt at his trial concerning the actual
circumstances of the victim's death; nevertheless the judge
recommended that he never be released. A moral panic
among the public, fuelled by press speculation, sealed his
fate. He was aware of the indeterminacy of the sentence but
he had proved himself by being a model prisoner. I felt that
at least he deserved to come 'off the book' and be de-
categorized from a category A to a category B prisoner. He
was now coming to the end of his first four years in prison
and was due for a transfer elsewhere. Category B status
would not compromise his sentence, but would allow him to
lead a more productive and useful existence while he stayed
incarcerated for the rest of his life.

It was the longest educational report I had ever written for
someone. It gave me great pleasure to be able to say
something worthwhile about a student instead of the usual
one or two lines ending with: 'this man is progressing well.'
I gave an overview of his educational background starting
with school, and how Bradley had gained qualifications
through part-time study. Bradley's exemplary attendance at
my current affairs class was carefully noted: the report
ended with a recommendation he be declassified, and he be

57

allowed to become part of a special tutoring scheme I was devising.

Prisoners learn most in an informal way from other inmates. The public has always believed that petty thieves only learn how to be bank robbers through their prison experiences. Prison officers regard mathematics teaching and literacy in general as a way of encouraging small crooks to steal property marked with higher prices. These animosities are not without foundation, but they detract from the civilising impact a better educated inmate can have over other men, especially where it is an older man teaching a younger one. I intended to formalize this fact into a procedure whereby inmates who could not read and write would be paired off with other men for whom they bore some respect. The simple philosophy so enshrined boiled down to the fact that prisons were failing the public, by encouraging what I liked to call preventable failures.

Ian Bradley had dressed up especially for his Board. The prison barber had cut his hair so he was left with a neat trim. The prison denims were carefully washed and sharpened with a crease. The shirt smelt new.

'Good luck,' I said to him as he sat forlorn on a chair in the Wing. Without his moustache he was visibly younger looking.

The Board Room was thronged with those who had come for Bradley's Final Board. Spicer, the tea boy, came in with cups and mugs and a plate full of biscuits; cups for the ladies, mugs for the gentlemen. Everyone laughed and joked. The Governor and the Chief were laughing with the Principal and Senior Officers. Two screws laughed about the tea. Three visitors from the Home Office laughed about the matchstick galleon on a shelf on the wall. The Psychologist, her assistant, the Chaplain and the Senior Probation Officer laughed about a programme they had seen on the television

the night before. All in all it could have been a splendid day.
Was it to be the last supper?

Bradley's file was unusually large. The Bradley archive of
human failure and human suffering was the Encyclopaedia
Brittanica of prison files. Bits of paper stuck out from the
corners of the huge tome. Only the cover gave it a
semblance of order.

'Let's begin,' the Governor said, as he swept away the
crumbs from the table in front of him, his cheeks flushing
and his mouth finishing the remainder of a McVities
Chocolate Wholewheat. 'The candidate for this afternoon is
P026357 Bradley. Category A prisoner. Been here for four
years as the first part of his life sentence. This is Bradley's
Final Board. Facts of the case are, on the night of the ...'

The Governor droned on and on with every detail of every
sickening offence that Bradley had ever committed.

'I took a sack of frozen peas with me once,' Bradley had
informed me during one of my evening classes when we
were alone together.

'What on earth for?' I said in amazement.

'To get the safe out,' he sniffed.

'How come?'

'Because it was too heavy for me to carry downstairs, so I
poured the frozen peas over the floor, tipped the safe on its
side and rolled it on the peas to the top of the stair. I push it
down and got it into the van. I was well chuffed, I can tell
you.'

We both laughed and laughed at this piece of ingenuity.

'You see, Bob, I'm a ducker and diver,' Bradley said with
swashbuckling bravado.

' ...the defendant grabbed his wife from behind and
exposed her to a vicious rape, and then rendered her
unconscious, before mutilating the body and disposing of it
in pieces.' The Governor came to the end of his introduction.

'There's some doubt about whether Bradley was capable of committing the rape offence, Sir,' the Chief remarked cautiously.

'How come.'

'Because Bradley admitted to being impotent.'

'Nothing about it in here. Let's look at the Medical Officer's report.' The Governor scanned the sheet. 'No comment here either.'

The Chaplain confirmed the Chief's point: 'Bradley told me that he couldn't get an erection even when he masturbates wildly.'

'Well, there's nothing in here to turn him on, is there,' laughed one of the screws, betraying his lazy, adolescent ego.

'Do you mind!' said Wendy from probation, who subsequently blushed very red, after reflecting on her faux pas.

The Psychologist said unkindly: 'He's dropped his habit of wearing lipstick and perfume.'

'Where did he get those from?' the Governor asked. 'Not from you I hope?'

The Psychologist replied good humouredly: 'No. Passed over on a visit I guess.'

The Governor gathered together his thoughts. 'Important or not, that point does not concern us here. We are the unfortunate ones who have to decide what to do with him, then send our recommendations to the Prison Department.' The Governor continued: 'I'd like you to comment upon your reports now. Everyone got a copy of them all?'

He glanced around. All heads nodded dumbly.

'First, you Mr Dodge. What is he like at work?'

The NCO, Dodge, sprang to mental attention for his Commanding Officer, and said: 'Very conscientious. Keeps himself to himself. A bit isolated, but no bother.'

'Chaplain?'

VOYAGE AND RETURN

The Chaplain's report was grave. Apparently, Bradley had shown no signs of remorse for what he did. He was not an active member of any church organisation. The Chaplain had little faith in the man, for he was not predisposed towards self-rehabilitation, as he saw it, and would not come to terms with his crime.

The report of the Psychologist was less involved with his behaviour and more inclined towards psychometric tests. Things called Raven's matrices and psycho/neurotic syndromes. The Board was too uninterested to make any comment, not even a sarcastic one.

Wendy from Probation, dillied and dallied over her judgements, referring to each meeting she had had with Bradley in his four years, and splicing this with verbal asides about how she found it difficult to get hold of the men when she wanted them. The Senior Officer made a remark about her timekeeping, and the Governor had to rapidly call the meeting to order, having listened restlessly up to this point.

I was optimistic that what I had to say would hit the right chord with the meeting. I carefully read my report and expanded it in places to confirm my belief that Ian Bradley should be decategorised. No one took any notice. I was not put out, because I thought a decision was still developing.

Then came a question from the Governor, directed at me, with the expressed intention of exploding my goodwill towards Bradley.

'Did you know, Dr Wildman, that Bradley had socialistic and inflammatory literature sent to him?' His head snapped round immediately and this time he gave me a full stare.

I didn't know, and didn't need to feign ignorance. But the thought of inmates being socialists was hard to swallow. You could only give them socialism in homeopathic doses, as I'd found out on many occasions.

'He is clearly not one of us,' he said with undiluted grimness, and his eyes flashed round the assembled company.

In my mind I could not see him for anything other than what he really was; a model prisoner bent on self-reform.

'Then you cannot see him for what he really is.'

'I believe so,' I remarked in a tone of abject confusion and a faint shade of sullenness. My voice for all its previous enthusiasm now sounded tired.

Thanking me for my contribution, the Governor referred to a slip of paper in front of him with the names of several prisons marked upon it.

He continued: 'Since Bradley needs a prison with a Medical Officer attached, I recommend Albany or Gartree. Any ideas?'

The Chaplain lightly pursued the issue of Bradley's uncommunicable state, but there was no dissent in the ranks.

'Okay, let's put it to him,' the Governor said, giving everyone a patrician look.

Bradley came in bright eyed and as clean as a new pin. I was proud of him. He sat upright, and said: 'Yes sir, no sir.' He even smiled at the civilians sitting around the table and gave a nod of recognition.

'Well Bradley,' the Governor went on, 'you've been here four years now, and how do you think you've fared?'

'Well Sir ...' He outlined his initial psychological weaknesses, the struggles within himself to forge a new identity, and his thanks to the Probation Department for their work.

Wendy sat beaming, for the first and last time.

He talked of his work and his education, the coming to terms with his crime, and how he could now see a way forward for himself. The Governor intervened and asked the Board whether they had any questions to direct to the prisoner. The Chaplain, ignoring Bradley's previous comments, asked him in what way he thought he had changed. Bradley became uneasy and shifted in his seat. He reiterated the point about his change of heart. The Governor looked up at the matchstick ship on the shelf above, and down into Bradley's eyes.

'Tell us about your education.'

Bradley expanded at length on his exam results and how he expected to get further exam passes. But he was never allowed to finish before the Governor interrupted with more than a wisp of his usual moral rectitude, and an indulgence in his face belying the sharpness in his voice: 'The Board have decided, Bradley, that you will not be decategorised. You will be sent, most likely, to Albany prison, where you will get adequate medical treatment for your condition. Do you have anything to say?'

Bradley's face visibly caved in. His nostrils twitched, his eyes pooling depths of anguish now, not hope. All his work was for nothing.

'What treatment? What rehabilitation have you given me?' he shouted, traumatised, as he lost his composure in the torment of the moment.

Bradley's face returned to its distorted look, and he put his hands to his eyes to mask a tear.

Visibly moved by the man's discomfort, and fearing an outburst Bradley might in future regret, the Governor asked him to leave.

The hunched prisoner was escorted to the door and was despatched tidily away.

I could compose myself no longer. I snapped, unable to control my mounting tension. I accused the meeting of cowardice, of inability to go beyond their brief. Slowly, balefully, I rose from my seat, my blinking eyes like a surprised owl on a dark night. I addressed them from a standing position: 'You fools. You silly fools. You have a moral duty to abide by Rule 1 of the Prison Rules, which says that the purpose of the treatment and training of convicted prisoners is to encourage and assist them to lead a good and useful life.' I had learned the rule off by heart from a book on .... 'You've failed miserably in every respect.'

The Chief exploded: 'Do you want a murderer living next door to you? He spluttered.

The man had missed the point. No one saw the point. I didn't want him to be released, just be decategorised, so he could say goodbye to the dog.

Mortified, I composed a letter of resignation from the Board that evening, and handed it to the Chaplain the next day.

I was unrepentant. I had no sense of remorse.

*   *   *

'How come the prison a man is sent to is all arranged in advance of Board Decisions?' I spoke to Jack Goodman next morning, as I breezed into the open door of my cell. Jack placed some books back on a shelf which had collapsed overnight on to the floor of the Education Office. Then he watered a plant with a jam-jar full of water. 'The Board has absolutely no say, whatsoever, in where a prisoner is sent. It simply rubber-stamps decisions made elsewhere.'

'What are you asking me for?' Jack replied, as he sat down and smoothed his nails with the edge of a Swan Vestas matchbox. 'I'm just a prisoner here – one of the hoi polloi.'

'Well, you seem to understand the dynamics of this place better than anyone I've met before,' I said in a complimentary tone of voice.

'It's an apron and white gloves job isn't it.'

'Stop talking in riddles.'

'Freemasonry of course.' He responded as if this explained everything. He put a scrubbed finger to his lips as though all the world was listening through the open cell door.

I'd grown tired of his games.

'Elucidate please.'

He continued with his toilet, put his hands up for inspection and said: 'The Governors here, and key members of the Home Office, they're all masons. They make the decisions themselves, based upon their own criteria, and judge's recommendations.'

'Go on.'

Jack Goodman stifled a laugh. 'No, I'm serious.'

'I bet you are, but it's far from that simple I'm sure. The Board was drawn from the Departments, and democratic, of sorts, anyway. Everyone had their say.'

'So it seems on the surface. You might as well have just had the Governor and poor old Bradley there yesterday.'

As Goodman was speaking an inmate eerily put his head round the door. We both looked up. Jack gave him a cold stare and the man disappeared sheepishly.

He continued: 'Though there are some gestures towards democracy at the present time, the outcome is the same as it always was. It's just that some participants are unwittingly involved, that's all.'

The head appeared again. This time at the bottom of the door. I got up and shut it.

'Who can say that the Governor's decisions are not arrived at without the collaboration of other Departments nowadays? But the same old people are making the real decisions, as they always have done. It cuts two ways you see. It's good for the prison publicity machine that they're a more open government, and at the same time the inmates are put on a merry-go-round of visiting all these civilian faces.'

Before I allowed him to continue I scribbled some notes down on a pad.

'Going back to what we were saying just now. Think of this. If an inmate's a mason, or on the square as they say, he can expect privileges. A better prison job or an earlier release date. Masonry is responsible for the sending of some prisoners to the most unlikely places. A sinister plot you might say. As you've often told us in your current affairs evening class.'

'And you're on the square yourself then?' I muttered wearily.

'I wouldn't tell you that, would I.' He regarded me with suspicion, and I didn't know whether he was joking. 'But when I was in the West End in the Sixties, all the men from the Obscene Publications Squad were in the same lodge as a right bunch of villains. No conflict of loyalties there. What!'

I declined to carry on the conversation until I had given it more thought.

'By the way,' I said, breathless with relief, and victory in my voice, 'I resigned the Board.'

'Good for you. You've only been chasing your tail anyway. Now you know you're not so indispensable after all. You realise your contribution came to nothing. It must come as a shock. What!'

There was a moment's silence.

'Now you can get on with some real work.'

'What do you mean, real work?' I heckled him combatively, annoyed at this new presumption. I eyed Jack Goodman unenthusiastically.

'You don't want to get stuck in this dump forever.' Jack gushed. 'You're wasted here in this hellhole. Get out there. Make something of yourself. You'll rot here. The Board meeting should have brought it home to you.'

Jack Goodman's face went stern. 'You don't want to be a Sixties leftover, disillusioned with the Eighties, now do you?'

I thought for a moment, and was guilty with myself that apathy had taken over my youthful aspirations.

'Write a book. Do some real investigative journalism and research. You'll make your name that way,' Jack harried me further. 'The world I come from is full of interesting material for books. I'll give you the codes and disguises you'll need to get by. Call yourself by another name. Everyone else does it. I don't know anyone in the acting or business world for that matter, who doesn't have an alias or two. All the world's a stage. Get out there and get on it.'

VOYAGE AND RETURN

I looked up and stared for a moment through the bars of my cell. I felt nervous and caged. I thought of the possibilities of getting more material for some great work of criminology or other. The world I lived in was restricted and perfunctory in its own way. I had exhausted it, like one does when squeezing a ripe orange. Jack Goodman was right.

Jack broke my momentary silence.

'I'll make it easier for you.' He took out a clean sheet of A4 paper from the pile on the desk, and tore it in half. He wrote a few sentences down, folded it several times, and stapled both ends.

'Here. Go to my Club, on the first floor of a building in Dean Street, Soho. It's got a narrow pavement entrance and it's up a flight of stairs. Go up the stairs and hand it to the guy who sits just inside the door on a bar-stool. I can't remember the bloke's name.

'What is this place?' I broke in.

'It's a drinking club. Just one room. Always full. I used to go there in the Sixties, when a woman ran the place. I think it started after the War for late-night drinkers. Artistic clientele. You know, painters like Francis Bacon, and actors?'

I didn't, but I nodded. I'd never heard of Bacon, and thought it was one of Jack's jokes - as in, save my bacon.

'Don't be afraid of the bloke on the door. Front him up.' Jack always talked as if a knuckle sandwich would be on the menu at a moment's notice. 'He's a foul-mouthed, belligerent bastard, a brandy-marinated barman. Give him the note and he'll put you straight.' Jack winked. I pulled a Cheshire cat smile. Time for a monkey, or even a pony.

*   *   *

Up the rickety stairs I trudged, round the dogleg to the top. I pushed open the door of the shebeen. Sure enough, the gatekeeper sat inside the door on a high stool; a man with a big, pock-marked nose and a grey beard. Knowing that I was new he asked who had introduced me, and where was my proposer. I just handed him Jack's note. He looked at it, tore it up, and threw it into the waste bin on the other side of the bar.

'I'll have a large ding dong,' he declared, 'and get one for the barman.'

Very soon, it was another short and another. I raced to keep up. All the while he said nothing to me, but kept conversation with a litany of the club's regulars. I stood there in my new disguise and tried to look at if I fitted in. I had ditched my waist coat and jacket style of dress for something more casual; more like someone who merged in, so I figured. These were clothes that didn't smell of prison; that dusty, raw, cabbage smell, the smell of decayed brickwork and disinfectant. Despite all that, it made me feel out of place, in thought, if not in fact. After an hour I'd drunk enough and had enough. I scrambled down the rickety stairs.

Next day I told Jack Goodman there was no contact of any sort. He stopped and looked at me perplexed.

Some weeks later the phone rang. It was from a girl named Pat.

'You're to meet me outside Wheeler's on Old Compton Street. I'll know you. You'll know me,' The phone slammed down.

'Where are we going?' I turned to Pat, and looked down at her patent leather, four inch heels, as she teetered along, and gave a furtive glance at her bum, one capable of stirring the emotions.

Pat looked down at the figure beside her for she must have been over six feet tall.

'To see Michelle dear.'

Clearly Pat was for business, not a temporary intimacy that couldn't commit itself to friendship.

'I know, but where, as in place?' I reiterated.

'Mayfair dear. We'll walk through Soho. No need to take a taxi.'

A mild Friday night and Soho was humming with life, even though it was late November. An incoming tide of football supporters had arrived in town early, ready for Saturday's big match. They were searching for the action, for some sex and the forbidden. If they could find it, that is.

The lights of Berwick Street Market were wild and inviting. We headed for Berkeley Square. Jones Street was a little street on the north side of the square. Pat marched up to a large black door and pressed a buzzer on the wall. No answer. She rang again. A voice croaked on an intercom.

'It's me. Pat. Open up,' was the sombre reply in the dark.

'You'll have to wait a mo darling. I'm not free,' Michelle's voice laughed wickedly through the miniature speaker.

Pat swore under her breath and went in the road to look up at the building.

'Lights on all right,' she muttered petulantly.

We both stood patiently waiting for ten minutes or more. Pat couldn't wait for a cigarette. She lit up a Gouloise and sighed deeply.

'What do I say to Michelle?' I asked.

'Whatever you like. Play it by ear. I'm only here to introduce you. Just relax. Stop being tense.' Pat straightened my shoulders. It made me feel relaxed, comfortable even.

Pat said: 'Michelle's a lovely girl.'

'Just introduce me as a friend of a friend.'

Pat nodded understandingly.

The buzzer on the door signalled that it was opening. We walked into the carpeted lobby and to the stairs. Our entrance was as smooth as geese in flight.

LIVING ON GOLD TIME

'Only two landings.' Pat threw the words back, and gave a premeditated wriggle as she climbed the stair.

Michelle was at the door of the flat.

'Hi! This is Bob. A friend of a friend. We're just passing through. Thought we'd pop in, ' Pat said confidently.

Inside Michelle poured two scotch and sodas and we sat in the lounge. The curtains were velvet drapes. The carpet was probably Persian, and the chaise longue smelt of new leather.

'Bloody Arabs,' Michelle burst out suddenly. 'They always want their money's worth. And more besides.' She pulled on a cigarette and tilted her head sideways and upwards, so the smoke eased itself away from her head.

Pat smiled. I smiled along with her.

Michelle was small and petite, with Chinese eyes and jet black hair. She had a regal, even saintly presence. Her good looks were slightly exotic with a touch of vulnerability. Sensing the direction of my gaze, and in anticipation of a question, Michelle remarked: 'I know, I'm half Chinese. Dad was Hong Kong Chinese, Mum's French.'

Michelle got up and pirouetted around the centre of the room, then glided and sashayed to a standstill. A girl able to walk between the raindrops no doubt.

'Well. Have you come to see it then?' she said at last.

'What?' I asked innocently.

'My workshop of course.' Michelle assumed the standing gate of a pubescent schoolgirl, then relaxed the posture. 'Jack always sends his special friends round here. Morbid curiosity I suppose.'

'Spreading a little business, if you ask me,' came Pat's reply, giving Michelle a furtive glance.

'He's not like that, is he?' I asked, not knowing what the workshop was, or what it all meant.

'Course not,' replied Pat. 'But he does like people to get the real flavour of the night life.' Pat took off her shoes and unceremoniously rested her feet on a glass table. She was heavy-headed from a drinks party the night before, and it showed. 'Bob's just here to do some research. That's all,' she told Michelle assuringly.

'Not from Mr Plod, or the Dirty Tricks Department are you?' Michelle asked directly.

I grasped at some excuse and said: 'No, I'm a sociologist.'

'C'mon then,' Michelle said. Leading me through the dining room to a room at the back, she switched on the light. It was a sparse room and on one wall was a one-way mirror that looked through into another room that housed a few props. Michelle switched on the sound system and disappeared, leaving Pat and myself alone.

Very soon Michelle and a man, the main actors, entered the stage of the theatre.

'Who's this guy? I asked Pat.

'His name's Sebastian.'

'That his real name?'

'What do you think?'

'Who is he?

'Can't tell you that,' Pat said, irritated. 'Don't ask too many questions. It was difficult enough getting you in here. Watch and learn. Take mental notes and write it down later.'

— The man poured himself a drink, emptying the contents of the bottle liberally into the tumbler.

'Got any more brandy, Babes? It's all run out.' He shouted out the words for Michelle to hear in the shower in a recess in the room. There was no audible reply, so he broke open the seal on a bottle of Scotch and mixed it with the brandy.

Michelle approached him silently from behind in her bathrobe. Her thick, black oriental hair, done up in a China-doll style bob, bounced on her shoulders. She had a diminutive but perfectly apportioned body. She was only just over five feet tall. The high cheek bones sat under sad, but inquisitively drooping eyes, that seemed to fall downwards on to an expanse of pure, unblemished, white cheek. Putting one bangled hand on each of his arms, she said: What'll it be today, Sebbie my little baby?

The man winced a little.

'Just the usual, mistress of mine, but I want to take some stills if that's okay with you?'

Sebastian liked to play games when he was with Michelle. Every Monday, on the dot, he appeared at her door, ready for an afternoon of high jinks. She was as always, happy to oblige. That day, however, he wanted something quite different.

Quickly, Michelle pulled out of the little game and her brow furrowed.

'But I don't want any pictures appearing in any of those Continental mags again without my permission this time. Understand?' She emphasised the word, understand. Sebastian eyes her respectfully.

'And I want the cash for the four hours' work, now. Four hundred and fifty to you.'

Sebastian bartered in a tantrum, but eventually capitulated and handed her the money in large denomination notes. She kneeled over and counted it on the floor, then placed the folded wad in a drawer out of sight.

On a previous occasion the tight-fisted Sebastian had got her to fill in the Model Release Form, paid her a miserly fee, then sold the transparencies to a foreign buyer. The photograph of Michelle appeared in several soft-core magazines circulating in France and Spain. One unscrupulous person had even photo-montaged her head on to a hard-core video box cover.

Sebastian unilaterally resumed the little game: 'No mistress, the haughty Sebastian promises this time they're for domestic use only.' He said this in the most obsequious voice.

Turning away from her he went over to his case, dug into it and brought out a single lens reflex camera with a strap, and some unopened boxes of Ektachrome and FP4.

'Okay if I put these in the fridge?' he asked, holding up the film for her to see.

She was pacing about. 'Go right ahead,' she replied nonchalantly, 'put them in the oven if you want.'

She permitted a smile. 'Give it a break Sebbie. Just for a while.'

He waddled off to the kitchen at the back. He returned fingering the flap on the back of the camera while loading it with more film. He stood still, looked around the lounge, and at Michelle, then announced tartly: 'Fuck ... I've forgotten the red-head. You see I need a tungsten lamp.'

She appeared put out. 'What, no flash?'

'No, I don't want the subject bathed in light. I want shadow, you see.'

'The lamp's no problem,' she said confidently, 'There's a spare in my bedroom. Another punter left it by mistake.'

Sebastian visibly sighed with relief. He went off and humped it in, positioning the tripod legs in a corner of the room. He then directed the lamp on to his subject, before switching on.

'Sofa shots first. If that's all right with you?'

'It's fine,' Michelle said with one, brief nod, 'but what'll I wear? She said it with the devouring anxiety of the insecure.

He produced his version of a large smile, a sort of sideways leer.

'You choose. Whatever you like, but make it sexy. The customer wants a turn-on you see.'

She scampered off and returned in a low cut black silk bolero and a broad leather belt with a gold encrusted buckle pulled in tight around her narrow twenty one inch Chinese waist. A mini skirt tapered down to a pair of seamed, black tights and high-heeled stiletto shoes.

'You want me to strip off gradually, open-leg shots, that sort of thing?' she asked, enjoyably worried.

'I'll leave everything entirely up to you. I just want some good shots, suitable for a British magazine. Make it artistic like, that's the only proviso.'

'Got it,' Michelle answered with more confidence.

He took a series of thirty six exposures with Michelle on the sofa. She let the silk bolero open to reveal her small Chinese breasts, then sat back, parting her legs slightly to give a touching glimpse of her white knickers.

Sebastian began winding back the film.

'You'd look great with a bigger breasted woman fondling those tits,' he announced with ease. 'Pity, but next time perhaps.'

He resumed winding then said thoughtfully: 'Hang on, I need to reload.'

He wiped some of the sweat from his brow and hung his jacket on the door peg. Circular patches of sweat appeared under his arms, staining his green shirt a darker shade of green. The heat from the tungsten lamp was intense. When the film was reloaded he snapped the back of the camera shut.

'This time I want you to remain seated on the sofa but put your hand inside your knickers, then peel off a bit from the shoulder.'

Michelle smiled indulgently.

With legs apart and skirt up, she drew one hand up the inside of her leg until it reached her crotch. She gradually placed the well-manicured fingers inside the frilly cotton knickers so her hand formed a little pouch between her legs. The knickers now pressed firmly against the outline of her fingers.

'Hold it there,' he ordered. He took several shots from one pose. 'Keep in that pose, but head back slightly, and mouth open a bit. Lick your lips.' He was not entirely satisfied with the choice, and adjusted her clothing with her permission.

She had done this routine so many times before, for so many punters.

More shots.

'Slowly, don't move too fast,' he implored.

The model kept two steps in front of him and assumed another pose, then another. Sebastian reloaded again, releasing each roll of film, placing it in a pod, then taking a fresh roll from the fridge.

By now she was virtually naked apart from the stockings and the high heels.

'Got a riding crop?' Sebastian asked, turning off the tungsten lamp before resting on the arm of a chair.

She returned from another room with a leather riding crop and riding hat.

'These any good?' she asked helpfully.

He got up, short, plumpish and concerned, and inspected the crop, whacking it a couple of times on his thigh.

'Feels good anyway,' he said with a little change to his normal anxious expression. He inspected the hat.

'You can try this on to see what it looks like.'

Turning, he pointed to a wall. 'Use the white wall over there as background.

She stood against the wall in a provocative pose, while he went to the lamp and lifted it gently before repositioning it. He undid the wing nut and retightened the head in a different position so that the light would bounce off the ceiling. He opened the barn doors wider before switching it on.

'Perfect,' he said to himself. First he knelt down, then he took shots from other angles, taking breaths to steady the camera before pressing the shutter.

'I've got ten exposures left,' he announced in time, 'how about posing in front of the mirror?'

The model obeyed, lifting a long mirror to the wall and placing it down gently. She repositioned herself appropriately.

'Ready?'

'Ready,' she tweeted.

This time he lay on the floor and focused it on the high heeled shoes to take in their reflection in the mirror. The angle was more difficult because he had to avoid his own reflection. Like a beached walrus he rolled around the floor, painstakingly clicking the shutter on the camera until the film was all but used up.

Eventually he finished.

'That it?' she said with relief, standing still. 'Can I rest now?'

'Fine. We've got some good pics there luv,' he said proudly. 'I'll use the black and white later.'

Michelle retreated and returned fully covered in a dressing gown, but still sporting the miniature size four and half high heels.

'Now for the other thing,' he chuckled, while making a face.

'Hold on a while,' she implored, poring herself a hasty Coke.

After a rest for her and a rapid march up and down the room for him, he said smugly: 'I'd like you in the black PVC outfit you had on before, and the long, black elbow-length gloves, the black bodice and the flaired PVC mini-skirt, and those lovely white knickers.' He seemed to be reading a list from his mind. 'And those black high heels again.'

Michelle emerged at the door kitted out according to Sebastian's instructions. In one hand was a riding crop. As she moved the PVC emitted a sticky, crinkly sound like sellophane being removed from a box of chocolates. Sebastian was naked on the floor, on all fours in doggy pose.

'Did I tell you to get undressed?' she yelled out at him in an uncharacteristically fierce voice.

'No mistress, no. I'm sorry mistress but ...'

'Little boys should only do as they are told, shouldn't they?' She went over and prodded the considerable white rump of the cowering man with the crop.

He said ingratiatingly: 'Yes mistress.'

'And what do little boys get when they are naughty, and they don't do as they are told?'

'A good beating, mistress.'

'Are there any reasons why you should not be given a good thrashing?'

'No mistress,' came the weak reply.

Michelle raised the crop and thrashed the white rump two or three times. Small weals rose along the surface and Sebastian scampered forward.

'Come back here at once.' The voice was high and shrill.

'Yes mistress.' His pitiful head looked round the corner of the sofa.

'Here, I say.'

'Yes mistress.'

Slowly he advanced on all fours towards her legs which were parted, the feet pointing firmly down into the shoe, the muscles tightening on the calves, the fierce legs like two straight sides of an isosceles triangle. Approaching, he saw the wet, white knickers twinkling beneath the skirt.

'You deserve a thoroughly good thrashing,' she commanded.

'Yes, please mistress ... please,' pleaded the voice to his dominatrix.

She leaned over his back and attacked the rump with the flailing crop again and again until her little arm was tired from the angle of the blows. The rump reddened appreciably.

'Lick my shoes.'

Sebastian obliged, simpering compliantly, sliding his tongue around the smooth surface, first backwards then forwards.

'Kiss the soles.'

He changed position to oblige her. She raised one leg slightly, and he kissed the underside of the shoe, while lying on his back and cupping the shoe between his hands.

She stood astride his prostrate body again as he looked up between her legs, begging for her chastisement.

'Do you deserve another thrashing?'

'Yes mistress, I do.'

The crop came down hard upon the flabby patches of his chest and stomach. Michelle then lifted her leg up and placed the point of the stiletto heel lightly upon his chest, drawing it along the abdomen.

'Is Sebbie a bad boy?'

'He certainly is … he is,' he said enthusiastically.

With that she rested the weight of her leg on his chest and pressed the stiletto down harder. The slave yelped with pleasure. Both his hands came up between her legs, the fingers wide, twitching in a wave motion.

'And now what does the naughty Sebbie want?'

'He pointed up towards her knickers.

'And will Sebastian stop being naughty then?'

'He will, he will.'

She moved aside and slipped her white frilly knickers down, stepping out of them with grace and precision. She resumed the astride position over the man's body, while holding the treat aloft.

'Is this what the naughty boy wants?'

Sebastian stretched up with both hands.

'Please … please.'

She dropped the prize towards his face and he hurriedly stuffed it into his mouth —

*   *   *

'What the hell was that all about?' I asked Jack, who was thumbing through his worn copy of the *I Ching*.

'Make of it what you want,' he replied secretively.

VOYAGE AND RETURN

We both laughed together as we were prone to do
'What did you get, some SM?'

'Something like that. That brass's not wet behind the ears,
but she certainly can make one wet between the legs,' I
joked.

'Didn't you believe me when I told you what it could be
like?' Jack asked. 'It's a theatre, not of war, but of love.
These people are sexually creative. Polymorphous perversity
it's called.'

He sounded like an entry from Krafft-Ebing's
Psychopathia Sexualis.

Some time later I decided, off my own bat, to go and see Pat
at one of her favourite Soho haunts.

As I entered I saw Pat's dominating presence
overshadowing the small group of drinkers at the bar. She
was a young and spectacular blonde, hair long and gleaming.
Generous, both as to bosom and gossip, she stood there,
giving pleasure to the pleasure-seekers, serving them with
automatic ease. The enigmatic smile, and the flowing body
lines, in a beautifully cut suit and creamy cleavage,
somehow appeased even the most unmanageable of the
Club's clientele. Pat was honest in all the minor ways and
unscrupulous in major. I observed her from the Club
entrance and realised how the part she played was tailored to
the visual collage of that underworld shebeen; a shebeen full
of thieves, hoisters and ponces. Pat could pass muster as the
warden of some social gas chamber. She could quite happily
load people onto a metaphorical slow train from whence
there was no return. My visual fantasy was heaped on to the
already well stocked and overflowing pessimism I felt at that
particular time.

'What have we got here then?' Pat said smartly, consulting
her memory, discreetly clearing her throat, lowering the
voice for the sales pitch and softening the natural bossiness
of her face.

'It's me. Don't you remember,' I replied, with melancholy pride and prompting obligingly.

'Suppose we've got to mind our P's and Q's now that … what do you call yourself … a sociopath, no sorry a sociol … ogist, is back in town?' Pat beamed with smugness and satisfaction to the amusement of the drinkers sitting with their noses in their glasses.

I took the banter with the sort of good humour one has to show if you are steeped in bar-room patois. Nevertheless, I gave an embarrassed laugh.

'I'll have a double whisky. Put it on the slate.'

'No you won't. You'll have a single. I'll have a treble. You owe me that. And more.' she snapped back.

I sat on a stool at the corner of the bar. Pat tilted her head over in mild conspiracy, out of earshot of the other drinkers.

'Michelle likes you. What is it this time … the workshop … a.k.a. the torture chamber?'

'fraid so.'

*   *   *

In a different location, at a different time of day, Michelle escorted me to a room and switched on the light.

'It's my torture chamber,' proclaimed Michelle proudly.

'My God!' The world inside the Sunday paper sex scandals was coming to life before my very eyes. Michelle was an upmarket brass and I was fascinated by this revelation.

'Too much, isn't it?' Michelle said, aware of my surprise. The room was equipped with what one might euphemistically call gym equipment. An exercise bike was in the corner, whips, chains, handcuffs and tawses were attached to the wall. In a locked glass case were rubber face masks with zipped mouthpieces and numerous gags and other types of restraints. They were props for the theatre. A rocking horse occupied the centre of the room. A thin mattress lay near a wall above which were exercise bars. Near the ceiling, and suspended from it, was a harness capable of supporting a human body.

I craned my neck up towards the leather straps and thongs. 'What's that for?'

'Well you might ask,' said Michelle. 'That's for a few of my special slaves. It's the modern equivalent of the Swinburne paddle for chastisement and correction. One Lord, the big knob, bless his little heart, just loves to get up there and stick his cock through that leather thong. I then give him a few swipes with this.' Michelle handed me a bull whip. I made a few feeble attempts to crack it. 'But that's not enough usually,' she carried on, 'so I get my maid to come through the door, and when he sees her approach he usually spunks all over the room.' Michelle made a flowing arc with her hand as if to indicate the spunk trail. 'A round of applause, don't you think, for a job well done eh!? ... Dirty beast. I never get fucked, you see. My customers prefer to hang from the ceiling or suck my cunt; if I let them, that is'

'You get paid well for all this?' I asked, with deliberate naïvity this time.

'Handsomely,' Michelle drew closer. 'Four hundred pound for an afternoon session with a Lord, would you believe. I'm your genuine deluxe, money-making machine'

Michelle drew me closer. 'I had one punter, a Labour Member of Parliament, who makes us whip each other, my maid and me, while he stands there wanking. The harder we do it, the more money he throws down on the floor. My maid's arse was red and blue. Poor cow. A road map of red lines'

Not knowing whether to believe her or not, as lies tripped off their tongues with the ease and lightness of birdsong, I mentally calculated the attractions of the work compared with teaching, and wondered about the inversion of human values. I then turned my attention to the centre of the room.

'What's that rocking horse for?'

'Oh! the horse. It's for the special treatment.' Michelle giggled and tossed her dark, black hair away from her eyes.

'You see, I get my maid to dress up as a little girl.'

'Then …?'

'Come closer.'

Michelle pointed to a dildo that was loosely fastened to the horse. She advanced and adjusted it so that the organ sat upright on the horse's back. Underneath, she fastened the clips until it was secure.

'My maid sits astride the horse and inserts the dildo in her cunt. She gently rocks back and forth.'

I wanted more: 'And so?'

'The client, one in particular that is,' Michelle giggled again, 'whips the maid with a cat-o-nine tails.'

'Bit sadistic, isn't it?'

Michelle was affronted and drew herself upright.

'Not my fault that these public schoolboys, and girls mark you, love giving and getting a good thrashing is it? Don't forget the maid comes off too.'

I was aware of my indiscretion and apologised. I then wandered around the chamber oblivious to Michelle. Nothing had quite prepared me for this. A whole world of sexual creativity came before my eyes. Jack Goodman was right all along about the possible uniqueness of these experiences. As a sociologist I had simulated detachment in the past. Now, that detachment had to be qualified, to comprehend fully the implication of the new findings. My thoughts filled me with excitement and anticipation at what I might find on my journey into the unknown.

'Another drink?' Michelle asked, at last.

'As you wish,' I said airily. The words were distant; away from my innermost thoughts. Just what type of world do these people come from, and the people who frequented that room?

I slid the dildo from the horse's back and sat on the seat, gently rocking to and fro. Michelle was away for an inordinately long time.

When she returned she did so hurriedly.

'I've got an unexpected punter,' she said jerkily, 'you're welcome to stay if you want, but you'll have to make yourself scarce, or something.'

I nodded approvingly.

'Go in there. You won't be seen, and it leads out into the lounge.'

Michelle pointed to some curtains that stretched from ceiling to floor. I parted them and stepped behind into a long box room. The other end had a door which opened into a similar room and into a lounge in which I saw Pat sitting. Michelle disappeared and I repositioned myself so that I had a full view of the room through the gap in the curtain.

A woman of statuesque proportions made her entrance into the chamber. She had strikingly large grey eyes, a long, thin neck and luminous make-up. Her clothes were chic: tailored suit, good shoes, neat felt hat at a becoming angle. An elegant, mature, sophisticated knock-out – thinking man's crumpet, at a push. From looks alone she was highly independent and self-contained. The woman placed her leather briefcase down beside the rocking horse and detached the hat from her hair. She marched up and down, hands on hips, stopping in front of a mirror for a while and turning to the side to admire her appearance. Michelle slid through the door and the two exchanged medium hello smiles. Michelle wore a skin tight rubber suit and high heels. I moved from side to side behind the curtain to get a wider angle of vision. I was expecting a man to appear, but non did.

Suddenly, unexpectedly, the two women engaged in provocative name-calling.

'Don't order me around,' the woman demanded, 'that's enough from you.'

'Don't you order me around either,' Michelle gushed, 'you're asking me for a damn good caning.'

'I'd like to see you try it.'

Michelle moved away and undid the straps on a long flogging bench, while the woman reluctantly and aggressively stripped off to her bra and knickers.

When Michelle had finished loosening the straps, they both engaged further in their quarrelsome dispute. Michelle marched over to a cupboard and returned with what I recognised as a flexible school cane.

'Get down,' she commanded.

'No I won't.'

'Down, I say.'

The woman meekly bent over in her humiliation, first kneeling on a pillow, then splaying her arms out so that Michelle could fix the straps securely to them. The victim pretended resistance and wriggled. Michelle administered the first blow with the cane across her buttocks. She yelled out at the stroke. The cane came down again and again and the woman resisted by wriggling her backside in the frenzy of the punishment.

Acting or not, I could stand it no more, and left the small room through the door, the sound of the victim's pleas and aggression ringing in my ears.

Pat was still sitting in the lounge applying nail varnish to her fingers, intermittently pulling on a cigarette, and making running repairs to her face.

'Do you know what's going on in there?' I directed the question to Pat.

'No dear. But I can guess' Her emollient, but nevertheless foxy eyes, caught my gaze.

'Some woman is getting her arse thrashed,' I stammered, 'and from another woman.'

'Think nothing of it,' Pat said, glancing at me forgivingly, 'she's a delicious masochist you see.'

I didn't see, and needed further explanations.

VOYAGE AND RETURN

'Well,' Pat drew in a deep breath. 'It's pretend, all play, a ritualized acting out of fantasies. In your terms, as women move more strongly into their recently won sexual freedoms, predictably they get domination fantasies of spanking and bondage more and more, either as active or passive partners. The woman in there,' Pat pointed a decorated finger at the wall, 'she's in a really high-powered job, so the more fully liberated she is in the work situation, the more she needs to achieve a counterbalance to it in her sexual life. Those who have emerged from being under male domination crave to return to it in bed, or wherever. See now?'

'No, I don't see,' I said candidly.

'C'mon, stop being so uptight. At least it's more civilised than the masochists who want to be dragged around the floor by their hair, or the masochistic men who eat used condoms.'

Pat explained with analytical superiority and mimickery : 'It's like one who melds into forgiving states and who experiences the cathartic release of confession. So there.'

*   *   *

Several weeks passed and I had put to the back of my mind thoughts about leaving the job which I had nurtured after the Bradley fiasco. I still held enough conviction to work on my research for a book; not one, however, that would give me entrée into one of London's fashionable literary salons. I had made some headway with preparations for the exhibition of prisoner's art. Paul Nerrity, Kenny Bruce, Ian Bradley and Ron Gifford had taken the plan to heart and had gathered a dossier of all the available work by inmates on the Wing. There were numerous paintings, a large portfolio of which had been provided by Jack Goodman. Model caravans and battleships made out of matchsticks were promised by several prisoners, as well as carefully sculptured cigarette tins, works of embroidery, and ingenious models made from scrap material and the casual detritus of the prison. Things that would elsewhere be useless were scavenged for to make exhibits – wood and card, drawing pins, containers, nails, twists of wire and odd bits of string. Two men were commissioned to draw cartoons and submit calligraphy. Even burnt wood from the pyrography class was added to the list of contributions.

'A champion idea,' someone had called it, although they stood to be convinced that I could pull it off.

I got a friend who had a small gallery to see whether the paintings could be sold. They could, without too much difficulty. Models were a bit more problematic, however, but I approached a shop which promised to buy the best work and sell it on their Saturday Market stall, provided it was of sufficiently high standard, that is.

The biggest hurdle was yet to come. I had figured that if the prison authorities would sanction an exhibition of art, competent judges could be selected from the Prison Visitors Association to give their approval for further developments of the scheme. The Burnbake Trust was already buying works of art from prisoners and crediting prisoners' private cash with part of the proceeds. I had calculated that the leap from the exhibition to an outright sale of the work to the public would not be too great a challenge.

Now that the concept was crystallized, and the men sufficiently fired by the idea, the first step was to get Prison Wing Management to give the go-ahead.

'I'd like to put on an exhibition of prisoners' art in the Wing, to encourage the creative talent that we have here,' I explained to the Wing Governor, who seemed to be cocooned in his office, sheltering from the incontinence of an over-regulated prison system.

'Let me get this correct,' he said discouragingly, getting up from a chair, at last ready to go. He went to his jacket hanging on the door. 'You want to exhibit these things in the Wing?'

I attempted to avoid any possible contact with his eyes for fear of a refusal, so I looked sideways out of the window.

'Yes,' I said.

Without turning his head he said: 'But where?'

I organised my thoughts before answering. 'There is so much room on the ground floor landing, that they could be put on trestle tables or mounted upright on display stands.'

The Governor put on his jacket and adjusted his tie in the mirror. 'Would it not obstruct the free passage of men and interfere with the arrangements to serve meals?' he said taughtly.

'They could be placed where they would not inconvenience anyone.'

'I am sure.' He made the final adjustments to his tie before going on,' but it's not possible for security reasons.'

I went icily cold. I had a horrible foreboding of what was coming next, but continued, nevertheless, to counter the man's in-built antagonism to anything that disturbed the custodial requirements of good order and discipline.

Eventually, under pressure, he relented. 'Okay, I'll give you the provisional go-ahead, but you must approach the Wing Chief and the Wing Security Officer for their approval first.'

This was more difficult than it sounded. These were men who didn't bend compliantly to any possible wind of change. Admittedly, they had their own and larger fish to fry than mine.

'But it won't interfere with anyone,' I pleaded to the Wing Chief. After much remonstrating he finally gave his approval.

Jones the Security Officer shook his head so negatively, it almost left his red, beefy face behind. He laughed, and settled back comfortably in his seat. Here was a man who seethed against the world – a true Lucifer. 'You what!'

'An exhibition of art in the Wing.'

LIVING ON GOLD TIME

'But we need all the paint we can get for renovating the cells,' he said sarcastically.

My impatience flashed. 'You know as well as I do, that our Department supplies all the materials.'

'They'll be defaced by other prisoners.'

'No they won't. They take pride in their work.'

'You're kidding! We'll have all sorts of problems with stolen material. Besides, they're not allowed such things in their cells.'

Jones could smell a Trojan Horse at fifty yards. He must have visualised it coming to the Wing. He imagined that out of the belly of this beast, and on cue, the world and his wife would pour; mostly the shirkers and malingerers at that.

I scanned the list of banned articles which Jones handed me. Most I had seen in their cells anyway.

'Basically, Bob, this could pose a security problem. I'm not putting the damper on it, but I would personally give the No, to this one. Mind you, it's not up to me. It'll have to go before the Wing Management Committee tomorrow.'

It did too. Much to my relief they all agreed, as long as they were given the details in advance.

My small group of men were more ecstatic than ever. Jack Goodman kept his reservations to himself. Later he confided to Kenny Bruce. He dare not venture to say it to anyone else, but he thought the visual image in particular, and hence creative art in general, was the only true revolutionary image, and for that reason the authorities detested and abhorred it.

Nerrity, Bruce and Goodman had filled the little Education Office with exhibits they had collected from the prison Wing. They had beavered away, bribing and cajoling the inmates to part with their treasures. Ron Gifford had applied that bit of extra pressure to be sure that every man felt that his efforts were for a good cause. Many prisoners gave willingly to public charities and appeals for the starving in

Ethiopia. They would give towards a life support machine for a hospital as atonement for the wrongs they had committed. But curiously, when it came to the Exhibition, some men could not see their giving as a way of aiding their own rehabilitation.

It was almost impossible to get into the Education Office for exhibits. Paintings and matchstick models were everywhere. Jack Goodman offered some of his best work, and was, not surprisingly, a bit contemptuous of those paintings that were mere copies of other works.

'Too many haywains and horses heads, 'he said in a ludicrously puffed-up and disparaging way, while casting himself in the most flattering light. 'Not enough creative work emanating from their own minds.'

His self-preening was ignored by everyone, for once.

There were several categories of work on display. Monies were set aside from Department funds to offer prizes to each category. No work worthy of commendation would go without a reward for effort.

Matchstick caravans, boats and galleons bristling with guns and turrets were willingly offered. One man had made a fairground ferris wheel. A number of tobacco tins saw the light of day. They were carefully concealed with matchsticks and painted, or inlaid, on the lids. There were one or two dolls and soft toys, an outline map of a futuristic home, pencil drawings and paintings on tiles.

I had encouraged the men to put prices on their work. On the whole these were rather modest, but some were well beyond their true value.

The original plan the men had formulated for selling prisoners' art with the hope of turning it into a prison industry were abandoned. The practicality of getting prisoners to produce work in sufficient quantity seemed an insurmountable hurdle, however. At the very least the Exhibition, and accompanying publicity and goodwill, seemed like a springboard for future development. My deal with my friend, that the best work could be sold to the public, cheered up the little band of organisers no end. If all did not turn out for the best, at least it had been an uplifting experience for everyone.

The feverish activity did not go unnoticed by the prison officers. While some admired it, a few of them sought to pour cold water on the project from the very start. Those responsible for security raised all manner of objections at every move. Having the full support of the Wing Governor helped, but there were secret fears, mainly given expression behind closed doors, that the inmates were running the prison, and that was not a good thing. Petty rules and regulations were discussed as a way of impeding the activities of civilian members of staff.

Thankfully, a date for the Exhibition was fixed. Judges had been contacted and Gate Passes and clearance duly processed. The judging panel consisted of a Senior Lecturer from an Art College, a member of the Board of Visitors, the Prison Chaplain, and representatives from Prison Industries, the Psychology Department and the Education Department. The Prison Governor agreed to preside over the panel.

All exhibits were numbered and labelled, and a small catalogue of the work distributed to interested parties. On the day before the Exhibition, tables and boards were arranged conveniently on the prison landing. All exhibits were locked away in the Education Office, ready for presentation on the big day. My class of five were beside themselves with joy. Only Ian Bradley felt despondent, as he was still smarting from the treatment meted out to him at the hands of the Training Board. I had to revive his flagging spirit with large doses of encouragement. Bradley remained visibly depressed and there was little I could do to retrieve him from the depths of despair. Melancholy already muted his face. He agreed to participate out of loyalty rather than personal commitment.

Jack Goodman, noting my higher spirits, commandeered me into one of his I Ching sessions.

'Time you had your future read,' he said.

I reluctantly agreed, as he promised that all the difficulties he had in the past had been ironed out using coins.

Jack sat down at the desk.

'Got three coins?' he asked.

I put my two-pence pieces on the desk. 'Anything else?' I said sarcastically, for I was far from convinced about divination.

'Right. Now throw down the three coins together. Each throw will give us a line. Heads, or even numbers count as Yin, with value two, and tails, odd numbers, count as Yang, with value three. From this the character of the line is obvious, since there are four combinations of Yin and Yang possible, having values four to nine'

I threw the three coins together six times and got one Yang, two Yins and three Yangs, which Jack assured me was hexagram Twenty Six, Da Chu or 'The taming power of the great.'

'So what!' I said. 'What the hell does it all prove?'

'Wait can't you!'

Jack picked up the I Ching for the interpretation and started to translate: 'This is what you've thrown: First line Yang: There is danger. It is wise to halt. Second line Yang: The carriage has its axles removed.'

'What does that mean, for Christ's sake?' I protested.

'Fucking wait, will you. Let me continue with the hexagram. Third line Yang: Fine horses surge forward. It's favourable to persevere. A well-drilled chariot stands guard. It's favourable to advance. Fourth line Yin: The young bull is restrained by a horn guard. There will be good fortune.'

I visibly brightened with relief, although I found the symbols in the interpretation antiquated.

'Fifth line Yin: The gelded boar does not use its tusks. Auspicious.'

'Thank god for that. Better still.'

'Top line Yang: You are on heaven's road. A blessed state.'

'That's as it maybe,' I said, reluctant to please the aspiring Buddhist master, but deep down perplexed. 'But I don't believe any of it.'

'You'd better,' Jack protested. 'Just wait and see.'

He shot out in a blur through the open door.

At least the divination game worked this time.

*   *   *

The big day of the exhibition dawned. The judges arrived on time and swarmed around in the Education Block outside the prison Wings. Coffee and sandwiches were handed out, and a general feeling of anticipation pervaded the small throng. I introduced myself to the guests and gave a short speech about the motives behind the project. A junior Governor suddenly came in, his face ashen white.

'What now?' I asked half-heartedly, expecting some minor problems over breakages.

'It's off,' he replied sheepishly.

Several voices chanted: 'But why?'

'There's a prison 'stand down.' That means no one can enter or exit the prison. Apparently Prison Security says that several pairs of scissors have gone missing and they fear someone will be stabbed,' he explained in a rush, before turning to me, 'they're blaming us for allowing inmates to have them in the first place.'

I fell back into a chair. 'They've done it deliberately. They've got an axe to grind. It's a conspiracy to thwart us.' I addressed the junior Governor: 'Can't you get it postponed until another day then?'

'I'll try.' There was a touch of bitterness, alloyed with nervousness, in his voice. 'I'll see the Prison Number One Governor now.' He loped off in the direction of his office.

Fifteen minutes later he returned, more agitated than ever. 'Prison Security wants it cancelled completely,' he said woodenly. 'They consider it a threat to good order and discipline and it should never have gone this far.'

'Sod them,' I howled, conjuring up some confidence from my own voice. 'More like carefully crafted callousness.'

I rushed down the corridor to the Number One Governor's office and burst in. The office was plushly comfortable, rather than functional, with a busily patterned carpet, several armchairs and many framed photographs on the wall. An immaculately dressed man, of easy charm and perfect English manners, sat beside a desk.

'Can I help you?' he said offhandedly, but not unexpectedly, with upturned face.

'Listen ... Sir,' the word, Sir, stuck in the back of my throat. 'You're supposed to be one of our judges, and yet you've let them sabotage the Exhibition with some cock and bull story about scissors being used as weapons.'

The Governor offered me a seat, then stood against the window, easing himself down slightly on to the radiator.

'I must get you to understand that it is a joint decision made after advice from the Prison Security Officer, and after consultation with the Prison Management Committee.'

His statement was typically elliptical, and he refused to explain the matter further. 'That's all I can say at this juncture. I must add, that we are not opposed in any way to your project, and we give it our full backing, but unfortunately the security aspect is too great a risk for it to go ahead in future.'

'Then why has it gone this far,' I wanted to know.

The Governor's eyes scrutinized me carefully, then they travelled through the window to the sun-dusted air outside, before he said: 'I'm not ducking the question, but you place too much faith in these men, and in the end they will let you down. Take my advice, there's only so much trust you can place in the criminal classes.' He paused as if to let me catch up with what he was saying. 'Psychologically they don't operate like you or I. That means you must have loyalty to the right people.'

'What then of all the talk of rehabilitation and reform?' I asked, 'How can you change men if you don't offer them an alternative, improve their self esteem, encourage them in socially useful ways of occupying their time?'

'All this is laudable, and we all support the philosophy of Rule 1, but the practicalities of managing the regime under such stressful and overcrowded conditions, means there are priorities to be considered. We haven't even got integral sanitation yet. That's a first priority before we can give away good-will. Besides, I've got the expectations of my uniformed staff to consider. The bottom line says civilian staff are here because the basic grade officer has the good-will to accept them unequivocally.'

The Governor talked fast, lagging behind his own breath. I was flabbergasted, wrestling with my own pain threshold. I felt I was indulging in some ham-fisted search for the holy grail.

'I'm afraid I don't agree,' I said.

'I didn't expect you to,' he said, glancing with dry understanding at my face, and taking a gentle glide down the thick carpeted hallway of his comfortable mental apartment.

'All I can say, is that I think you are making the men worse, contributing to crime, and turning those men into a threat to the public.'

The Governor's composure subsided slightly and he grasped the radiator lightly with both hands. I sensed that my protestations were useless, falling on deaf ears. This was the signal for me to go. I made towards the door. As I opened it he said acidly: 'Take the day off, go and get drunk or something.'

VOYAGE AND RETURN

There was an element of good riddance in this statement. I left for the lavatory, washed my hands, and stared long and hard into the mirror – why was I there, why was I punishing myself, why was I running up the down escalator?

*   *

Preparing for the Current Affairs evening class was difficult: a labour of love, more disagreeable than of late. The visitors to the Exhibition had left, promising to meet at some future date. The anticipation of the previous day had dispersed. The clock was not speeding up but slowing down; the same numbing routine, the same deadening torment. The missing scissors had been found, the guilty processed with a visit to the punishment block. The exhibits in the little Wing Education Office remained in place, ready for distribution back to their makers. A few hard hearts were well satisfied with the day's work. They had behaved as if some unwanted fresh wind had blown through their fetid swamp.

Cautiously, I arrived ten minutes late for the class, looking rested and cleaned. Two figures sat poised at their desks – Jack Goodman and Kenny Bruce were there.

'Where is everyone?' I asked fearfully.

'They're not coming.' Kenny mysteriously beamed as if sucking in every detail of a dimming situation. He could afford a little humour at least. 'They won't be coming again. They blame you. They feel you've let them down.'

I fumbled with the mucky residue of my own thoughts, and said: 'It's hardly my fault. It was a security problem.'

Kenny was uncharacteristically forthright, adding gritty reality to the waking nightmare. 'That's not the way they see it. They think you led us all on, raising hopes, making promises and trying to achieve the impossible.' Something like regret touched his mouth.

I put Kenny on the spot: 'Do you believe that?' I was beginning to feel martyred.

'It doesn't matter,' Goodman inveighed, being a more shrewd, but morbid judge of character and human weakness. 'Everything assumes unmanageable proportion in here anyhow. The lesson to be learned is that you can't do anything for anyone until they are capable of helping themselves. The screws are cunts, anyway. You did your best Bob. Trouble is, prisoners don't think for themselves.'

'Leave me out, will you,' Kenny said in a grating voice.

'I'm not including you.' He gave Kenny a glazed look. 'Point is, where do we go from here?'

'Nowhere. I think,' I reflected.

Goodman said: 'I think you're right. At least on matters of prison reform. It was a noble gesture on your part, Bob. There are, however, other battles to be won.'

Any further attempt on my part to pour balm on the raw nerves of my remaining charges, failed. I turned to the board, picked up some chalk, and wrote in quotes – Philosophers have only interpreted the world; the point, however, is to change it.

'That's the topic for tonight's discussion,' I said dryly.

*   *   *

I took a week's leave after my ruckus with the Management. It was planned as a recuperative break, away from the humdrum and the status quo to a place that allowed for a liberty of spirit. I could imagine those I left behind having unsuppressed smirks of satisfaction on their faces. Upon my return I discovered that the 'old firm' had been 'ghosted out.' The five prisoners on my Current Affairs class were no more. For me it was adios, goodbye to my philosophical jam sessions with them. It seemed that the art Exhibition was just a bit too successful. No one seemed to know where the men were.

Many months later, I received a Visiting Order, straight out of the blue, from Nerrity, the scallywag. I was in two minds as to whether to take it up or not. However, curiosity got the better of me. I fancied a visit to Peterhouse Prison anyway, even if it was to listen to a dogged story of social descent.

On arrival we were escorted to the visitors' waiting area, before being allowed into the Visitors' Room. It was a room that reeked of ash. Two screws sat at the door, near the alarm bell. Another one sat in a wooden box, about seven foot high, from where he could view the whole room. Tubular steel chairs clattered as visitors drew them back.

There he was, the scallywag, resting his elbows on one formica-topped table. Far from being down in the dumps he looked as bright as a button. So would you be if you had unlimited effrontery like his.

'Fuck ... in ... Ada!' Nerrity said, stretching out the first word and sharply uttering the second, 'so you came. I didn't expect you to, you cunt.'

I bought him a tea from a serving hatch and sat down across the table to hear the news. From my pocket I withdrew a packet of twenty cigarettes and put them on the table. Nerrity took one for himself and we smoked calmly together.

'Is this where you were ghosted to?'

'No, I was sent to Newnham. Doing bird there was a piece of piss. Then I was released. I was fitted-up for that offence in the first place, you know. The bastards.'

I was perplexed. 'But why are you here?'

'I'm on remand. After release I went on a job. We did a safe deposit place in Belgravia. I went with a little firm, four-handed with pieces'

This didn't sound like Nerrity, mixing with across-the-pavement artists and local faces, tooled-up and everything. I was sceptical. There again, one doesn't question these things. I imagined him as the guy outside, in the street, as the lookout, ready to have it away on his toes.

'I've got some news to tell you.'

'What?' I said, expecting some fairy story.

'That robbery I went on opened my eyes. Do you know what I mean?'

Anything could have opened his eyes, for sure.

'To what? I asked.

'To what these rich people are up to, of course.'

'What's that?'

'Remember, we talked about it on the Current Affairs class?'

I searched my inner filing cabinet to think what he was talking about.

'What are rich people up to?' I asked.

'Listen.' Nerrity, still with his elbows on the table, leaned forward, conspiratorially, and lowered his voice.

'When we opened the safe deposit boxes they were crammed full of loot: papers, house deeds and personal documents, but also large quantities of diamonds. By large, I mean, large. And paper money in all denominations, all currencies. I'm telling you, Bob, these cunts are fucking up to it alright. Several boxes had passports in. Two or three passports in one man's name. What do you make of that?' he asked.

I thought for a while, and came up with an answer: 'They must have bought some passports as an insurance policy, so they could do a runner from the country in times of trouble.'

Nerrity nodded, then said: 'And that's not all, Bob. There was porn. Lots of it. These rich geezers are into that as well. Big time. Not just the bum and tits stuff. But with kids.'

Nerrity emphasised the word 'kids' as if it held a common meaning for both of us.

'So what. They're paedophiles, or something,' I said.

'I'm telling you, Bob. I was really gutted. They need a check-up from the neck-up, Bob. To think those rich nonces were playing with kids and getting away with it. You know the sort of treatment those guys get in prison, Bob.'

I did. The nonce was the most ostracised of all inmates.

I downplayed his 'news' a bit, by pretending it wasn't news at all. 'You brought me all this way just to tell me this?'

It wasn't 'news' for me, but he wasn't crestfallen. I had to admire his general resistance to being buried alive. The robbery had certainly opened up a new vista in his otherwise monotonous, rudderless life, lived well below the horizon, and he was likely to trade on it, with other willing ears, for some time to come.

I left the irreverent Nerrity on good terms.
'Good luck, you cunt,' he said, as he shook my hand.

I looked back at him as I walked through the visiting-room door into the fresh air. I waved, and he waved. Perhaps we would never meet again, who could know. On the train home into town, I mulled over what Nerrity had said. It was time for me to move on as well, and get a new vista like his – re-invent myself on a road to Damascus somewhere; somewhere where my memories were not so clamorous. Possibly, I'd get by on a monkey or two, even a pony or a cockle, ha, ha!

When I left the riotous embrace of Wadham Prison, a month or two later, I felt bereaved, but also cleansed. In a strange way I was pleased, since it's no good hankering after pixie dust is it?

Postscript

Along teak-inlaid corridors, and in corniced offices with antique furniture, where the 'small change' of power is swopped, and where ruddy complexions, instinctive tact and polished manners rule supreme, serious issues were being addressed.

Fingers of London rain drummed against a window pane as heavy as lead, and extended down. A small man with a pencil moustache and a grey, sharpish face poured brandy. A tall, hunched man, considerably older, with a military bearing, sat easily in a rich leather-backed chair. He wore a pin-striped suit and a lopsided smile. He was a man brought up as a good dresser, one adept at small conversation, and a good judge of fine port.

The hunched man picked up a glass, pressed it to his lips and drank slowly.

The other cupped his glass and rolled its contents. He walked towards the window to observe the rain outside, then turned and addressed his colleague: 'You know Graham, I don't like this one little bit,' he said in a distant manner. 'It's all been terribly badly handled.'

'Well Charles, how was I to know the bugger would make it a wet job,' Graham replied, with a voice like gravel being tossed into a path. 'Can't you get your lunchtime chums at the Club to sort it out for us?'

'Possibly. But for heaven's sake, don't inform The Office. They'll say it's my turf, and it's best left to me as the person responsible.'

Graham looked discouraged.

Charles added: 'What is more, we've got this added complication of this other chap. What's his name?'

'Robert Wildman,' Graham ventured.

'What do you know about him?'

Graham looked deep into the brandy glass. 'His file's pretty thin, he replied smoothly. His tone hardened: 'But getting bigger. Rum and unbiddable I'd say'

'My dear child, what are you on about? For goodness sake. What's his background I mean?'

'Inauspicious beginnings, you know. Plateglass university in the Sixties. Teachers' certificate. That sort of thing. Pretty run of the mill.'

'What the beastly fellow is doing isn't run of the mill,' Charles said in a disapproving manner. 'In fact, he's going well beyond the line of duty.' He walked over to the window again and was silent for a while. 'Was he positively vetted?' He at last asked.

'He was. And he's clean. Only one small thing against him.'

Charles raised his eyebrows and consulted the ceiling for a moment.

Graham continued: 'Party Piece showed that his father was a member of the British Communist Party for a spell in the nineteen thirties.'

'So were a lot of others. And a lot of shirt-lifters and Bolo's, too, supposedly on our side,' Charles said heavily.

'But these were agitators in the ranks, and cryptos, not officers and gentlemen.'

But Charles had the look of a man who could smell red meat; a ravenous, voracious look. 'Nevertheless we can use that to some effect. We'll get someone on to it,' he said.

'We think he's doing some sort of research work. Thesis maybe,' Graham said.

'What does that mean?' Charles asked in genuine surprise.

'Social survey of sorts.'

'Listen. It's beyond me. I'm old school. I read Greats, not the *Guardian* letters column; that tribal notice board for the liberal elite.'

"Quite so, but I must admit, though, if we didn't have the *Guardian*, we'd have to invent it. It's A1 for tracking and information gathering.' Graham said.

But what does social survey mean?' Charles reiterated the point bluntly.

Graham stuttered momentarily, lost for words. 'It means he's trying to understand the buggers, not just teach them to use a knife and fork.'

'We can't expect him to come up to anything then, since his loyalties are elsewhere?'

'Afraid not.'

'It all depends on how much he knows. If anything at all.'

Graham's face was grim. 'I think he knows a good deal more than we think.'

'What about, Goodman?'

'That's right. We've no reason to believe he's going to give up either.'

Charles's voice dropped into a low monotone. 'Then there's nothing else for it, he's got to be stopped.'

The telephone rang. He picked it up, listened, mumbled a few words and put it down.

'You see Charles,' Graham went on, 'at present he's done nothing wrong. Broken no rules really. We haven't got a watertight case against him that would stand up to the scrutiny of a jury, theirs or ours.'

'Can't you find some pretext?'

'We'll have to. But the bottom line means he might then come back to Rule 1 and give us a hard time, especially if the press get hold of it. Besides, we don't know what are his personal feelings with regard to the business.'

Charles grunted. 'Put a List D-Notice out on it.' Then went on: 'I'm more interested in the killing of our man, not some silly prison rules. Rule 1's no argument. It's of absolutely no consequence. It's a pious hope. No one believes in it. Besides, it's been revised to prevent it being used as a charter for the do-gooders like him. Rule 1s are meaningless.

It's what he knows about the operation I'm concerned about. It's all the fault of that man Goodman. He's a thoroughly bad lot. We should never have used him.'

Graham chimed in: 'There was no knowing that he would renege on the agreement and set up in business alone. The man let the side down. Didn't play the game.'

'Too true.'

'And had brought some worthy chaps right out into the open,' Graham said earnestly. 'Causing an appalling stink.'

'Listen.' Charles downed another brandy and lit a cigar. As his head was wreathed in a halo of swirling smoke, he said: 'I want his place under surveillance, old chap, burgle your way if necessary, and letters, telephone taps, eavesdropping. The lot. Prepare him for a life completely in the shadows. Understand? What you might call Still Life.'

Both men guffawed heartily; Graham grinned.

'I'll inform The Office then and get clearance.'

Part 2 **The Way Back**

LIVING ON GOLD TIME

Cast of Actors in Order of Appearance

Jack Goodman	Pornographer
Bernie Mason	Technical Wizard
Joyce Adams	Actor
Barry Adams	Actor
Bella	Porn Actor
Richard Hanlon	Max Miller Impersonator
Geert	Barman
Julius Hoogstraten	Businessman
Danny Daniels	Gopher
Roger Utley	Producer
Toni Khan	TV Hostess
Trevor	A Friend
Walter Nagel	Businessman
Bob Wildman	Narrator

Life is a tragedy when seen in close-up, but a comedy in long-shot – Charlie Chaplin

1

A big fat green book, heavier than a brick, landed in my lap as I sat in the armchair.

'Take a butcher's at that,' came the voice.

It had 'Spotlight' written across the front, and 'Actresses' written in black type at the bottom. I opened it and peered at all the faces: all nice middle-class girls with names like Georgina, Trudie, Imogen and even Zulema; all hoping to catch some casting director's eye.

'Do they do a turn, do you reckon?' I asked.

'Could be. But what do you think, for fuck's sake,' Jack replied. 'Haven't you heard of the casting couch treatment? Anyone will do anything at the right price. Don't you know that the film studios are whorehouses?' Jack said unrepentantly.

Another thing I was missing out on, obviously.

I gazed on page after page of beaming faces and thought of what they might do for money. I reflected back upon a film I had once seen in the Sixties, called *The Magic Christian*. It had a glittering cast and showed the moral effects of money, avarice, and the greed that it elicits. The closing shots had a million pounds being dropped into vats of sewage, urine and pigs' blood and offered free to city gents, who took the plunge in order to scoop up the readies.

'Don't be mistaken,' Jack said. 'Financial gain is not the motive of blue-film actresses. They do it because they like it.'

As a novice, I still had to have proof beyond all reasonable doubt.

'Besides, the film business calls actors cattle; those who wait in line to be chosen. The bastards. And take my word for it, film directors won't get up off their fucking arses until they're given a suitcase full of used readies.' Jack was at his most instructive. 'Take those misogynist male directors who show women being stabbed. That's what the director would like to do to a woman. You mark my words. The knife is his cock going in.'

A poignant moment had come and gone, and I paused for a breather from the conflagration I had started.

'Fancy a tea?'

How did I manage to meet up with Jack Goodman again?

Well, some months after I'd left Wadham Prison I received a letter at my home address. It had taken a long while to arrive, as no one at the prison knew where I was. The contents read: 'Meet me at the Coach and Horses pub near the Moor Street area of Soho at lunch time on January 15th.'

It was already March and I thought our rendezvous was missed. I went to the Coach and Horses pub a couple of times in passing, but no Jack Goodman. By chance I met the culprit one night at the Soho Brasserie in Old Compton Street. He was sitting in the corner near the door which opened out onto the pavement. He sported a piece of arm candy, a twenty something girl dressed up to look fifteen. Uncharacteristically his hair was short, almost a crew cut, although the big moustache was still there, and the prison pallor had worn off.

'Nice to be out, son?' I asked.

'To tell you the truth I've been waiting for some weeks for you, to make you an offer you can't refuse.'

He went up to the bar for my drink.

'What's that?' I asked him on his return.

'Why don't you join me for a while and we'll make some great films together? Give you some of the realism behind all that book knowledge. Take it as a learning experience, or at least material for that book we've talked about.'

I told him to give me time to think about it. He handed me a telephone number.

'Don't think for too long,' he said smiling.

LIVING ON GOLD TIME

He left promptly with the girl for Raymond's Review Bar. I watched them walk down Old Compton Street. The girl's skirt was so short I saw her knickers peeping below. Her sexuality seemed to give her a special glamour and exemption.

Since I had time on my hands, and felt duty-bound to keep faith with myself in doing what I said I wanted to do all along: that is, taking advantage of the chance to gather evidence on the domestic production of blue films. I didn't need much convincing. Jack would be my deft and purposeful guide to jump-start a study of sex in general: a John Milton's angel, or more realistically Dante's Beatrice. If calamities ensued, then I'd be Voltaire's pilgrim, Candide.

*

It was a beautiful summer's day; it gaped upon us like the mouth of some great oven. Jack and I were walking down the Uxbridge Road in West London, near Ealing Common.

'Where we going?' I asked him.

'To see a bloke called Mason.'

'Don't tell me, his first name's Free.'

'Belt up for a bit. I make all the jokes today. He's got a licence from Old Bill.'

'Licence to thrill?' I added in my mock naïve and off-beam way. The comment fell upon deaf ears.

At the common, we made a beeline through the sun-dusted air, across the green towards a group of Edwardian houses; the type that well-heeled Londoners, the urban gentry, like to buy. Ealing's a place where such people boast about the elegant opulence of their private lives.

Jack rang the bell. Soon, a small, balding man appeared and he greeted Jack with the words: 'Long time no see?'

'I've been doing a bit of HMP,' came the gloomy reply.

'You haven't asked me yet.' The balding man said.

'Asked you what?' Jack seemed puzzled at his friend's little game.

'Asked me how's business. Go on, go on, ask me.'

'Okay. Have it your way. How's business?'

'Oh dear,' came the man's reply, said with a hand on the forehead and a shaking of the head. 'Don't ask me.'

Both men fell about laughing as if it was some strange blast from the past

Jack addressed the man when the merriment had died down: 'I need some gear to start filming.'

Eventually I was introduced to Bernie. He treated me with cold-eyed indifference and turned back to my friend. After some more bantering Bernie led us through the hallway of black and white mosaic tiles, and through an entanglement of rooms to what he called his store.

The store room was loaded from floor to ceiling with equipment of various ages: row upon row of lamps and cables, piled on shelves up to the ceiling, used VHS cassettes and metal film cans scattered about, and an editing suite stretched down one wall. I walked around, poking about.

I'll need a camera,' Jack said.

'Here's a JVC KT2700,' said Bernie with authority, heaving it down in its carrying case from the shelf, and blowing the dust from the top. 'And here's the cables, batteries, charger and a Sennheiser microphone and boom.' Bernie produced these effectively and efficiently like a human fork-lift truck.

'And lights?'

A blonde, two redheads, a hand-held spot and three lighting stands appeared at our feet.

'What about the U-matic recorder?'

'Give me a week and I'll get you a JVC, high band deck, charger and mains unit. How about that?'

LIVING ON GOLD TIME

Jack was well pleased. We shook hands, left, and thought about our first production. About ten days later we drove the car over to Ealing and collected the equipment.

Back at the flat we unloaded and spread everything out on the floor. Jack showed me how to connect the boom and keep it above my head, parallel to the floor, and out of camera shot. We went through the rudiments of camera work, checking sound levels with the mike and U-matic recorder, adjusting barn doors on the lights, and finally loading the still camera with film. We were ready for the off.

*

At one in the morning the door bell rang at Mr and Mrs Adams' home. Their house was difficult to find and they were expecting us at nine. A light went on in the hallway and a bolt slid back with a rattle. The door opened to reveal a prematurely balding man with a halo of curls encircling his head, reminiscent of a monk.

'I'm Jack,' Jack said in explanation, oblivious to the late hour.

'Yes, I realise that. But the time!'

To our annoyance the door still didn't open. Then a woman's voice called from behind: 'Let him in darling.'

In the hallway of the house was an attractive blonde-haired woman of ample proportions. Her large breasts were accentuated by the black night dress which she wore. She stooped, then bent down and kissed Jack on the lips.

'I'm Joyce,' she introduced herself, drawing back. 'and this is my husband Barry.'

Barry stood there in his pyjamas. 'I didn't think you were coming,' he said.

'I've got a girl with me, a model, and Bob the technician.' The two of us shuffled into the hall and left the girl in the doorway. Jack had brought the experienced Bella to coax the new actors into being uninhibited.

'Bring her in then. Barry will love that. Won't you darling?'

Barry leaned against the stairs blinking and mute. 'Yes,' he at last answered, in a matter-of-fact tone. 'I would enjoy that. I'm going upstairs to change. I'll be right down.' Barry's pyjamas disappeared around the curve of the narrow staircase.

'I'm in here.' Joyce's voice came from the open doorway of the living room. 'Do all of you want something to drink?'

When I entered the room she was seated at a table upon which stood a bottle of spirits and some glasses. It was too early in the morning for me, so I politely refused.

While speaking I assessed her face and body. She was not quite as pretty as the slide she had sent us, but she was photogenic. Her breasts were large and her legs long. An image flashed into my mind of the colour slide she sent us. Without modesty she had sat with her naked thighs wide apart, one leg over each arm of the chair.

It was time to bring in the equipment and lighting from the car. That was my first job.

Outside, the night air was cold. All around the identical houses stood in marshalled rows, their roofs covered in a glistening shroud of early morning dampness. They all had the uniform dullness of a council estate. The illuminated blinds of Barry's house were down, so no one could see in. It was a perfect place in which to shoot a film, as a long narrow lounge ran through the width of the house. In the boot of our car was a tripod, the video camera and other lights, recording deck, cables and boom.

Once indoors, Jack screwed the camera into the tripod as I arranged the lights, untwisted the cables, and attached the boom, before going to the car for what was left. Barry came down the stairs into the garden dressed in a pair of grey trousers and shirt.

'You have some impressive gear,' he mused sombrely, passing his hand over the lens cover of the Pentax still camera. Barry helped collect the electric junction boxes, still camera, and some spare magazines, and went inside.

The three of them Bella, Barry and Joyce, sat on the sofa facing the camera.

'I take it,' Jack said, talking to Joyce and Barry. 'You've never made a film before.'

'No. But Barry's taken a few photographs of me. How did you like the one I sent?'

'It was beautiful. I like the pose.'

It was possible to detect a London accent in Joyce's voice.

'Where do you come from Joyce?' I asked.

'Harrow. In North London. Know it?'

'Really!' I said. 'I come from West London. Acton to be exact. What's it like to be up here in Yorkshire. A bit dull after London isn't it?'

Polite conversation was one way to get the performers to relax.

'Oh! you'd be surprised to know what goes on up here ... wife swopping ...the lot.' Joyce's eyes were watery and mellow.

Barry nodded his head and turned to look at Bella, before pointing his face in the direction of the camera. We all noticed the look as his eyes had taken in the attractive Bella. Bella was sexually very attractive indeed. The red suit which she wore that night showed off her girlish figure, her small breasts, long legs and natural blonde hair.

Joyce's knees were parted slightly and she was wearing stockings. Her face recorded the direction of my gaze.

'Do you want to come up to the bedroom for a bit of fun Bob? Barry won't mind, will you Barry?'

Barry was absorbed with Bella. 'No I won't mind.' His face showed neither approval nor distaste, and his reply was vague and non-specific.

Jack remonstrated: 'No, we can do that after, or during the film. I want to get this in the can, start the film now.'

Just then, Joyce stood up and walked over and offered me her hand. 'Come on.' Her arm encircled my waist. She looked at Barry who was still sitting there with a glass of whisky in his hand. Bella smiled at him not saying anything. Joyce left me and went over to Jack. She was eager now and rubbed gently against him.

'You'll find the best way to enjoy yourself is to just let things happen.'

He moved out of her reach. She was very insistent though, and moved after him, grasping at his clothes in the region of his genitals.

'Come on. Just a little game first. There!' she whispered, as her hand grasped his penis through the material of his trousers.

'Look, we can film the action now,' he said. 'But before I go any further, I'll put the agreed fee over here.' Jack looked at me still holding the boom. I took out an envelope from my pocket and placed it behind an ornament on the mantelpiece. Joyce sat down.

'Joyce, I want you to go upstairs and change into some ordinary clothes. The kind of things you wear in the daytime.'

Joyce's face almost collapsed with disappointment.

'Wear the stockings under a skirt and tight jumper to show off those beautiful breasts.'

At the mention of this prominent part of her anatomy Joyce got up and kissed Jack.

'Okay. I'll go upstairs and change.'

'Right Bob. Whitebalance'

I held up a white board in front of the video camera for Jack to make the necessary camera adjustments. Then I reset the still camera and tripod until it faced squarely on to the sofa. It was a large room, so decent long shots were also possible. When the lamps were turned on, the room and its occupants were brilliantly illuminated.

Soon, Joyce emerged wearing black, high-heeled shoes with straps at the ankles, and a black knee-length pleated skirt with a white woollen sweater to complete the outfit. It reminded me of the girls I used to go out with in the past who had dressed that way.

'You look lovely. Really sexy.' I said.

Jack continued. 'I always have a story line in my films. So when I have finished the action I will take some shots of Bella being welcomed at the door by both of you.' He paused during this announcement. 'This is the story: do you know the adverts in that magazine I advertised in?'

'The personal ones you mean?' Joyce whispered.

'Yes,' he continued, trying to include all of them in his gaze. 'Imagine you, Barry, and Joyce, are highly sexed and adventurous.' It was a cue for them to giggle and they looked around them smiling. 'Which of course you are. Well, imagine you've been fantasizing about having a threesome and decide to put an advert in a contact magazine. Bella here answers your advert. Do you get the picture?'

Joyce, Barry and Bella all laughed.

'Right. Get yourselves ready, and don't look at the camera.' Jack emphasised this by repeating it once again. When they were prepared Jack bellowed, 'Action.'

The lights were hot now and the trio writhed madly around in a frenzy of ecstasy. Joyce lay on her back on the sofa with her legs drawn up. Barry knelt on the carpet in between his wife's legs, while Bella put two hands around his penis and guided him in and out.

'Cut,' came the instruction. 'Now Bella, you suck Barry.'

'Action.' The camera zoomed in for a close-up, Bella's eyes closed in abandon; her long tongue slid up and down Barry's penis.

Joyce then sucked avidly at Bella. Shortly, and without warning, Bella's eyes flicked half open. Her eyes were turning upward, her face contorted. She gasped with little

116

short intakes of breath. Jack took some close-ups of the ecstasy in her face, then the writhing of her hips.

'Bella. He's nearly coming,' he shouted.

Bella quickly turned around and guided Barry's penis out of his wife's vagina. She opened her red lips and began to suck it, pushing the foreskin back and forth, stretching it, until Barry, unable to control himself any longer, began to jerk. The rectangle of the camera lens was filled with Barry's penis and sperm ejaculating in short spurts. Bella smiled delightedly at the thick spurts of semen.

'What a lot you come,' she said with a twinkle in her eye and a pure smile.

Barry looked sated and he let out a satisfied sigh.

'Right. Cut.'

Jack looked exhausted from holding the video camera on his shoulder. He handed it to me.

'You'd better lay down some bars Bob. It'll make editing easier, later.'

Afterwards, I switched it off, before resting it on the carpet.

'Okay. Let's take a few stills in the bedroom, 'Jack said.

Barry pointed to his deflated organ.

'I won't be able to do anything for a bit.'

'Okay! Don't worry, you're doing fine.' He went over and picked up the Pentax.

'I just want to get a couple of shots of you welcoming Bella at the door. Now tidy yourself up a bit.'

'Don't make a noise though, because of the neighbours,' Barry implored.

Jack took a few still shots of Bella ringing the doorbell, while I lit her with a small hand lamp; then a shot of the door opening from the inside and Joyce and Barry greeting her.

Everyone was now back in the house.

'Right. Upstairs for the bedroom scenes,' said Jack.

Everyone laughed and ran excitedly up the stairs.

LIVING ON GOLD TIME

Both he and I hauled the heavy equipment up the stairs, and I set the lights and put a new camera master in the recorder. I labelled the old one and closed it inside its plastic container. The recording deck was a box with shoulder strap at the end, which the camera and boom plugged into.

Jack filmed Joyce and Barry in bed reading the magazine and fantasizing about a girl in bed with them, while Bella stood by the edge of the bed.

This time Bella was on top and astride Barry. Her buttocks were facing the camera and she was bouncing up and down. The camera couldn't see Barry's face, only his penis, as it moved with ever increasing rapidity in and out. His breath came in short gasps, his penis thickened and writhed as it was filmed at the point of ejaculation.

'Cut.'

Barry lay on the edge of the bed. Bella stood up and his limp penis slid out of her and lay red and shiny alongside his thigh.

'You get up Barry, and I'll take your place.' Jack said.

Barry obeyed. He stood there watching while the two women waited expectantly for instructions.

'Here Bob. It's your turn. Your chance to use the camera. Just take the shots that you think will turn the punters on. If they turn you on they'll turn them on. Don't forget to compose the shots you take, like I have told you. And don't be afraid.'

Before I could do this I had to fix the boom with gaffer tape on one of the pieces of bedroom furniture. Then both girls and Jack jumped on the bed.

'Kneel down and play with my penis both of you. And face the camera, but don't look at it,' he said.

Soon their tongues flicked over his body. Bella enveloped his glans with her lips. Joyce kneeled upright as Bella guided him into her body. She began to move up and down gyrating her hips from side to side.

'Oh! I love being fucked,' she said. Her eyes were closed in blissful surrender. She was moving very fast. When he was about to come I saw Barry standing by the side of the bed masturbating wildly.

'I'm coming,' Jack yelled.

'Oh! yes, you dirty bastard. I am too.' Joyce burst out in a rush.

*   *

Jack was thumbing through the mail at the office when I arrived. We had hired a couple of rooms above a shop and entered via a door on the road and a long, internal passageway.

'What do you think of this?'

He handed me an envelope. It was one of those letters from models and would-bes looking for work. We had had many of them since we started advertising in the monthly Video View magazine. Often they sent photosets and the odd one hour video and a letter with their CV attached:

Dear Sir,

I am writing in connection with your ads in the video magazine. I wonder if you require girls for glamour work. I have done three videos: one as a nurse, one as a schoolgirl and one lesbian.

.........Hope to hear from you soon.

Trixie ....

The letter in my hand was from Trixie. It showed a girl of nineteen, who looked much younger than her age, sitting on a bed with legs splayed apart and wearing white stockings, white knickers and stocking suspenders.

'Yeah. She looks okay.'

'She's sent a telephone number. I'll phone her and tell her we're coming over. We'll use her place as a location. She wants glamour shots but we'll take the video equipment just in case there's more. I'll get her to dress in school uniform and school tie. It'll be our first Lolita style video.'

*

It was a house in Milton Keynes, the spitting image of Joyce and Barry's. Since it was a summer afternoon the sun was out. Dennis came to the door before we had even come down the path. Dennis was a Barry without the monk's haircut, while his wife Trixie looked even more glamorous than the photo she had sent us.

After the introductions Dennis went off to sort out his record collection, so he told us, while Trixie was instructed to pose wherever in the house she felt most comfortable. This she did with consummate skill. After the living room it was up to the bedroom. Meanwhile, Dennis could be heard shuffling around in the loft. Trixie posed with her teddy bear on the bed as a developed fourteen year old would, first with finger in mouth, then more seductively, by kneeling with bottom raised.

Just then there was an almighty crash in the loft above our heads that shook the ceiling light. Jack pointed to a small letter box style hole in the ceiling above the foot of the bed and behind our heads. Dennis had keeled over in the loft above. He had fallen while wanking at the sight of his wife on the bed in the room below.

*

Not all domestic locations for glamour shooting had G-plan furniture and wall-to-wall carpeting. Tina's sumptuous pad in Hampstead Garden Suburb, with Panther sports car outside, had all the accoutrements of well-off professionals:

colour co-ordinated, though minimally furnished, but with all the necessaries. But somehow it didn't look lived-in. It was a film set she personally appeared at on a weekly basis to look at herself. And look at herself she did. She was a born exhibitionist. Tina was already at the door when we arrived, dressed in nothing but PVC mini-skirt and upper-arm length PVC gloves which crinkled as she moved; flaunting herself, a fiery temptress, insolent and immune. A striking brunette, her high heels were not of the thumb-pricking variety, more meaty, and businesslike. The final product was a half hour of voyeuristic pleasure and sophisticated eroticism. The difficulty of shooting in an apartment bedecked with mirrors was immediately obvious; at all costs one had to avoid getting the camera and equipment in shot.

Jack liked the older woman and young girl scenario so off we went to another location. The script involved an older girl teaching the younger one, the novice, to strip for the camera. Once they were scripted the actors were left to work through the scenes themselves.

At one location I had the tiresome acting task of spanking a brass's arse.

*   *

The daily routine of would-be, blue-film moguls, is not all hard cocks and compliant fannies. There are the daily routines to perform and the blizzards of paperwork.

The 1980s was the age of the videocassette recorder, or VCR, which recorded from TV and played back on signals transmitted to magnetic tape. Even by the late 1970s this technology had achieved mass market success. The impetus for all we did was selling mail order videos to customers who either wanted the standard JVC VHS cassettes for their video players, or those in the minority who had bought, and preferred, Sony's Betamax format. It was argued by many that the Beta version was technically more sophisticated in recording quality, although many users didn't perceive a visual difference.

To get to the VCR owning market we needed to advertise. It was advertising that constituted one of our biggest costs along with point of sale material and printing. To keep costs down we planned and set our own advertisements, often by using the time-honoured method with Letraset. What I learned from our advertising experience was the link between big business and newspapers and magazines. Generally, the advertiser always dictates the editorial regarding his/her products.

Then there were the mail shots to customers on our expanding mailing lists. I never realised how time-consuming folding paper and sticking stamps on a thousand letters could be. Auditions had to be arranged as films piled up in the office waiting to be despatched to the censor.

After a new film was shot, edited and certified, it was advertised and orders would roll in. The first customers were always the pirates, especially the blue-film pirates, who'd get their copy and sell duplicates to their friends or business contacts. The more they sold, of course, the worse the quality of the duplicate. The duplicated films in turn would be duplicated by someone else. Since they didn't duplicate from a master, our films could be fifth, sixth or even more in generation, with attendant drop-out from being copied on machines with worn heads. No doubt this affected the customers' perceptions of our films. Poorly duplicated porn films, played into the hands of those people who did their damnedest to find evidence that porn film-making was an underground and disreputable activity. We paid dearly whenever we got our work duplicated from an untrustworthy source.

The technical language of film and film-making tested my poor understanding to its limits, especially still photography, which I found to be a nightmare. Regularly I'd pop down to

Joe's Basement in Wardour Street but always had to write down the order as I couldn't distinguish between cibachrome, tungsten and daylight film, contact sheets, E6s, EPTs or FP4s. All I could comprehend was that film had to come out of the fridge to guarantee colour quality. At Stanley Productions, up the road, there were E60s, E120s, KCS-20 U-matics and Gaffer tape to consider.

The most nerve racking job of all was seconding Jack on the editing suite. Two monitors on either side and in front of us, were complemented by dials for winding backwards and forwards tape from the camera masters. The more masters there were, and any lack of sequence therein, increased the bill we had to pay at the end of the day, because the suites were hired by the hour. All this proved the necessity of editing as much as possible on the camera. Besides the film itself, there were credits and captions to put on, dubbing music, copying U-matic masters, or transferring to low band. Oh! and on top of this there were cut-aways, fades, jump cuts and voice-overs to consider – mind boggling for a novice! Furthermore, not having one's own editing suite was a ghastly and expensive mistake.

Reading customers comments and correspondence arriving daily by post, could be either an uplifting or disheartening experience:

Dear Sir,

The video I received from you I thought was of good quality, but unfortunately I found it to be very tame.

Yours Sincerely

This was a frequent complaint. Censorship rules meant customers could not get what hard-core material they wanted, and more often than not they sought out German, Swedish or Danish videos instead.

LIVING ON GOLD TIME

Dear Sir,

I am only interested in <u>hard</u> not XXX or XXXX videos.

Yours,

This comment was a by-product of producers over-selling a tame or inferior product. Although we tried to be as radical as possible, frequently we fell for our own publicity or 'rave reviews.' We even came to believe our over-selling in the publicity game. Some purchasers complained that it must contravene the Advertising Standards Authority code.

A few videos would disappear, or go astray, or get mislaid in the post; most likely stolen by postal staff who coveted what they imagined were illegal (not certificated) stronger products.

Some customers were confused, because they did not know whether the video they purchased was an R18 version or not. That means one which was saleable only in a sex shop.

Please mark my package 'private and confidential' some implored.

The possibility of being 'ripped off' was strong, as some correspondents hoped we would not do the same. That means not selling 'cut' films.

Some of our films must have been used for teaching purposes for they were in demand from schools or by medics in hospitals. Videos sent to hospitals might have been objects of delight for those with erectile dysfunction.

The films most in demand were always the ones with Lolita in the title:

THE WORLD IN CLOSE UP

Dear Sir,

Thank you, Thank you, Thank you. I have just watched the film *Lolita X* and I don't think I have ever been so turned on by a film as much as I have by this one. My only criticism is that it could have shown more, especially where she is masturbating. If this could have been a great deal more explicit the film would have been even better. Other than that it is a wonderful film.

Sincerely

Dear Sir,

It was well worth the wait for *Lolita X.* Excellent.

Thanks

Lolita aficionados were not without their technical criticisms however:

Dear Sirs,

...... *Lolita X* was only spoilt marginally by her not having regulation black or navy school knickers. Usually I am badly disappointed by material I have bought, since some people describe their offerings as schoolgirl stuff simply because the girls are young and not in uniform at all. Other 'schoolgirls' are dressed in stockings and suspenders which is totally unrealistic also, and other material I have bought has the girl ending up nude, or out of uniform after the first shot. If people want nudes or stockings and suspenders let them buy that St.Trinians material, but us schoolgirl freaks basically just want girls in uniform with socks, short skirts and black school knickers.

Yours Sincerely

That letter must have been sent by a male teacher. What do you think?
The attraction of older men for young girls is a rarely discussed, but widespread social phenomena:

Dear Sir,
      I'm writing to you regarding a fantastic Video that I got from your company, a homemade type.

Sincerely

By 'homemade type' he meant non-violent, and therefore not American, with British locations and British social scenery.

Satisfied customers were not without ambitions and self-promotion:

Dear Sir,
      ……. But my reason for writing to you is because I would like to please ask you if you would please place my name on your list for being <u>in</u> your films. I'm 5′ 11″ tall, 28 years old, short hair and good looking.

Sincerely

One in particular showed deep anatomical leanings:

THE WORLD IN CLOSE UP

Dear Sirs,

      ...... What I now seek is of one girl, on her own, in her own bedroom or bathroom, doing all the things they do and which you never see unless you live with them. I run you a short list so you can see what I mean: -
Alone in the room she looks at herself, breasts, nipples and vagina. Trims pubic hair, urinates standing. Body, leg and hip movements to show change and shape of vagina......
The whole action centred on the girl, without outside help as an appreciation of her body and all the secrets it holds.

Faithfully

We offered to make this film for him personally if he submitted a full script and agreed to our payment, with part-payment up front.

Finally there were letters from the indomitable spirits:

Dear Sirs,

      Please send me the four adult videos...... I am 82 years old with still some life left in me and plenty of lead in my pencil.

Regards

*

Our last film in the glamour mould was, I think, our best. Astrid was a writer of porn for women. Although beautiful and oozing with sex appeal, she admitted to being celibate. She lived alone, but her life was a constant frisson of sexual pleasure. As she wrote her sexy novels, she acted out the

127

fantasies by watching erotic videos and playing with her own body.

Our making of the film began like this:

One day I jumped into my old banger with Jack, off to one of our locations together
'Where are we going this time? I asked.
'Norwich,' he replied, grinning.
'Christ. You never told me that.'
'She rang up last night.'
'Who did?'
'The model, you fool,' he said with cheeky confidence.
I fumbled through my tatty copy of the AA Book.
'But it's miles away.'
'Just get going,' he remarked in agitation. 'I've got the script here.' He patted his chest. 'I've built a story around the location.'
Out of his breast pocket he produced the film script, neatly typed.
As the car clattered along, loaded with equipment, Jack read aloud the script. He stopped and turned to me saying: 'You're a reporter on a famous newspaper.'
I shrugged in acceptance
'You've come to interview a gorgeous blonde, Astrid, a writer of erotic novels.'
'Is that all?' I said in disappointment.
'If you like ...' He hesitated in mid sentence.
I eyed the script with side glances while driving, feverishly learning my lines.
We arrived. There she was, the ravishing Astrid, waiting at the door. I unloaded the equipment while Jack took a look at the location. There was plenty of light, plenty of room, and a whole day ahead of us.

THE WORLD IN CLOSE UP

Well, Astrid stripped off, following her clues slavishly.
She had a shower and we retired to the bedroom.

By six o'clock there were eight reels in the can.

'A little gem,' Jack said.

I looked at him bewildered. 'Are you sure you can say it's that good at this juncture?'

'Of course. Just give us to the end of the week to edit it.'

That Friday afternoon we had a few drinks, sat down in front of the TV and put on the VHS. After an hour of seeing it I really didn't know how we achieved such results.

'So, it's magic after all,' I said with exhilaration.

Production values in this film were our best, and although it was relatively 'soft,' I liked the creative potential in the direction in which we were travelling. The film was overlaid with hypnotic, electronic music and sound effects. Colour mixes and colour changes created a dream-like effect. There was nothing formulaic, repetitive, or anything lacking in stylistic presentation about it. When Jack overlaid the shots of Astrid with shots of a large vibrator massaging a vulva, the effect was mesmerising. The viewer was enchanted by a lattice work of image and background music. The film posed interesting questions about female eroticism.

As for the lesbian film, one Dutch customer said: 'It's not hot …it's red hot.'

I didn't believe that at all until I saw his letter.

'Aren't some of features of this film degrading to women?' I asked Jack.

'I didn't write the script,' he explained.

'Then who did?'

'The girls did. They're into that sort of thing. Not me.'

'What! with clothes pegs on their nipples?'

'It seems so,' he said nonchalantly.

*   *   *

LIVING ON GOLD TIME

The biggest blight on a movie maker's life in the 1980s, and the source of all our woes, was the 1984 Video Recordings Act. Quite easily it could have put us out of business. The Act made provision for regulating the distribution of video recordings; it received the Royal Assent on 12th July 1984, and commenced August 1985. Its intention was to regulate the classification by certificate and labelling of video works supplied in the furtherance of a business, save those concerned with sport, religion or music, or those that can be properly described as being designated to inform, educate or instruct. After video recorders were first introduced in about 1978, there was no legislation at all which governed the kind of content which could be distributed on video. Hence the makers of big budget productions, which were being shown using 35mm film in the cinemas, were wary of the use of video as they felt that their distribution would have an adverse effect on the number of people wishing to view films in the cinema. The market was left open for low budget material that principally depicted sex. These low budget companies were free to do this as there was no legislation banning films which did not carry a classification, or films refused a certificate, being released on video. The British Board of Film Censors (BBFC) had been instrumental in the certification of motion pictures since 1912, and was designated as the classifying authority in 1985. Video works were to be classified by them under an age-rated system; and so it was an offence under the Act to supply video works to individuals who were, or appeared to be, under the age of classification designated. Under section 8 of the Video Recordings Act, classification 18 meant a video film was suitable only for persons of 18 years and older, and was not to be supplied to any person below that age. A restricted 18, or R18 video could only be supplied in licensed sex shops to persons not less than 18 years. A video work was defined by the Act as: any series of visual images, with or without sound, produced electronically by use of information contained on magnetic tape and shown as a moving picture.

The insidious nature of this Act was evident in the fact that the BBFC changed its name to the British Board of Film Classification, to convince everyone that that is what they did. It was to have special regard to the 'likelihood of video works being viewed in the home by persons who have not attained a particular age, or whether no video work containing that work should be supplied in a licensed sex shop.' It tried to make out that the law was designed specifically for the protection of children. But its framers were more interested in treating the whole adult population as if they were children, and alleviating the imaginary danger to social order. Remember the Lady Chatterley's Lover Obscenity Case in 1960, when Mervyn Griffith-Jones prosecuting counsel said: 'Is it a book that you would even wish your wife or your servants to read?' Patrician attitudes of master and servant still existed twenty years later, as they still do today. The framers of the Act were obsessed by the masturbatory potential of sexual imagery and were devotees of the 'hands off cocks, on socks,' view of human activity in the home. Therefore the criteria for classification were much tougher than for the cinema.

The question remains: how did such a draconian piece of legislation come about, where every story-teller has to submit his or her story to a censoring body, and pays to have them check it? The story is then checked against a secret set of guidelines drawn up by state prosecutors and sent to the censoring body to tell then how to operate. Their contents are a closely guarded secret. If you submit a story they don't like, or does not meet the criteria, you won't be allowed to tell it.

'How do you think they decide which bits to censor in our films?' I asked Jack one day.

'Easy. When the Censor gets a hard-on, he cuts it.'

Absurd as this may sound, this is not so very far from the truth, because, although the Video Recordings Act was applied to what were publicly hailed as 'video nasties,' it was obvious that it only applied to sex. How come?

Some say that the Act was a legislative reaction to a moral panic at the time concerning violent videos and their effect on children, and sparked by tabloid newspapers in Britain. I think, from my experience, the motives go far deeper than this.

Videos which were felt to be in contravention of the Obscene Publications Act of 1959 were put on a banned list, often referred to as the 'video nasties list.' The main problem with it, however, was that a work could only be prosecuted once it had been released. The authorities thought that appropriate legislation was required.

More pressingly, advances in technology caught the mainstream film industry with their trousers down; while the authorities were losing control many people didn't want to go to the cinema if uncensored sex films could be viewed on video at home. It was boom time for small film-makers as they required a lower investment in camera equipment. The Act was there to neutralize this threat. The industry put it about that 35mm film was superior to video, which Jack and I had our doubts about.

'Too many talking heads on TV and film. It's not as flexible as video,' Jack said.

Big business therefore needed a moral imperative, combined with a penal punishment, or at the very least a punishing fine, for uncertificated publishing. The Video Recordings Act supplied the means of coercion to keep everyone in line and intimidate or seduce the gullible. It was a tactic used by the giant telecommunications company

AT&T for the best part of a century – cleverly manipulate the regulator and crush the competition.

Here you have it then. From 1977 onwards, Britain's overzealous, American-educated Censor, was an American TV and theatre director and one-time member of the US Air Force. Little wonder then, given the power of the film industry as a corporate venture, that our American Censor was head of a British non-governmental organisation, the BBFC, funded by the film industry itself, less as a form of self-censorship, more as a technique for keeping others out. The mafia did not want porn legalised in order for them to keep the market price up, and the Video Recordings Act saw to this. The British Censor's job was to secure the British market, the biggest domestic market in the world, for foreign porn, by eliminating British competition through censorship of home-grown products, hence keeping up the black-market price. If porn was legalised, British products would sell at a fraction of the black-market price. Of course, the corollary of illegal porn was police corruption.

In addition, the US controlled the international film industry. Its existence allowed the indiscriminate and unmolested portrayal of violence on film to justify US foreign policy. It had been the case since the Second World War and it was so in the 1980s. Capitalist society was forever portrayed as a pathological death culture where violence is the norm. A soldier going to war could see a violent video but could not have a woman.

In Wadham Prison when I was there, every weekend they showed violent American films to violent prisoners. Now what sort of rehabilitation is that?

Many of these films depicted the torture and mutilation of women in a sexual context. For those who saw them they must have had a tendency to deprave and corrupt, as they deliberately associated sex with violence in a repeated pattern throughout the structure of the film. As an entertainment genre this body of films could cause an aversion to the sexual completion of erotic encounters and psychologically displace sex by violence. The simple enshrined message was that the sexually liberated woman will suffer horrific torture and death for being what she is. The autonomous sexual female should really be morally and socially acceptable, and the supreme function of film-makers should be to show that the source of violence is repressed sexual emotion.

Therefore, the 1984 Video Recordings Act, and its censorship priorities, had a two-pronged effect, whether its promoters were aware of it or not, or whether they were just ready to be willing dupes. It kept the price of American porn up, and because of the dearth of erotica, violent American films in constant demand: little to do with morals but everything to do with economics.

Deeper down in the British people's psyche festered the remnants of the Victorian purity movements. Established first in the early nineteenth century in the Society for the Suppression of Vice, later on they crystallized into the late nineteenth century fanatical purity campaigns. In their twentieth century form one offshoot was the National Viewers and Listeners Association. At every turn the moral re-armers saw the necessity, universality and the eternity of sexual vice assumed as a basis of action and legislation. In late Victorian Britain it was increasingly urged that, if the British Empire was to survive against the tide of sexual chaos, the imperial race had to exercise sexual restraint and the government had to intervene to enforce it. In other words, sexual opportunity had to be reduced. At first a ferocious purity campaign was launched against the Contagious Diseases Act on the grounds that it regulated, condoned and licensed prostitution by seemingly making it necessary and ineradicable; but multiple assaults on sexual life in the 1880s followed, attacking the easy-going attitudes of the working classes and adolescent sexuality. This outburst of neurotic Puritanism resulted in repressive sex codes and the reduction of sexual opportunity. The age of female consent, raised in 1875 from twelve to thirteen, went up to sixteen. By comparison, in the United States, ten had been the usual age, though in some states it was non-existent. The 'solitary vice' of masturbation became a symbol of catastrophe too, because it was believed to be a cause of degeneration in the next generation. With pornography Lord Chief Justice Cockburn produced a famous working definition of obscenity in 1868, as 'that which had the tendency to deprave and corrupt.' But the Customs Consolidation Act and subsequent Acts went further, and empowered officials to seize prints, books and photographs. Apparently prudery was an establishment defence against enormous increases in literacy consequent upon the 1870 Education Act. Even nude bathing came under the excessively prurient searchlight of the purity campaigners. These people changed the visible face of British life as well as many of its inner attitudes to the advantage of powerful economic interests. Despite the liberating atmosphere of the 1960s in Britain, the legacy of purity, parochialism, was enshrined in the 1984 Video Recordings Act and the penalisation of everyone's harmless pleasures.

The 1984 Act was the biggest growth of British censorship rules for many years, bringing in new controls on what people might be allowed to see. It was a success for the Conservative government, rightwing moralists and purity campaigners, who, with frenetic speed and secrecy, publicly orchestrated opposition to video imagery. They even referred to the Obscene Publications Act as a 'flawed instrument.'

LIVING ON GOLD TIME

There were three standards of assessment to be made for some films: the cinema standard, TV standard and harsher video standard. Thus, films could be shown in the cinema, cut for TV, but be illegal on video. It showed the uniquely powerful influence of video, resulting in an image of it as, almost by definition, corrupting. Surprisingly enough, the words 'video nasty' did not appear anywhere in the Video Recordings Bill at all, although the whole campaign centred around the corrupting effects of these supposedly nasty films and their influence on children. Although the bill was called the Graham Bright private members' bill, after its initiator, the Conservative MP for Luton South, it was really a government bill which had the support of the churches, the Conservative Party, the Nationwide Festival of Light, and the *Daily Mail* newspaper. Umpiring came courtesy of Mrs. Mary Whitehouse, President of the National Viewers and Listeners Association and part of the 'clean-up' TV pressure group. And yet the public image of the nasties campaign was one of simple concern for children. Threats of political censorship were disguised, of course, by moral protection.

The nasties were used to win support for much wider, and publicly far less acceptable, views about the media in general, especially the corrupting effects of popular entertainment. The old right wing arguments about videos on sex education stimulating sexual activity in under age people were resurrected, as was their corrupting influence on illiterate minds. In fact, most people, despite the rhetoric of the moral crusaders' clamorous and unproven insistence on the 'incitement effect,' use sexual imagery to relieve frustration rather than encourage it.

The ideology of the purity campaign amalgamated a powerful anti-intellectualism of 'nanny knows best,' with the new language of sickness and corruption. Really, what would Mrs Grundy say? Since the whole package was marketed via the idea of the child, such an idea is, of course, always a powerful one. Horrific content was 'gratuitous,'

and 'protection' stood between us and the end of
civilisation. But, as always, the problem was with the
working-class children. For the right-wing mind, working-
class children meant working-class adults.

The vital and inalienable rights of artists, whether painters,
novelists, playwrights or film-makers, to freedom of
expression and to create nightmares as well as dreams, was
lost in all of this.

*   *

The British Board of Film Classification at 3 Soho Square
London, had a special tariff of fees: £6.0 a minute for
viewing the first hour; £4.50 per minute for the second hour
and £3.0 per minute thereafter. By 1989 it had gone up to
£7.50, £5.0 and £3.0. This amounted to a demand for money
'up front' in the form of a tax, before a state licence was
issued. They offered a business service in their advertising
literature but were loath to extend the usual thirty days'
credit. The BBFC's decision was final, pending an appeal,
but they even had the temerity to charge a fee for appealing
against their decisions. Furthermore, they were always
pleading poverty, carping on about the fact that they had no
recourse to public funds and being a non-profit making
organisation. Trading standards officers must have been in
great demand because the BBFC whimpered over the
escalating costs of providing certificates of evidence to
them.

All our films had an average running time of fifty minutes,
except for a couple of feature films, not that the censors
actually sat for fifty minutes watching a fifty minute film.
They fast-forwarded through the film until they reached the
sex and most probably, then, rushed out to the toilet for
relief. With the huge quantity of violent films the job was a
synch, and a real money spinner, as they must have fast-

forwarded at double the speed and tallied the time at the end to see how much they'd collect.

Whenever the word Lolita appeared in any film title it must have caused pandemonium down at Soho Square. First they wanted the title changed as they declared that they took a firm line on material which appeared to encourage the idea of under-age sex (poor Nabokov), then they wanted evidence of the age and marital status of the main actress. To satisfy this request we had to send Model Release Forms, contracts of employment, and marriage certificates to headquarters. Not only visual imagery but dialogue had to be cut and made good with music according to their instructions. 'Licking and sucking of nipples' was apparently abhorrent (poor baby), although 'kissing could remain.' 'Evidence of spanking' had to be reduced. 'Any suggestion of a woman urinating on a man's face' was removable (presumably the double standard for reverse domination). The BBFC standard for sex images, for an 18 classification, were the innocuous and puerile films trading under the name of Electric .... something or other. Censorship not only applied to films themselves, but included the packaging. Since we sold by mail order, rather than display, this did not concern us greatly.

Such was the nature of the bureaucracy, mutilation and delay of the cuts process, that Jack and I decided to mount a challenge and Go to Appeal. It was a lonely guerrilla war against prudery and for hand relief and happy endings. We chose one of our films on the cuts list which had an Interim Clearance Form, although it wasn't the best, quality wise. The Board had imposed a forty two day period in which to lodge an appeal from the receipt of that form. We attended the hearing of the Video Appeals Committee on a deliciously warm day in May.

The grounds for our being aggrieved was that one of our films was given an R18 classification, rather than an 18 one, which meant it could not be supplied other than in a licensed sex shop. *We mounted a challenge to the authorities by wanting much stronger sex in our film for the 18 certificate.* We didn't want our film in a sex shop, as there would have been no sex to speak of in it after their cuts for an 18R, and we didn't want to be party to ripping off customers with deception as to its content, especially foreign tourists from countries where censorship rules were non-existent.

As appellant, we believed the Board was wrong in regarding the film's content as there were no acts of cruelty or harm. All acts depicted mutually pleasurable behaviour between consenting adults. It portrayed no acts which if imitated would lead to any crime. This point is important, because very few sexual acts are criminal in themselves. In one part of the film compilation the behaviour was light-hearted, satirical and humorous, in keeping with the traditional iconography of British eroticism i.e. Thomas Rowlandson and Aubrey Beardsley. The fact that the Board was prepared to grant an R18 certificate showed that there was no question of the material being refused a certificate. In other words, the material was lawful regarding the Obscene Publications Acts since the Board refused certificates to material which it believed contravened those Acts. We also maintained that we should be granted an 18 certificate because from a conversation I had with a Director of the Board we had complied with the Board's request to produce a film without depiction of explicit sexual intercourse , fellatio, cunnilingus, erection, ejaculation, penetration, or extreme close-ups of human genitalia. The imagery was to be even less specific than in 'girlie' magazines lawfully sold in newsagents shops to which minors had access. That our film was unsuitable for minors was a further argument for 18 Certification. Since the Board member refused an interview with me, and a list of objective criteria as to what was and what was not permissible, the Board had acted in an arbitrary and unreasonable way, we thought. Even though we requested an 18 Certificate, the

Board consistently refused to issue one on grounds that: 'Cuts for 18 would be extremely difficult in most of the sequences.' This was tantamount to admitting that they were censoring ideas made visual. We noted to the Board that American 'hardcore' films had been issued with cuts lists to bring their films to an 18 standard. We felt that we had been singled out for particularly harsh treatment. We appealed to the Committee that to limit our video recording to an R18 Certificate meant they were pushing us towards insolvency, as sales restricted to sex shops would be economically unviable. Besides, how could we trust sex shops not to pirate them? Unless our video was allowed <u>more sex</u> for the R18 classification, and, or was, allowed an 18 certificate in its present form, marketing the film would have been uneconomic.

Our most powerful argument was one that I had hinted at earlier in discussing the Video Recordings Act and the BBFC. It had to do with the economics of the film business internationally.

First, we stated that our market research showed that while severe censorship of 18 and 18R material was restricting sales of lawful erotica, the gap in the market was quickly being filled with European, and particularly American 'hard core' videos; lawful in their countries of origin but not in the United Kingdom. Such material could be obtained through illegal Soho bookshops, even offering a half back on exchange, or by mail order. We had, prior to the Appeal, submitted a catalogue in evidence. In fact the implementation of the law, and in particular the application of the Video Recordings Act, had reduced the whole situation to the absurd and encouraged corruption, pirating and crime on a massive scale, as demand will always be supplied in a competitive society at any price. The only losers were the film-makers who do not get any royalties, and the British public who are forced to buy inferior, pirated videos at inflated prices.

Second, the UK being a member of the European Community was obliged to aid the harmonization of business between member states. The standards that the Board sought to impose were completely out of line with those of other member states, which were far more liberal in their treatment of video recordings where sexual material was concerned.

With that prescription the Appeal ended. We both knew that it was all a waste of time and that they had made their decision in advance. The nightmare of the inquisition had ended.

Some time later we had a written reply from our tribunal or protagonists where, somewhat mysteriously, it used categories appropriate to civil law rather than criminal law. Apparently, the principle it adopted to determine whether a video work fell within the R18 category was whether unrestricted availability with regard to its sexual content would be offensive to reasonable people. If the video work appealed to the prurient interests of the viewer, namely, those having an unhealthy obsession with sexual matters, its availability had to be restricted: what healthy young persons didn't have them? If it was offensive to reasonable people, were it to be on display and available for supply in ordinary video shops (this depends on packaging) to which all members of the public, including persons under the age of eighteen had access, then it had to be restricted. How it defined the reasonable person was beyond me. The man on the Clapham omnibus, I suspect, or a member of the National Viewers and Listeners Association, most likely – certainly not 'reasonable' in the general sense.

The word 'prurience' concealed an abiding fear among the upper classes for the uncensored behaviour of the poor. Deep down lurked fears for the virginity of their daughters, and a psychopathic distaste for erect phalluses and masturbation on the part of the poor, who might use the females of the 'respectable classes' as the objects of their obsession. This is not a modern fear by any means, but one that goes back to the era of slavery, masters and servants.

The Board therefore believed that the sole purpose of our film was the sexual arousal of the viewer, consequently it had, for them, no plot, no character development or narrative. It did convey, however, a strong sense of reality:

'...in none of the sequences is any aesthetic distance established between the actor/performer and the viewer; there appears to be no mediation interposed to distance the viewer from the reality of the sexual activity of the performers.'

'...this work gives the sense of being a private rather than a public event, with the viewer a voyeur of a private sexual transaction.'

There is a whole wealth of possible criticism here of their definition of a dramatic performance. It resurrects an older set of anxieties too, about obscure texts which were thought to violate frequently the distance thought to be necessary for separating subject, and representation, from their object. But as media and communication technologies became more widely understood as part of the fabric of ordinary life, there had been a general blurring of the 'real' and the 'representational.' The Censor felt that we were breaching the demarcation lines between real sex, and simulated sex. Since sexual imagery is often seen as disturbing the boundaries between reality and representation, fact and fiction, isn't this the real reason why it arouses such concern?

They did not think our work was a humorous, light-hearted, playful fantasy but:

' ... apparently serious, realistic sexual activity at times bordering on the deviant.'

To be truthful I'm sure the Censor got the hump when our hero in one sequence turned out to be a Colonel with unusual sexual habits. What really got the Censor's goat, was that in the Colonel's flat two women were invited to dress in military uniform, while another, a school mistress, masturbates with a cane in preparation for giving the man a damn good thrashing. Deviant sex is more than just unappetising, as exposing the sexual deviations of the ruling classes is obviously forbidden territory. The deviancy was not in our work, but in the social relations that a class society perpetuates.

The Board was aggrieved by such realism, preferring the elements of fantasy, stylisation, exotic locations and role playing in order to distance the viewer from the action.

With regard to our reference to harmonization within the European Community, the Board was of the opinion that its classification did not violate the obligation of the UK as a member of the European Community since Article 36 of the Treaty of Rome, allowed state controls on the grounds of public morality and public policy, permitting each member state to regulate itself.

Remarkably, despite all the bad news, the Censor stated:

'...more sex would be allowed in the R18 Classification if he (I) so wished.'

What an amazing proposition given all that we had been through. However, the caveat was that Classification would still have been on a film's merits. There was no escaping the power of censorship.

All in all, the Appeal was a no-win situation for us. We didn't expect anything else, considering that the home addresses of our combatants were all vicarages and manors.

LIVING ON GOLD TIME

The result of the Appeal was that the customer still couldn't get what he or she wanted from British films even from sex shops, where standards of control meant certificated video films on sale had no sex in them. To have a licensed 'sex shop' without videos that contain explicit sex, defeats their object. Members of the public entering licensed 'sex shops' and buying videos from which all explicit sex had been censored, would feel cheated as victims of hypocrisy and deception. The primary effect of the R18 category was to create a monopoly for the one or two persons who own the few licensed 'sex shops' all under 'front' companies.

The purity campaigners, including the BBFC, drummed on about minors and the sexual protection of the public all the time. Sexual exploitation of minors seemed to be one of their greatest fears, or, more sensibly, what they were addicted to themselves. They wrestled and fought with their guilty consciences and repressed natural desires with hair-shirts and tourniquets.

The Video Recordings Act replaced the old Obscene Publications Act with draconian censorship which would never have been thought possible before. It reached far beyond the criteria of the Obscene Publications Act. In effect the Act was being used by the BBFC to enforce censorship from above, in the wake of too many acquittals by juries when cases were brought against films under the Obscene Publications Act. Where our films were concerned the BBFC was particularly severe, possibly because it was a very rare example of English eroticism, perhaps the only English eroticism on video. But censorship of this depth cuts deep into the subjective area of freedom of expression and the censorship of ideas. The paternalism of the Board towards adults affected their capacity to discriminate.

What is an R18 adult and an 18 adult? It is not good enough to say that each film should be judged on its merits. This means that a civil servant can be the sole judge of what the rest of us see, or what films film-makers can make that will be available on the free market. Similarly, it is not good enough for the Censor to award an R18 certificate to sex movies. A majority of the public didn't wish to go to sleazy sex establishments to buy films to consume in the comfort of their own homes. The public wanted them by mail from respectable companies, or to hire them from their local video shops. There should have been an objective list of things we could or couldn't show. Saying that a film is prurient or sleazy says more about the person making the remark than anything else. Not to give a list was pure deception. Of course, they understood and I understood, that once it was written down I could take them to the European Court of Human Rights under Article 10 'freedom of expression.'

Sexual pleasure should be a perfectly legitimate subject matter for films. Legal acts do not become illegal because they are shown on film.

If the government sincerely wanted to ban 'nasties,' why haven't they got R18 Violent Shops, run by authoritarians, where only violent films could be purchased?

*   *   *

Our customer correspondents were a worldly wise, hard-bitten bunch, and it was not so easy to pull the wool over their eyes, honed as they were by years of censorship repression.
They were our private anti-censorship campaigners.

Dear Sir,
          You have my fullest support in your certification battle. This sort of meddling in one's right to choose merely creates an offence where none existed before. Taken to extremes no freedom is sacred – these busybodies take

everything to extremes! The main consequence will be to drive even innocent adult material underground with all the scope that offers to the rip-off organisations, blackmailers and malicious informers.

Sincerely

Dear Sirs,

I agree with your views on censorship of violence, but do not think legal sexual acts should be censored (There is less sex crime on the Continent.)

Yours Faithfully

Sirs,

...... Is it a video where all the sex scenes are hidden? You never see a penis or a vagina. All you see are a couple going through the actions, and what I want to see is I want to see the sexual organs in the act of having sex. I can see wrestling anytime on TV and the films I have bought recently are just videos of a couple wrestling. All you see is her head going up and down ... In plain words I want to see the lot, not imagine it. If I have to use my imagination I can read a book.

Sincerely

Dear Sir,

...... I for one will certainly not be purchasing any further videos which have been 'got at' by the BBFC and the now infamous 18 symbol. Good Luck, but at this moment of time I'm afraid the vocal minority are in the driving seat.

Yours truly,

THE WORLD IN CLOSE UP

Dear Reader,
After reading your advert in the video magazine, I felt I must write. I am a member of the RMAC that stands for Responsible Majority Against Censorship. There are other such organisations, which are also against this outrageous dictatorship, that this minority of the so called 'new right,' or ban brigade, have been doing in the last few years ......I agree with you, most of the European countries allow their people over the age of eighteen to view sexually explicit material, and so should we. I think you will find also that Denmark have just brought that age limit down by two years. It must be nice to live somewhere that treat their adults as just that, instead of this country where a small minority of dictators feel they have some right to tell the rest of the people what they can and can't view. Again, I agree with you when you said that the law was first of all brought about because of the so called video 'nasties.' I think that most responsible people agree that violence is a different matter, but what angers me is the way that people like Mrs Whitehouse have put sex and violence in the same category. A scene of a sexual nature is a thing of beauty, but violence is ugly. I think even video shop owners would agree with that. But of course, as usual, there were a few irresponsible ones who didn't think, and sold the 'nasties,' and of course that's just the action the ban brigade wanted ... They had to over-react. Instead of being reasonable about the matter, they banned everything they disapproved of. In your campaign I hope you will remember to fight all the censorship that goes on in the arts, and by that I mean television.

I look forward to your letter.

Q: Dad. What's the difference between a pornographic
   film and a ordinary film?

A: In a pornographic film, son, all the sex takes place on
   the set.

2

He came through the curtain which hung over the door: a
long fur coat covered gaudy plus-fours, a rainbow creation
of silky material which shimmered in our spotlight. He had
on a white trilby hat, kipper tie, two-tone co-respondent
shoes, and a diamond-topped walking stick.

'Who on earth is this?' Jack said, addressing me.

'Miller's the name. The one and only. There'll never be
another. They don't make 'em today.'

'It's a Max Miller impersonator if you ask me.' I said in
semi-hushed tones.

The man pulled two books from his pocket, one white, the
other blue.

'In the White Book they're all clean jokes and in the Blue
Book there's all the others. Which do you want – the White
Book or the Blue Book?'

'The Blue Book, Max – the Blue Book,' the small
audience shouted. Max had a touch of the matinee idol about
him.

'Did you hear about the fella who came home one night
and his wife had two black eyes? He said: 'Where did you
get the black eyes?' She said: 'The Lodger gave them to
me.' He said: 'The Lodger?' She said: 'Yes.' He said:
'Where's the lodger?' She said: 'Upstairs.' He shouted
upstairs, he said: 'Did you give my wife two black eyes?'
The lodger said: 'Yes.' He said: 'What for?' The lodger
said: 'I found out she was unfaithful to us.'

We all fell about laughing.

'It's all clever stuff you know. No, listen. I was up this
mountain and I was edging along this narrow ledge – it was
so narrow there was only room for one – side-saddle – so
anyway, suddenly I saw this beautiful girl coming towards
me – along this ledge. There was no room for her to pass.
Honestly, I didn't know whether to block her passage or

toss … …

I know what you're saying. You wicked lot. You're the sort of people who get me a bad name.'

More laughter.

'Can he sing a song?' Jack asked.

'Sing us a song Maxie.' I called out, pushing the new performer to the edge, to see what he was capable of.

Without a mike, or backing music, he sang a song about his old Mum, the finest friend a fellow ever had.

The song went on and on, and the audience were spellbound. At the end there was not a dry eye in the house, as they say. It was a moving elegy to a lost form of entertainment, unmolested by time or tyranny, and Miller was the emissary from that vanished civilization.

'Yes. We'll have him.' Jack at last said. He was reluctant to dismiss anyone.

'But how'll we use him?' I asked.

'Just wait and see!' he replied, as he shot me one of his most sanguine looks, almost cocksure. He had a more sunny faith in humanity than I had, and an unvanquishable spirit, but I agreed in a small voice.

Max's audition took place in a derelict pub we hired from an Islington pub theatre. We had put an advertisement in Stage newspaper, asking people to turn up for auditions at a certain time and place. Surprisingly, we had a generous turnout.

On the second day of auditions we saw a few coma-inducing, anodyne performances. One was too dull, even for moths. Another girl, impressively statuesque, with bright eyes and pale, flaxen hair, inspired everyone with her honeydew voice when she sang an unaccompanied song. Unfortunately her acting turned out to be below par; and that was a compliment. Some actors were would-bes, who had been sent by the acting establishment to the back of the acting queue in steerage, along with the forgotten people. As in all talent competitions, just when the judges start to get worn down, someone appears to impress them. One chap, in weather-beaten trilby hat, and a long gabardine raincoat, who maintained he had just been busking in Trafalgar Square, materialised with a look-alike, who metamorphosed into a 1950s variety act at the touch of a button. The gabardine raincoat played a creditable few numbers on a saxophone. The man's general chippiness made him a worthy contender for stardom.

The third day raised our hopes of discovering talent by a meaningful leap.

A Prince Charles impersonator appeared from behind our curtain, followed by a black, comedienne; probably the only one in London at the time with stand-up comedy experience. But the prize went to a diminutive street dancer and his side-kick, a twenty four stone, black wrestler.

When a Texas cowboy, in cowboy hat and boots arrived, with a pocketful of songs, a guitar, and a sob story about separating from his wife, two film scripts were already in Jack's head.

'I could really do something with this guy, based upon his life story alone,' Jack said, with an air of reckless abandon. Given my amateur hands, there was nothing for me to do but agree.

The auditions were an eye-opener. So much unrecognised and dormant talent lay neglected in London's crevices and cubby-holes. It was surprising how a small advert in a theatrical trade paper could bring it to the surface. No doubt the authorities kept a lid on this by creating entry restrictions, overseen by the actors' union engaged as gatekeepers. In other words it amounts to a closed shop. Theatrical and screen royalty carved up the pitches for themselves and their friends. There again, in other respects the business is not all it seems to be. There are a limited number of job opportunities for actors. The supply of actors for stage and screen far outstrips the demand. Places are not open to competition. It is not a meritocracy. Sons and daughters of the middle classes must be catered for first. The rest are left with the crumbs. Heavy competition for the little that is left means the numbers of casualties are high.

Throughout the summer months of that year, Jack and I produced two feature films.

The first was the usual rags to riches story of a former millionaire, now penniless, who decides to make a comedy movie without any cash. He tours London with only his still camera. Basing this story line on the reality of what we did ourselves, the penniless director puts an advertisement in a showbiz paper, to find an amazing pool of talent in London waiting to be discovered. It was a metaphor for the then Prime Minister, Margaret Thatcher's New Britain, and the spirit of free enterprise. We hoped to tune into the 1980s' zeitgeist.

All through the film there was a merging of fiction and reality. The viewer was prompted to ask – have the incidents been staged, or are they spontaneous – do the actors believe the film will ever be made? Throughout, the camera was used as a paintbrush across the canvas of reality. In fact the viewer becomes involved in making decisions about the film by becoming part of the action.

Suitably emboldened, the theme of the second film, like the first, was about being successful. A Texas cowboy comes to London by mistake. While there, he decides to see if the streets are paved with gold. After frequent returns to his residence under Waterloo Bridge – the cardboard hotel or Hotel Carton - he eventually cuts his own record and enters on the conveyor belt to fame and fortune.

Here we have it then, two films with the hardcore cut out by the actors themselves: so, no enemas and no water sports; a triumph of prudence over passion, no doubt.

THE QUEST

Putting on big productions was attended by a welter of new problems, not the least of which was checking that the continuity was precise, which means checking whether actors' clothes etc., had changed when moving from one scene to another. Then came the search for appropriate locations. That wasn't so difficult, after all, as we centred most of the scenes around London. Post-production work revealed the biggest flaw in our technique. The number of camera masters was too great, because we had not made the required camera edits. It was the inevitable result of the way the films were made – unscripted and on the hoof. Jack kept the scripts in his head most of the time, linking scenes to create a story. Then tendency then was to walk a narrow line between chaos and order. As a consequence, the film riffed, and when it seemed that the theme was veering off into randomness, he had constantly to bring it back again to unite it with the visual melody.

The final edited version exposed the flaws. Scenes were often too long and needed re-editing. We had Bernie Mason's antique equipment, so sometimes the sound was poor with background sound not isolated; and yet sometimes it was very good. Outside shots, at night, suffered from poor image quality at times. Being on the move meant the camera became unsteady in some scenes. I noticed, though, that as video camera footage became more popular in mainstream television camerawork, the images created by the professionals were as unsteady as ours.

Apart from this, the films were an accomplishment. I learned about linking shots, splicing, sound dubbing, burnt-in timecode, and placing music over images, as our original songs were produced and edited at a recording studio in Denmark Street. The actors were pleased at earning £50 a day; in a few cases just for short performances.

LIVING ON GOLD TIME

Dear Reader,

You may still be thinking film-making is a piece of cake. No such luck I'm afraid. Achieving the right mix of eroticism is an art in itself. Pick up your video camera and try it. Think of a script. Take an everyday situation. Build a story around it. Arrange your actors and actresses, locations, lights. Get the actors and actresses in the mood and get them on location at the right time. Shoot. Cut. Edit.

Not easy is it? What! You tripped over and fused the lights. What! No props. You left the lens cap on. Someone knocked at the door. It poured with rain. You ran out of cassettes on location. The camera angles were rubbish. There's no continuity in the dress code. It's out of focus. Your lead actor wasn't in the mood for the bedroom scene.

Never mind. Your problems are just beginning.

Bob

*   *   *

I don't quite remember all the details of how it happened, but we were awarded an exhibition stand at Cannes international festival.

I arrived early at the office one day. Mysteriously, Jack was already there.

'We're going to Mipcom at the Palais des Festivals et des Congrès,' he blurted out, while jumping up and down. 'I phoned the Board of Trade and told them we are young entrepreneurs keen to break into the European Market. And they agreed, by letting us take part in the British Overseas Trade Board Subvention Scheme. That means we get a four-unit exhibition stand with a Board of Trade Subsidy.'

THE QUEST

'Wait a minute. Hold on. First things first,' I said exasperated. What's Mipcom for a start?' I couldn't believe we had come so far so soon.

Jack picked up a book he had put on a shelf and read out: Mipcom is an International films and programmes market for TV, Video, Cable and satellite. He put the book down.

'If we go there we've made it. At the very least we'll pick up customers and plenty of info besides.'

'The next big question is: 'What are we going to sell?'

Jack thought for a moment.

'We can't take the sex films as we've still got to get full BBFC classification on most of them, but we'll take the publicity material for them, as we're bound to find dealers in the hard stuff there.'

He thought again.

'We'll take the feature film we've just made. That's an 18 certificate and that should attract the customers.'

'What if they don't want to buy that?'

'Use it to sell the hard stuff. All big companies have an interest in earthly delights. Believe me.'

'And where's Cannes for Christ sake, and what is this Palais des Festivals?'

'It's in the south of France on the French Riviera. The Palais is a convention hall virtually on the beach. We've got two months to get our act together. Six weeks to be precise.'

Jack went off and made a cup of tea. On returning he said: 'Cheer up Bob. We'll be millionaires. We'll be standing our ground with the likes of Walt Disney and MGM.'

I had some misgivings. I thought for a moment about all the problems of getting there and back on our limited budget, and paying for a week in Cannes.

'Think of all the sunshine.' He was trying to raise my spirits. 'Think of walking along La Croisette with a nice girl on your arm.'

I couldn't.

'Take a doss at this map.' Jack said as he spread an AA road map out across the table. We'll take the ferry from Dover to Calais. Here.' His finger marked the spot. 'And take the A26 and A1 down to Paris. The problem will be getting round Paris. We'll pick up the A6 all the way down to Lyon, and the A7 towards Marseille in the south. After that it's easy-peasy along the south coast to Cannes.'

I saw Monte-Carlo along the coast, and immediately thought for a moment about some comedy film title from the 1960s, called *Monte-Carlo or Bust,* based upon the Monte-Carlo Rally. The plot was about the disastrous adventures of rally enthusiasts.

'Alright, alright! You've convinced me,' I said reluctantly. 'But I'm sure it will bankrupt us.'

'All the new orders we get should cover us.'

This turned out to be but a frail optimism.

'Where do we stay?'

'A lot of the incidentals we'll know when we've signed the contract; and more about the stand as well.'

Over the next few weeks there were lots of preparations to make. It was impossible for just the two of us to do anything on our own, let alone going all the way to Cannes. We had to get a film crew together, or at least more hands on deck. We needed a salesman, primarily. Eventually we got a friend to help us who had sales experience, but who was temporarily unemployed. Then we trawled through our portfolio of models and would-be models, and selected the four best looking girls to back-up work on the stand, and generally to look pretty for customers. After some phoning around, two of them enthusiastically offered to come, as long as we paid the expenses for food and accommodation.

Other expenses followed – insurance, rental of extra VCRs, AA five-star service, Board of Trade expenses, print costs for mail shots and paperwork etc., etc. On top of all this, we needed something called a carnet, or list of all that we intended to take through the customs. It allowed for the temporary importation of goods free of Customs Duties. It required the submission of serial numbers and model numbers.

'We'll have to take the video camera, U-matic recorder, lights and some equipment,' declared Jack. 'Although we're on a selling spree you never know who we can use to make a film. Besides, filming in Cannes is good publicity material.

Later we were sent the technical file of the Cannes exhibition area by the Board of Trade, with all the details, dimensions, even location of electric plugs on them, and furniture or plants we could use to decorate the stand we had hired.

When the big day arrived we loaded up two cars while the girls sat in the back of one making their faces up.

Getting to Paris on the ferry and by road took eight hours. Then there was an eight hour drive to Cannes. A few times we drove the wrong way around roundabouts, and hence the wrong way down motorway slip roads.

Upon arrival the air in Cannes was fresh and warm, even though it was early morning. We drove down La Croisette waterfront avenue with its palm trees, restaurants, cafés, boutiques and whitewashed buildings. The exhibition organisers had allocated apartment accommodation near the seafront for the week. Next day we dressed our stand next to CNN's. All in all the week passed relatively uneventfully, even though it was Cannes. We had an article about us in Mipcom News. There were plenty of visitors to our stand. We handed out wads of publicity material, exchanged numerous business cards, and the girls, in between times, frolicked and posed on the beach for the locals.

When we arrived back in London there was plenty of correspondence on the mat from all over the world: Brazil, South Africa, Italy, Sweden, the Philippines and such like. Some potential foreign buyers wanted 'screening cassettes' or soft-sex titles (soft-core) which were possible to rate 16 with the German Censorship Board. Since we already had a battle with the British censor, we were hardly in the mood for more confrontation. However, we sent them a VHS viewing cassette, compilation or demo tape, but we had to be careful who these so-called 'buyers' were; whether they were just pirates; especially the ones who wanted all our packaging and point-of-sale material as well.

Some potential buyers considered that they would manufacture under licence, or make an outright buy-out. But, preferably, we were not willing to supply unless they were looking for a sole-rights deal for their own territories, or were seriously interested in the rights, and would sign a clause in the contract that they wouldn't re-import into the U.K.

We figured this would see the sharks off.

One piece of correspondence did attract our attention. It was from The Black Eye Production Company of Naples, Italy.

'Here you are. You've got an offer you can't refuse. It's from the mafia,' I said, handing it to Jack.

'A black eye. That's what you get if you don't do what you're told.'

We both fell about laughing, but pulled ourselves together to be more serious.

'Of course you realise the Italians can't make sex films.' Jack said. 'It's all dubbed with Oohs! and Aghhs! It's only the Americans who can make films with all the right production values and cinematography.'

'Be that as it may,' I protested, 'this letter says that one of the Italian film representatives will be in London. They'd like to meet us with a view to buying the rights on our films.'

'What do you reckon?' Jack said.

I was game for anything.

'Okay.' I agreed. 'I'll write back and arrange for a meet.'

THE QUEST

'Make it in that coffee shop in the corner of Soho Square. We can always send the bloke along to the censor at number 3 Soho Square to iron out our differences.'

More hilarious laughter.

'But perhaps they've been mates all along.' I conjectured.

'Then we'd better be sure he doesn't iron us out.'

We sat in the café in Soho Square the morning of the meeting. Spot on time a man appeared in a sharp suit with a coat hanger in his jacket, or overlarge shoulder pads, anyhow.

'Bit small isn't he?' I said.

'Yeah! But his body's as unyielding as a brick shit house.'

After the initial introduction and handshakes, and the orders, he disappeared into the gents' toilet.

I came back with his coffee. 'He's been away for a long time. Where the hell has he gone?' I said.

'To put the gun behind the cistern in the bog I expect.' Some muted thoughts followed. Then he returned. It transpired that he wanted to see several potential clients that morning. So when he left, we left with a promise to mail him demo tapes. We had no idea at this juncture of the outcome of this meeting.

Next day I had booked my first flight to Amsterdam. Lo and behold, at the transit gate our friend appeared with a sharp-suited girl in tow. I kept my eyes on him throughout the whole flight. At Schipol airport I looked behind me until I was well out of his sight. I let him take the first train to Central Station. Suspicion is good for the soul.

*   *   *

After the fiasco of the Appeal I researched the possibility of acquiring a sex shop in Soho. It wouldn't have been economically viable to place our films in someone else's sex shop, as we couldn't consent or conspire to defraud the customer or innocent tourist. Having our own shop might have opened up new opportunities and ways to avoid the pirates. However, Westminster City Council Regulations made it difficult to open such an establishment unless we agreed to be driven down into presenting sex as a degrading and degraded activity, on a par with shops which had blacked-out windows and over-censored displays. Presumably, they expected us to skulk in the corner. For them, all sex was dirty, and every participant had to look degraded and be invisible to passers by. On top of rules and regulations, our costing showed that it would require an initial capital input of £10,000 (high by 1980s' standards.)

Really, we needed a duplication bank, editing suite, vehicles for location work, and money for publicity. But this was all beyond our means at the time. We had a skirmish with Equity, the actors' union, as well. They told us not to use non-Equity members, although we paid everyone Equity rates and we didn't discriminate. That went down well with those actors bent on getting an Equity number. Equity was really a form of closed shop, run by those doing very nicely indeed; a conspiracy against the poor in fact. The biggest hurdle for film-making outsiders was monopoly control of outlets and distribution networks, which were practically leak-proof and unconquerable. Frankly, we produced films for less than the film establishment stick up their noses while partying on Saturday nights.

We decided to concentrate our energies in other directions. We had already established another office in Fitzrovia, and decided to take out classified ads in national newspapers. But first we had to be members of MOPS – the Mail Order Protection Scheme; a body set up by the national newspapers to protect themselves and the public from unscrupulous behaviour when customers sent cash by mail order. MOPS checks whether the applicant for membership has a character reference, an official address, and the necessary stock to fulfil orders, and makes sure advertising is vetted prior to publication. We were accepted and became members.

'We'll get an ad in the News of the World,' Jack said.

'Wait a minute. Isn't that the underworld's trade paper?'

'Don't be so negative. So what! We're protected by MOPS too!'

Our first ad was a small piece, six by four. Centimetres, that is. It brought in a postbag of enquiries. Apparently national newspaper advertising was the answer. Shortly, we began to realise that national exposure also had its drawbacks. One day a complaint came in from Trading Standards saying we were selling uncertificated material. A customer was pursuing an issue, or vendetta, far beyond any reasonable brief. We saw him off.

'Don't you find it strange?' I said to Jack, 'although we've jumped all the hurdles with the BBFC and all that, and even become members of MOPS, the authorities always seem to be one step ahead, ready to set up other hurdles?'

Jack nodded.

'And they always know what we're doing. Do you know what?'

'What?'

'I think that the News of the World is the Old Bill, the police in print. The News of the World acts as a trawler, setting out to sea to capture all manner of deep sea fish.'

Jack stared at me without speaking.

'This place is bugged. By whom I don't know, but we've had plenty of actors and odd characters coming through here.'

Jack walked around the office and looked out of the rain-speckled window. 'If you're right, what are we going to do about it?'

'We've got to set up in Amsterdam. There's no alternative. At least we'll begin on a level playing field there.' I said.

'I'll go along with that.'

LIVING ON GOLD TIME

'One last gesture before we do,' I added further, 'I'm going to send a copy of our feature film to East Germany. They'd appreciate its subtleties, especially the bit in the film where our actors are driven to sleeping in boxes, under Waterloo Bridge, and busking for a crust. That'll foil the authorities and stir things up a bit.'

*   *

I opened up the map and spread it across the table in the railway carriage. The small print was difficult to see as the train pulled out and proceeded through a tunnel. The flight had been delayed by an hour at Heathrow and it arrived at Schipol, at four o'clock, London Time.

When the train eventually burst out into the fading, but natural, winter light, the map was easily discernable. The orange and blue of the buildings and canals formed concentric circles around Amsterdam's Central Station. I glanced from the map to the monotonous, flat landscape, outside, then down again to the list of people and places to go, which I had sketched out on a piece of notepaper. I thought about that evening, and how I would feel, and what I would discover in a city whose contours I was barely acquainted with.

Twenty minutes, and the train slipped passed Sloterdijk into Amsterdam Central Station. Trams, those perambulators of the people, queued in the forecourt of the station. A hurdy-gurdy man played 'roll out the barrel' as he turned the wheel of an ancient organ. Slotted cardboard sheets, like computer cards, powered it into greater life. A ragged group of street musicians thumped out their harmonies to some attendant tourists and a solitary dog. Everyone appeared to be heading straight on. I followed, clutching a small weekend case, but came up against the tidal wave of people leaving the city via the station. The Damrak was crowded. Flotillas of tourists were replaced by the earnest faces of

Dutch commuters. I stopped at a small cabin to eat a fresh herring before searching for an hotel.

'Turn left off the Damrak into the Zeedijk area,' the station porter had said in punctilious English, 'down into the Warmoesstraat.'

I swivelled the map in my hands, flexed my stiffening fingers, and made my way passed a garishly lit porn shop. Then another porn shop. Then another. Anal, oral, wet sex, lolitas – the varieties of sexual pleasures were endless. Gadgets Michelle would have been proud of, adorned the window displays. There were porn videos in garish boxes, whose point of sale material and quality we could only aspire to. Giggling knots of women inspected the windows with ever ascending eyebrows. Familiar as I was with London's Soho, I still felt slightly apprehensive in Amsterdam's notorious red light area, like one who had lived fiercely in the emotions but had no real experience of life.

A flag with three black crosses on it fluttered over a little hotel called The Mercury. The hotel catered for all. Its rooms were small but clean. It had a bar and tables for breakfast set in the window. The tables were covered in what appeared to be carpets or rugs. Loud disco music blared from the coffee shop next door. Young Dutch boys and girls sat pressed against the entrance, and the murky light was dimmed even further by the brown varnished paintwork inside.

'What's the sweet odour coming from the coffee shop next door?' I asked Geert, the barman of The Mercury.

'Don't you know?' he answered stolidly. 'Why it's hashish! Smoking is tolerated here. The Dutch police have regulated its use. The price is twenty five guilders and it's the same all over the city.'

I pressed the barman further: 'Does this happen throughout Holland?'

He wearily cleaned some glasses with a cloth. His conversation was hesitant, the English gentle, undogmatic, brooding.

'Yes. But Amsterdam is Amsterdam. It's unlike anywhere else in Holland.'

I nodded. The man's thick black moustache made his eyes look even heavier, and emphasised the brusque military exterior.

'The Amsterdam police, when they go on strike, walk about naked in protest.' He stopped cleaning, and treading a temperamental line between charm and rage said: 'Heavens, what is Amsterdam coming to?'

'Yes. What?' I said mimicking, then commiserating and confusing my own apprehensions with the barman's conservatism. I felt that he must be politically conservative with a big C.

I remembered a friend saying that when he did National Service he noted that the Dutch army was anarchic and disorganised by English standards. Hair over the collar and all that, even in the nineteen fifties.

'Do you know these Brown Bars have a menu of available dope?' the barman continued gloomily: 'Give me the menu, everyone demands when they come in here.'

'No!' I mixed understatement with pleasure.

'One night we had two English boys in here. They both had enough dope to immobilise a horse, on top of which they'd both been drinking.

'No!' I said again.

'Burnt the bed they did.' He retained his pained expression.

'Golly.'

This would sound great in my book I thought. Yes, a book it was going to have to be. The unpredictability of my adventures demanded it. I visibly cheered up, despite the weather.

THE QUEST

*   *

Meanwhile, two suited figures stood in the foyer of the Ambassador Hotel. The taller of the two downed his Scotch in one gulp.

'He's here. That little upholder of the rules,' he protested in a boyish, hoodlum way.

'How d'ya know?' the other man enquired.

'He's been seen.' He put the glass down purposefully on a table. 'We'll have to tell him something sooner or later. He's one of … well … them … impeccable credentials apparently.'

'Only tell him enough to frighten him off. Freak him out if you must. You know the guvnor's not going to be pleased by any of this,' the other man said with cowboy manners.

'Fuck him. He's on a right little earner and expects me to do his dirty work for a monkey.'

'Don't grouse,' the other said, as they both trudged upstairs. 'He'll pull you out with early retirement whenever you want.'

*   *

Saturday it rained: pounding, uninviting rain, like London. The neon sign winked through the sodden panes of the Hotel Mercury's windows.

I read out the first name on my list of contacts. I had gathered them from a businessman I met in Cannes. My job was to search out potential buyers, or distributors, for our films.

'Julius, Julius Hoogstraten? My name's Bob Wildman. I'd like to come and see you. I was given your name by a contact in Cannes.' I said the words quickly, as if by filling the listener's brain with information it prevented a refusal. I held on to the receiver for a moment, listening, then slapped it down. A man in a trench coat stared at me from across a table. I looked over my shoulder. Around, No one else there. Onset of doubt? 'I think not,' I reported to myself.

Vinkenstraat the street sign displayed. Number eighty two was written on my paper. The door with its spy-hole, was imitation Georgian, improvised for the purpose of excluding unwanted guests. A girl with heavily made-up eyes opened it and stood back.

'Julius Hoogstraten. I've an appointment.' I was abrupt, almost rude.

'Upstairs please.' The girl spoke broken English.

The lights were dimmed and I bumped into customers at the top. My eyes were as yet unaccustomed to the ultra-violet and red light. Customers leaned on girls at the bar. Other girls sat in armchairs. 'A brothel.' I rehearsed the words to myself.

'He'll see you now.' A girl's voice answered crisply. I followed her down some steps and into a room. A wiry, broad-shouldered man in black track suit and Chinese slippers sat, arms folded, on a straight-backed chair. The man was handsome, high cheek-boned, maybe fifty years of age, or perhaps thirty five. His expression gave very little away. I eyed him with chilly respect.

I stretched out a hand: 'Mr Hoogstraten?'

'Not me. He's there.' He clicked his tongue reprovingly. The man switched his gaze and pointed to a curtain, behind which another man of about sixty five, military looking, small moustache, and grey on top, washed his hands.

'Aha! He ventured, turning. 'You've come to see me.'

'Are you Hoogstraten?' I was still uncertain.

'Correct,' was the reply. Hoogstraten walked across the room drying his hands on a towel. He spread it on the back of a chair and sat at his desk.

I drew up a chair a few feet away from the man in black. 'Who sent you?'

A Mr. Jack Goodman. Do you know him?'

'Heard of him,' Hoogstraten said.

'Still smudging is he?'

A quaint English term for a foreigner to use, I thought. 'No. Its video and feature films.' I said proudly.

'So,' Hoogstraten said with faint contempt.

'I'm looking for potential buyers or distributors for our films.'

'Well. Amsterdam's the right place.' He said. 'It's not my game. But I know a man, Walter Nagel, who'll help you in a big way.'

Hoogstraten's face was blank, revealing nothing. 'He's frequently a visitor here. A client, of course.' He huffed and puffed a little in irritation. 'But I only know him as a client. He never informs me when he visits. He just arrives.'

I was eager: 'Do you know the place he frequents?'

'Danny knows of such places. Don't you Danny?'

Hoogstraten pointed to the man in the track suit, then corrected himself. 'Sorry. You aren't acquainted. This is Danny Daniels. English like yourself.' He was all charm again.

I acknowledged the man with a smile, a small uncommunicative smile. He grinned back, but his grin was tough.

Suddenly the door opened. A man in a Fair Isle sweater lumbered in. Hoogstraten spoke at length to him in Dutch with a few words in Russian. Hoogstraten had a deep claret voice with rich brocade tones, like a man who had passed a dizzyingly varied career in the theatre. I thought of the port in Amsterdam: the sailors, trade delegations and the comers and goers on the fringes of respectable society. Hoogstraten carried on the conversation as the man hunched over the desk.

I glanced at Daniels' face which was expressionless, then surveyed the room, its clutter and memorabilia. It was heavily draped with velvet. A wooden chair disappeared out of sight in one corner. Faded newspaper cuttings were pinned to one wall. Above the desk, on a shelf was a new pile of books. I craned my head forward and sideways. Freud and Jung were printed down the spine. A tattered carpet covered the floor, but worn linoleum was visible at the edges.

The phone rang. Hoogstraten answered it. The man in the sweater turned round and smiled. Hoogstraten moved his chair to face me but continued speaking in Dutch. His eyes challenged mine. As he replaced the receiver the man in the sweater backed out through the door and left.

'He's my odd job man,' Hoogstraten eventually said abruptly, referring to the visitor. 'A Russian. A relation of mine.'

Hoogstraten slumped back in the chair, picked up a cigarette from his desk, lit it and blew a smoke ring in the air.

'I'm sorry I can't be of more help to you.'

As an afterthought he asked for his visitor's name again and wrote it down on a notepad.

'Danny here will take you to some of Walter Nagel's watering holes.'

Danny nodded assent.

Watering holes. I thought for a moment about another particularly English phrase.

I didn't know it then, but I was to meet several of the Hoogstratens of this world in my stays in Amsterdam.

That evening I arranged to meet Danny Daniels in a coffee shop in the Voorburgwal Oudezijds. Even in the early evening the prostitutes in their cabins along Amsterdam's canals were opening up for business. A few older, male tourists and some young couples ambled by, judging the quality of the product for sale. A man of about seventy five rode by me on a white bicycle. He parked it against a railing, took off his cycle clips, disappeared into a cabin and the curtain was pulled across the window. Very civilised, I thought.

THE QUEST

Danny Daniels was waiting outside the coffee shop. He had an overcoat over his black track suit, but still wore the improbable Chinese slippers. Inside, the atmosphere was rendolent with the sweet smell of hashish. We sat at the bar.

Danny ordered: 'The menu please. And two coffees.'

The barman opened a file with plastic pages. Each page contained sachets of different herbs – Moroccan, Afghan, Nepalese, Lebanese, sensimilla. Danny gave the barman twenty five guilders for a small plastic packet of sensimilla.

'The best, this is,' he said, turning to me. 'Skunk, it's known as locally. Home grown. From the top of the plant.'

Danny placed a large cigarette paper on the wooden ridge on the edge of the counter and broke the herb up along its length. He fashioned a cardboard filter and made it into a cigarette, twisting the end to prevent the contents falling out.

'What! No tobacco?' I exclaimed.

'No. It spoils the taste.'

Danny put his head back, lit the joint and inhaled the smoke deep into his lungs. He passed the joint to me.

I pulled a protesting face. 'What do I do with it?'

'Smoke it.'

'But I don't smoke.'

'Never mind. Take a deep puff into your lungs.'

I was frightened of the possible effects; but I had come this far, and I intended to see my mission through to the end, despite what I might have to endure. The smoke made me cough and I quickly handed it back to him. I expected an effect. There was none.

Danny smiled wryly, then said: 'Never smoked before?'

'Never.'

'It's the same high as alcohol, but clearer,' He replied.

'Oh!' I said, anticipating some instant physical reaction.

Danny sat back, contented. 'Do you know,' he began, 'Amsterdam is a huge theatre. People from elsewhere come here, to these coffee shops, and think that everyone inside is a tourist or stranger, and no one knows anyone else. In fact we know everyone. Only the visitor is a stranger. The visitor comes to Amsterdam and enters the stage of our theatre. You can get everything here. The police run them as information exchanges, and to keep an eye on new arrivals. The authorities use them to distribute social welfare. You can even get your hair cut here, when the barber comes on a certain day. Notice that there are children around. It's like a social club.'

I stared at Daniels and thought for a moment. Of his background I knew little. He was not particularly forthcoming either. He told me he had worked for Julius Hoogstraten for some months and had a part share in an Amsterdam jewellery shop. He had lived in Amsterdam for two years, and was wanted by the British police for jumping bail on a charge of smuggling cannabis. Although I expected him to know of Nagel's whereabouts, he knew nothing of that either. He even seemed a little vague about his full description.

I withdrew a piece of paper from my pocket and looked again at Jack's list of people and places to visit. Danny glanced over my shoulder at the writing on my notepaper.

'The Meridian, that's a disco,' he said, pointing to one of the entries. 'I'll take you there tonight. But it's not for the squeamish.' He looked at the other entries. 'The Glove. That's a porn shop. We'll go there tomorrow. But the Pretty Face ...' It was the last name on the list. 'That's closed.'

Casually I asked: 'Have you met Walter Nagel?'

'Once or twice. When he passes through. He's a small guy who lives, I remember, in a Crombie-style overcoat. Bald on top, black hair on the sides. Hoogstraten thinks I know more about him than I do.'

Danny stopped talking for a moment and looked to his right and left. 'See that guy on your right?' There was a crumpled figure sitting on a stool next to me. 'There's something odd about him.' Danny put his hand down the front of his tracksuit trousers. I could see the hilt of a knife.

Suddenly I became scared. Was it the dope or the fear of a
threatened attack? The music seemed to get louder and
louder. I felt the blood drain from my face and my breath
getting shorter. An uncomfortable anxiety welled up inside
me. Voices were speaking, giving me contradictory orders. I
compromised with them.

'Let's go,' I said, agitated, and walked out with a brisk,
fluid movement.

Danny was unprepared to leave but sensed my unease and
followed me out of the bar. He stood beside me as I took
some deep breaths.

'Can be scary if you're not used to the smoke and
atmosphere.' His smile was warm and embracing.

'Certainly can. I'm not sure what you gave me entirely
agrees with me.'

I looked into the canal, at the shimmering water and
around at the neon lights. The fresh air brought relaxation.

'You ready for the disco then?' he whispered cheerfully, to
arouse new life into me.

'Okay,' I replied, thinking objectively now of my sudden
lapse into paranoia again.

The lights of the Meridian added a new dimension to my
delusions. Amsterdam's night life and underworld seemed to
be crowded around the disco bar. Danny rolled another joint.

'Not another. I don't know how you can take it,' I said
amazed.

'By not drinking alcohol, mainly,' he replied. 'Look over
there.' He gestured towards a group of girls seated around a
man of Middle-Eastern appearance with matted dreadlocks.
'That's a coke dealer who knows Nagel. The girls appear in
some of the porn movies you'll find in the shops in the
Zeedijk. Wait here. I'll talk with him.'

I dutifully relaxed at the bar, watching the girls serving
sparkling water and cokes, and the odd customer smoking a
joint.

LIVING ON GOLD TIME

Danny moved over to the group of girls and pulled up a chair next to the dealer. The man with the dreadlocks dipped his head to one side to listen to his conversation. The disco thumped out the monotonous tones of House Music, and a film projector cast psychedelic patterns on the wall. Striking blonde girls kissed and canoodled with their mates at the bar. I drank two glasses of sparkling water and ice before Danny finally came back over.

'He met Nagel two days ago,' he whispered. 'That means he's in town. You're nearly there. Prickly characters though, these coke dealers. They all carry guns. Are as paranoid as fucking hell. They shoot each other out of greed rather than necessity.'

I thought for a moment, London was easy; all rules and nothing could be done, but Amsterdam was blindingly difficult – no rules, so where do you start?

I slept in late Sunday morning. The disco closed at six in the morning. The walk through the town to the Hotel Mercury had been particularly cold.

Despite Danny's optimism, Nagel's whereabouts seemed as far away as ever. I decided to see my last contact at The Glove. A funny name for a pawnshop, but perhaps he was a useful contact.

As I left the hotel on Sunday afternoon, the same man in the trench-coat sat at the table in the window of the hotel. Coincidence, perhaps, I thought to myself.

The Glove was difficult to find. It was tucked away in a side street, away from the main thoroughfare of the canals. The windows were full of books, many privately published. Collectors' copies of old Travellers' Companions, and others with cover illustrations of men and women in leather harnesses and straps, sat side by side with cleverly illustrated video sleeves. Copies of English Sunday newspapers hung outside on a rack. I pulled out a copy of the News of the World and went inside to pay.

The shop was empty, but for a tall, thin man with a goatee beard placing some paperback books in an air-bag ready for dispatch.

I plucked up the courage to speak: 'Walter Nagel. Mr Nagel please.' I was suitably earnest.

The man was silent. After he took my five guilder piece for the newspaper, he placed it in the till and held the change in his hand.

'Who sent you?'

'No one. But Mr Hoogstraten said you might be interested in selling our films; English soft and hard-core.'

The man grew uneasy and peered over his glasses.

'You work for him,' he frowned.

'No. But he works, or he did work for a friend of mine, an Englishman, Jack Goodman.' I tucked the rolled-up newspaper under my arm confidently.

'I'll need a demo copy of the films, then the U-matic master for viewing.' The voice was diamond hard.

I felt triumphant that the escapade was reaching fruition. The man moved away from the till and began stacking video boxes on the shelves. He returned from his task. 'The shop doesn't close till five. Come back and I'll talk then. What's your name?' A note of irritability crept into his tone.

I gave him an alias, thanked him, and left. Nagel had an American accent. It played on my mind. Few of my contacts in Amsterdam had seemed on the face of it to be Dutchman. Hoogstraten could have been an Englishman who knew fluent Dutch. Danny Daniels was supposedly an Englishman, now Nagel was an American, or a Dutchman who had lived in America. At least I had found my quarry, despite the unanswered questions. Jack would be pleased. The job was part finished. It was all downhill from now on.

The man with the goatee was locking the porn shop door when I arrived.

'Good business today?' I asked lightly.

'Okay. English tourists as usual. The best time for them of course is high summer. It's almost exclusively tourist trade. That's why the prices are so high.'

'We'll be going then?' I probed.

His face was stony.

'As you wish.'

He led me up a side street past a group of heroin junkies on one of the bridges over the canal, and through the Nieumarkt to a tall house facing the Geldersekade. He pressed a bell on the door and a buzzer released the lock. We climbed three flights of steep stairs and headed towards a room with the light on. Two men stood near the window. One wore a commodious brown overcoat. The smaller man greeted me.

'Ah! … Mr Wildman, or should it be Dr Wildman?'

I was visibly startled; my dismay palpable. He knew my real name. But how?

'You're very brave coming here alone.'

I nodded, swallowed, and gave a half smile.

He gave a shark smile back.

'You're visit has been a fruitless waste of time I'm afraid.'

The statement confounded me.

'But why?'

The man stopped me in mid sentence and said tautly:

'Come over here to the window.'

I complied, and looked blankly down to the cobbled street far below.

'That's where Walter Nagel landed last night. He fell from this window.'

My mouth sagged open.

The tall man laughed.

*　　　*　　　*

The envelope was franked with the words: Perspective Films Ltd. It read:

THE QUEST

Dear Dr Wildman,
Toni Khan, the American Television
hostess, would like to have you on her forthcoming show
TELL ME ANOTHER.

If you would care to take up this engagement please contact
this office without delay.

Yours Faithfully,

Roger Utley

I was overcome. It must be to do with my prison work I
reasoned to myself

   Before I could respond to the news I had to get to the
office to chat with Jack about the visit to Amsterdam. In
spite of the incident with Walter Nagel, the trip was amply
productive. I had established a new business address near the
Vondelpark in an attractive part of the city. The famous
gathering place, the Leidseplein, was just up the road. I
made a trip to Den Haag to chat with a buyer and I had
become familiar with ways of getting around the city centre.

   'Whatever you do we mustn't give them U-matic masters,
in case they disappear with then.' Jack said. 'There's thieves
everywhere. Give them the compilations and get them to
respond. And don't spend too much time with this Channel
Four nonsense. I need your help in the office here.'

   I told Jack about the incident with Nagel. He said they
were trying to faze me out and not to believe anything. And
besides, Amsterdam was not for the faint-hearted. I felt
mollified.

LIVING ON GOLD TIME

I danced out of the office door at the new prospects.

*   *

In the back streets of London's Tottenham Court Road,
where it is mandatory to get lost and wander, bistros and
wine bars bristled with New Year Life. Lorries unloaded
barrels, young men hurried in and out of doorways, and
pedestrians dodged mountains of black, plastic, rubbish
sacks. The four storey tenements had newly painted railings
and big white doors bearing the names: Premier Films, Astro
Video and Reckitt and Maybury Financial Consultants. The
doors huddled together, warm in the knowledge that they
represented the comfortable yuppiedom of Britain.
Strategically positioned around the headquarters of Channel
Four Television, it was an answer to the Government's
directive to 'buy in' from the independent film companies;
hive off your film producers, set them up in private
companies, buy their products, and all would be well with
the status quo.

I approached the door that bore the legend, Perspective
Films Ltd, and rang the bell. A prim, ineffective junior
opened it and announced herself to be a secretary. The
secretary, with sharply pretty face and gentle hair, directed
me through to a waiting area. The renovated building was
painted harshly white inside. I passed a camera on a tripod,
eerily silent before a colourama screen. Hasselblad was
written across the front of the camera's box.

'Miss Khan will be with you in a moment,' squeaked the
secretary.

She left, and returned almost at once with a white coffee. I
stared into the swirling liquid and wondered what she had
stirred it with.

A pallid man in a worn leather jacket, white trousers and
baseball boots, came in, and beckoned me towards another
room.

176

'I'm Roger Utley, the producer,' he announced.

I nodded appreciatively as I was led into the room. We both sat round a table. From my pocket I removed an ageing box of cigarettes and a lighter that I kept for emergencies like this. I took a cigarette out, lit it awkwardly, and placed both on the table. I slid an ashtray across to my side of the table with a finger.

The producer spoke reassuringly: 'In case you don't know Tell Me Another is a ten part series which will be televised on Channel Four. Miss Khan interviews people with interesting jobs who've got a tale to tell, so to speak.'

'It's not live then?' I remarked, pretending I had knowledge of the way television programmes are put together.

'No.' He seemed a little deflated, but brightened up with the words: 'We'll shoot on location in two weeks and the first show will go out pronto in February at nine thirty. Your name was given to us by someone from the Prison Visitors Association. It seems that your efforts in prison have hit the right chord with a few people, and we think that they should not go unnoticed.'

I visibly beamed. I said: 'You mean my work with the prison art exhibition?'

'I think so,' he announced vaguely.

The door opened and a woman in her late forties rushed in.

'Ahh ... a cancer stick,' she said, disarmingly forthright.

She picked up the ageing pack on the table. After removing a cigarette, she slapped the pack down, put the cigarette between her blood-red lips, lit it and breathed in, sighed, then tightened the belt round her fetching green dress, before planting herself in a chair.

'Hi. Sorry, I'm Toni Khan.'

We both rose slightly from our chairs and shook hands.

'Roger, you just take notes,' the woman directed in a strong East Coast American accent.

LIVING ON GOLD TIME

I smiled amiably at the effervescent personality sitting in front of me.

Toni Khan now said: 'Do you want to come on the show?'

'Of course,' I admitted, 'but what'll I have to do?'

'Well, we know you've worked with prisoners for a long time; you've therefore got considerable understanding of the criminal mind, and the right academic credentials, so the audience will believe you. You've organised exhibitions for them, and doubtless you've got the sort of information that'll be of interest to the audience.'

Toni seemed to have acquired a short curriculum vitae on her prospective interviewee. 'You see, the show's built around me,' she pointed a finger proudly at her flowered green dress, 'I bump into these people who have interesting occupations, but who never appear in the limelight. We're trying to get away from Mr. and Mrs Average, you see. Your slot will be for fifteen minutes. One show runs for forty five minutes, so I'll be interviewing two others besides yourself. The thing is, I've got to bump into you, so we've arranged to meet at Victoria Coach Station. I go to the buffet for a coffee and you're there. Hey presto. Okay?'

I moved my head in agreement.

'Dress as you like. Say what is interesting. We can edit out anything that goes wrong. We'll pay expenses and a small fee. Talk to Roger about that.' She gestured towards the silent but forgiving Roger Utley.

I carried on nodding while thinking of the potentiality of the part.

Toni continued against Roger's silence: 'If you're writing a book or something, you can advertise that, but keep it low key. I'll frame a few questions about crime and prisons and have them sent to you beforehand in preparation.'

With that, Toni rose from her chair and Roger and myself followed suit.

'Got to split. Sorry. This is going to be the best show of the year,' she effused, 'It'll be a riot. Don't worry.'

THE QUEST

Toni left and disappeared to another room.

Roger escorted me to the door and showed me out. We exchanged pleasantries. I was visibly walking on air down the street.

It all happened, just a bit too fast.

*   *   *

The January afternoon closed early as though it were anxious to be quit of the day. The sky was a strange combination of deep midnight blue and fading yellow like a nasty bruise. As the plane rapidly descended, the lights at the end of the wingtips flashed on and off; a beacon against the dark cloud overhanging Schipol Airport.

Upon disembarking, the man hurried through the terminal building to an awaiting train, then on to Amsterdam's Central Station. With haste he booked into the little hotel, The Mercury, where he had stayed on the previous trip. Everything appeared as it was before, only this time the adventure was less well defined. There was no itinerary either. People and places had to be sought out willy-nilly. The objective, however, was the same, to expand the portfolio of contacts for our films.

Amsterdam comes to life at night, around midnight to be precise. On Thursdays the shops opened later, throwing hordes of people on to the streets, to shop and to laugh, and to sing into the early hours. On Friday and Saturday nights sex-starved Englishmen, humiliated by the rip-offs and fake bed shows in London's Soho, throng the Zeedijk for some real sex action, or stare up at the huge advertising hoardings for women's lingerie, where models in their underwear are escorted by similarly attired young female children: eye candy, banned in the UK. The coffee shops seem never to close. Long past the bedtime of respectable Amsterdam citizens, groups of night people sit on stools, or stand around bar counters, sipping orange juice or beer, occasionally rolling joints and negotiating the sort of business deals which the Dutch are so fond of. At Irish bars like Chico's, pints of draught Guinness line the counter amid Irish accents and the drawl of American visitors. Chico's never closes, but sustains an eternal vigilance against the conventions of normal society. At three in the morning, the Rambert next door, opens its doors to the city's fubsy, and not so fubsy, transvestites, who whoop and scream to the resounding delights of popular music. The pilgrimage for the world's wearisome outcasts is complete. Everyone finds a safe haven, washed up on the shore of this flat land. When they settle in Amsterdam they do so promiscuously: a prostitute in the basement, an old lady on the first floor, and a family with children at the top. Amsterdam is a pagan society rebelling with pagan practices against the racket of the cross; a licentious, hedonistic, and some say, heathen, world. It allows everyone a cultural shopping spree of gargantuan self-indulgence.

In one coffee shop in the Leiseplein a figure dressed in black, with close-cropped hair, lifted a lightly packed chillum to his lips and lit the bowl with a lighter, swirling the flame around in a circle to ignite completely the glowing embers. I sidled up beside him.

'Hi, Danny!' I said cheerfully.

Danny's eyes swivelled down as he continued to hold the chillum up and breathe the pungent smoke into his lungs. Eventually he rested the pipe on the counter.

'Hi, Sherlock Holmes! Back again?' he said.

'Afraid so,' I gasped, still short of breath from the run from the station and hotel. 'Still got to meet a few people. I've still not got what I wanted to know.'

I was loath to tell him everything about our business, and chose to be elliptical and open-ended as the Dutch appeared to be with me.

'Why are you pursuing your enquiries so vigorously?' he sniffed; his face stiffening. 'What's in it for you?'

'Selling films. I'm in it now just for the hell of the ride I suppose. I've started and I might as well finish it. Whatever I thought about it initially, doesn't matter now. There's a story here, as they say.' I spoke in a low, even tone, carefully judging the impact of each well chosen word on my acquaintance.

'What, Nagel you mean?'

'That's right.'

Danny rolled his eyes melodramatically and said: 'Did you find him?'

'No. It's inconclusive. He's dead apparently. Fell from a window I believe.'

He coughed from the smoke and viewed me with a certain resigned sympathy.

His voice was unhurried and unemotional: 'Do you believe that?' he said.

'I suppose I've got to,' I shrugged, 'although I'd like more information. More background details. That's why I'm here again.'

I watched as Danny emitted a cackling laugh and then said: 'Good for you.' He lit the pipe again. 'So you've come to me. Honest Danny. To find out some info?'

'Not info exactly, whatever that might mean. Just any details you might have to fill in.'

'I'm only what the English call a gopher, you know, and a small time dope dealer. Anything else is out of my league, although the police occasionally suspect me of being behind the bodies that now and then can be seen floating in the canal. But that's just a civilised society doing away with its local waste.'

He obviously tried this out to see whether I'd recoil at the remark. I didn't.

'You don't mean to say Walter Nagel was into the big time then?' I said with a grin.

Danny refused to answer. But we both exchanged expressions. Whatever comment he might have made had to be left unsaid.

He prepared to leave. 'Come with me and I'll see what I can do.'

He carefully emptied the chillum, blew the residue from the bowl, and packed his materials about his person. He had sounded to me like the complaints' manager in a department store when a disgruntled customer comes in.

'Where to now?' I added respectfully.

'We'll spend the rest of the night at the Moulin Rouge, for a few beers and some entertainment at least. But I'll have to walk the dog first.'

Walk the dog! I thought this was a euphemism for something else.

We weaved through the town, and Danny told me to wait on a street corner. Sure enough, five minutes later, he appeared with a mongrel on a chain. We went through the back streets to what I assumed was his flat, the dog preceding us by paces. Once through the flat door, we went through another locked door to the back room. I noticed a gun on the table. In the corner of the room was what I can only describe as a large trunk. He opened it with a key. I stood back in silence. Inside was the largest cache of dope I had ever seen. Huge blocks, various sizes, each block neatly wrapped in plastic. I stepped back and said nothing. He said nothing. Within minutes we left for the Moulin Rouge. Either he trusted me, or he was trying me out with this new piece of information.

Outside the Moulin Rouge police were jacking up an elongated, black-windowed Mercedes saloon on to the skids of a police tow truck. Two parallel lines of bullet holes stretched the length of the car.

'Machine gun holes, I suppose,' I remarked.

'You're probably right.' Danny moved closer to inspect the holes. 'An Uzi submachine gun I think. You see, the bullets enter the car then ricochet all over the place. Guaranteed to kill the occupant, if there's no armour plating, that is.'

I peered, childlike, through a hole in the glass, to see if I could see blood.

The Moulin Rouge faced one of the canals in the tourist heartland of the Zeedijk. I followed Danny to the entrance, keeping as often as was practical at a physical, if not emotional distance from him wherever we went.

'Live sex show ladies and gentlemen,' blurted out the little doughy-faced Greek man at the door. Danny paid the entrance fee and we climbed a squeaky back staircase into the auditorium of the converted cinema. Danny spoke a few words of Dutch to an usher who showed us to a special table reserved for his exclusive use.

The auditorium was packed for the floorshow. Males and females, mostly gaggles of female tourists and groups of bronzed Spanish men crowded around. As the lights dimmed a spotlight searched the room and came to rest on a small hillock of animal fur on the stage. The mound parted and a girl sprung into a classical striptease routine, discarding her clothes until she was fully naked. The audience clapped appreciatively. As one act finished, another began. A girl with a feather boa placed two white balls into her vagina and teased a motley looking Spanish youth in the front row to remove them. He completed the task amateurishly, much to the delight of his companion. A plump, black stripper, with little potential as a true body artist, enlivened her act by placing a peeled banana between her legs and coaxing volunteers to eat it while she was spread-eagled on the floor like a beached whale.

I homed in on Danny, when the music and entertainment had ceased for an intermission, and regarded him accusingly.

"What about Nagel then?'

'What about him. It's all history now, isn't it?'

LIVING ON GOLD TIME

I grumbled bitterly: 'Couldn't you tell me a little of what you know about him at least?'

'I'll be honest with you Bob, he wasn't an easy person to follow. He had a few shady business deals on the boil. Exactly what. I'm not sure. He regularly came to Hoogstraten's place though.'

'For the girls?'

The busy eyebrows frowned: 'Not really. More to talk and play cards with Julius. I make him sound like a high roller. Excuse me, cos he wasn't. One thing he did do though, he was shrewd enough to be an odd job man for the Mafia.'

'Suppose they gave him an offer he couldn't refuse?' I said, sardonically and unthinkingly.

'More than likely,' quipped Danny, amused.

As the word mafia sunk in I thought of the guy in Soho Square. If Nagel was one of them and they found out I was asking questions, I feared I might be shipped back to London in a wooden overcoat.

As if to confirm that what I had heard was of no importance, I asked timidly and with a weak voice: 'The Mafia operate here then, in Amsterdam? I thought they only worked in Sicily or the States?'

'Sure they're here,' Danny said confidently, 'but not in the way you're thinking, not all random vendettas or Godfather thuggery that you read about in novels.'

I felt partly re-assured.

'They're into legitimate business operations. Like yours, the porn business for instance. It's open, legal and honest. And so are they.' He hesitated and qualified himself 'Here at least.'

On this point I kept my doubts to myself. Perhaps in future our main competitors would be the mafia.

'What precisely then does being an odd job man entail?'

'The mafia are up to all manner of scams, particularly off-centre business deals, which earn them more money than gambling and prostitution.'

'Go on.'

'One of the classic ways of raising substantial sums is to secure a loan on stolen, or what they might call 'borrowed' securities. The trick is for a plausible businessman to approach a bank and ask for a loan, which he covers with collateral in the form of share certificates. He deposits the securities, which the bank checks out, and, finding them genuine advances the loan. In fact the share certificates have been 'borrowed' by a person placed by the mafia in a stockbroker's office or somewhere similar. This is what Nagel would do for them because he had some office experience. In due course the person who got the loan returns the money and is given back the share certificates. The sting comes when he returns to the bank and asks for another substantial loan, and offers the same share certificates as security. Only this time the shares are counterfeit, the originals have been returned. Of course the bank has already checked the securities and doesn't check them again. The loan goes through. By the time the mistake is discovered, tracks are covered, and the bank is too embarrassed to make a fuss.'

'Incredible,' I breathed deeply. I'd heard some stories while in prison but this ranked as a real goody.

'And Nagel was into this?'

'It appears so. He just did the borrowing. Probably didn't know what it was ultimately for, anyhow. He got paid, that pleased him, on top of which he earned a bit of goodwill of course.'

'How do you know all this Danny?'

'Don't keep asking,' he replied angrily, jumping down my throat and losing his temper.

I sat in awe for a moment, conscious that Danny's mood could ebb and flow bewilderingly, but also aware that he was truly a suspicious character. There was so much that he really knew about the film business in Amsterdam that could be useful to us, but it was too premature to ask.

185

The music started up again. It was grand finale time.

'The Sultan and his Ladies,' the master of ceremonies announced.

A half-caste man in Turban and sarong paraded round the stage in time to the music. He loosened his sarong and withdrew a long flaccid penis. Two beautiful and lithe girls entered and strategically placed cushions on the stage. They danced with their master and stripped naked. He obviously had trouble getting an erection and the audience stared, faces wrapped and enthralled.

Danny remarked: 'He needs a fluffer. The silly sod.'

When at last his penis was erect, the girls kneeled on the cushions facing one another. The Sultan penetrated each girl from behind, in turn, after stretching a condom on his penis. I looked at the women in the audience. Not so much shock but curiosity gripped their faces. The Sultan repeated the ritual several times until the spotlights faded on the scene. To my dismay the audience clapped wildly in appreciation.

Danny turned to me: 'Listen, I'm off now. You stay.'

I didn't want to stop him.

He stood up. I glanced up at him and said: 'I'm going to The Glove porn shop in the morning to do some business. Do you fancy a meet?'

He thought for a moment.

I made a histrionic plea: 'Do, or don't you want to come?'

His aloof expression sharpened with the hardness of my voice. His face was then set and passive.

'Okay then, at eleven.'

'Okay, eleven it is,' I affirmed, smiling a pale smile.

With that, the man in black hurried away into the night taking his life, as usual, at a trot.

In The Glove a man stood behind the counter.

I addressed him in a schoolmasterish voice: 'Walter Nagel please.'

'I'm sorry no person of that name has ever worked here.'

THE QUEST

I was taken aback.
'But I'm sure he was here only a few weeks ago.'
You're mistaken then.'
The man turned and served another customer.

Outside the shop I waited for Danny. I was accosted once or twice by pushers and walked up and down trying to merge, chameleon-like into the background. It was twelve thirty. Danny hadn't appeared and it didn't look as if he was going to either.

*   *

The letter said: Victoria Coach Station, call time 10.30 a.m. on the morning of January 29th. An attached sheet had a series of likely questions that Toni Khan might want to have answered.

I peered down the sheet. There was nothing too difficult there. In the few days prior to the interview I began rehearsing appropriate answers. In readiness, I prepared replies to any possible trick questions I knew might be sprung upon me. I still had a tactless disregard for beating about the bush. Some might say this is my strength. I wasn't so sure.

I arrive at the Coach Station at ten o'clock. A section of the station buffet had been cordoned off. Endless cables snaked towards a mobile television unit outside, where technicians sat before a mixing desk and monitors. Confused customers tiptoed with their trays across the floor like captives in a snake pit. Roger Utley in his baseball boots bounded towards me with a greeting and some news. We shook hands perfunctorily.

'Good, you've arrived,' he gasped, 'some delay I'm afraid. Another interviewee has arrived late. We're shooting now. You won't be on for a while, however, so loosen up somewhere. Food and drinks are on the firm. Don't disappear, we may need you at any time.'

Although Perspective Films had devised some pretext for my meeting Toni Khan at such an outrageous place, my nervousness began to show. My hands were clammy and I kept moving about unnecessarily; first to get a coffee, then a sandwich, then a newspaper and finally another cup of coffee. Reservations, big reservations, welled up. I fought heroically with them, took deep breaths and wondered why I should be alone even at a time like this. I made a show of bluff contentment that really didn't reflect the anxiety underneath.

At eleven o'clock Roger Utley escorted me to an improvised interview area where there were two large studio couches. Toni, beaming face, approached from behind a curtain. She came with eyes sparkling, white teeth gleaming; wearing a red full-skirted dress and shoes with high heels.

At the interviewer's presence, the first overwhelming promptings of fear were beginning to die down and I answered with only minimal hesitation.

Toni said soothingly: 'You okay?'

'Just.'

'A few preparations and we'll be ready.'

A make-up girl applied powder over my face with a large floppy brush. A microphone was placed over my head and attached to clothing by adjusting and re-adjusting it with assiduous application to detail. My panic resurfaced. The heart raced so completely I hoped the heartbeats would not be picked up on the microphone. Three cameras pointed at the studio couches from their tripods, and the lights lit the area brighter than day.

'Ready everyone? Quiet please.' Roger Utley commanded in a distinct, loud, edgy, pub voice.

'Ready,' Toni said levelly.

'Roll 'em.'

THE QUEST

'This is it,' I mumbled silently to myself. 'No going back now.' I crossed my feet and placed my hands neatly on my lap.

The interviewer ignored formal introductions and headed directly to the point. She smiled sweetly. 'Dr Wildman you have gained for yourself a reputation as a teacher and criminologist.'

'Criminologist, I said to myself in my head, this is flattery indeed.'

The interviewer was saying: 'But principally a reputation as a person with forthright views on the penal system. From the inside so to speak. Would you agree with that view?'

'I wouldn't put it so strongly,' I spoke as if compelled, 'but my job did bring me into daily contact with men who have fearsome reputations; men who have carried out crimes from the most trivial to the most heinous. I myself have a reputation among my colleagues for my outspoken criticism of the criminal justice system.'

After these few words I forgot about the cameras, the director, the crew and the few newspapermen who were in the small audience. I rallied myself and argued beguilingly and compellingly, even being disarmingly forthright.

'Prison is a degrading, brutalizing and squalid place,' I said, 'there is a permanent simmering resentment among staff and prisoners over the deadening, mundane routines and the assaults on human dignity, despite the wishes of the prison staff to do a more humane job. This does not make headlines, largely because of the prison's obsession with secrecy. Prison overcrowding is only a part of the issue. Britain locks up more people than any other country in Europe into a great prison machine, a human warehouse in fact, a cauldron of resentment, bitterness and violence.'

Toni Khan asked innocently and without malice: 'Don't people deserve to go there, only for the protection of society, if nothing else?'

I pondered, looking again at the patient questioner.

'Possibly,' I said testily, 'the sentence of the court is to deprive the guilty of their liberty. They go there as punishment, not for punishment. We deprive them of their liberty, but in doing this we must not deprive them of their dignity. Although we don't know a lot about the prisoners, despite bundles of Home Office statistics, in my experience most of the men are either on remand, which is a scandal in itself, petty offenders, or those with a drinking or a mental problem. All of them are overwhelmingly of one class. I like to call them the pathologically unsuccessful. These are people who, no matter what they will do, will always make a mess of it. They are predisposed to getting caught.'

'If crime seems to be getting worse, isn't it right that the numbers in prison should be rising?' Toni asked, attempting to disarm me.

This was a difficult one. I thought hard, while momentarily glancing up at the ceiling. The answer came: 'Yes, but the number of men with previous convictions is falling, therefore the offences are not more serious, and they don't commit any more of them,' I replied submissively.

Insistent, with stony contempt, mean of spirit, she said back: 'How do you know? How do you then? Why are you so definite?'

The mouth twitched nervously, I grasped at a half-truth: 'I've seen the statistics.'

Toni Khan sulked: 'Are there alternatives to prison then?'

'Sure, a pantheon of alternatives: fines, probation, Community Service Orders, suspended sentences, part-time prison. All these remove the stigma of a prison sentence, but few are tried properly.'

'Why?' she said brokenly, disconcerted.

I looked down at my hands and up again. 'Sentencing policy I think. A great taboo inhibits the discussion of sentencing policy. It's a trade secret, you see. A sentence is carried out in an individual way which makes it resistant to persuasion from policy makers like Home Secretaries.'

'How do you mean?'

'Sentencing is a culture of its own, conducted by magistrates, or judges in their particular court. There's no mechanism for translating policy into practice. It has an historical root, for fear is the cement of the social order. The criminal law has to do with authority, bonds of obedience and deference and such like. The criminal law has much of the psychic components of religion. It's there to frighten the population into submission. Prisons do that. They don't grind rogues honest, as the Victorians thought. Judicial discretion is what is important. The criminal law is a selective instrument of justice; operated to maintain the fabric of obedience, deference and gratitude; to prevent popular outrage from going too far, in fact. Government policy therefore prefers to keep sentencing as a discretionary tool. It is warm to the idea that wicked people must be hurt and humiliated, and who better to do that than the local potentates?'

Toni Khan became uneasy at the serious aspect that her show was taking on and she gave me a loaded expression. Although primed beforehand to blow my kneecaps away, it was becoming a show about me, and not about her, as all TV really is. Desperate to steer the conversation in new directions she said: 'Let us avoid politics for a moment, for the sake of our viewers. Let me ask you what you think traditionally have been the objectives of the prison system?'

I felt the anger of my opponent falter and evaporate. I rewarded Ms Khan with an answering glint in her eyes: 'Retribution, deterrence, containment and rehabilitation.'

Toni leaned back on the couch, looking at her guest assessingly. She jumped into the gap that had been opened for her: 'Ahh! ...rehabilitation and reform is of particular importance to you I believe?'

'Yes. Particularly rehabilitation. Deterrence doesn't work in the long term, and containment is warehousing,' I answered, white as the driven snow, then continued: 'I like to think that Rule 1 of the 1964 Prison Rules is my bible.'

'What's Rule 1? Tell the viewers so that they will understand.' The woman's smile became warm and embracing. I thought about Rule 1. Rule 1, like all prison rules, is a dubious, dangling, article of faith, a diluted mission statement rather than a policy carved in stone. However, I began:

'Rule 1 is about encouraging and assisting prisoners to lead a good and useful life. It sets the tone for all prisons and particularly my work. Although rehabilitation is now thoroughly out of fashion, it was formulated because enlightened people believed that if a hospital could treat and cure, so could a prison cure crime. The prisoner was in some way sick. This has been shown not to be the case, of course.'

'So, in principle, there is something very wrong with the idea that those who get sent to prison are sick and in need of treatment?'

I shook my head. 'No,' I exclaimed, enjoying the drama.

Came the astonished reply: 'Why not?'

I instinctively sought to outmanoeuvre the interviewer whom I began to see as an adversary.

'Yes, I agree that they're not morally sick, and 'treatment' won't cure them either. But I believe the philosophy of treatment, or rehabilitation, has never been allowed to work. The people who run prisons either don't want them to work, or they haven't got the ingenuity to set about making changes. They're only civil servants after all. They do what they are told, for a good pension, like any servant. They're not great thinkers or doers, and they're certainly not in the mould of the nineteenth century Victorian prison reformers, or those who framed the borstal system.'

'But how can you train people for freedom by putting them in captivity?' she asked.

'Simple.' I trumped the remark.

'But how?'

192

THE QUEST

'Cutting the prison population and integral sanitation on its own is no answer. Humane containment and positive custody are simply words that have been used in place of Rule 1. First, ration the intake to prison with deferred sentences until accommodation is available, like Holland. Institute the 1987 European code of minimum standards in prison to enhance self respect: don't censor letters, have telephones and longer home leave, lengthen visits, prepare men for release.' I stopped before going on: 'Have an ombudsman to adjudicate grievances and oversee prisoners' rights. Make the rules legally enforceable. Stop building new prisons and empty out the remand prisoners. Staff must be free to experiment by reinforcing the old local prison with its roots in the community. Even mixed prisons.'

What I said was a shock of cataclysmic proportions.

Toni was annoyed: 'So there's been no prison reform for a hundred years then, from when the prisons were first built? She answered, righteously indignant.

'Humane concessions have passed through the Prison Department's needle eye. But few are earth-shatteringly ingenious.'

'So you believe, Dr Wildman, that the prison system as it stands does not work, it doesn't prevent crime, nor make it more difficult for people to resist the temptations of crime and lead a law abiding life?'

'Of course not. Incidentally,' I added, 'prisons are schools of crime as everyone knows. They have not affected crime rates for the better at all. They make people worse. Sending fewer people there would have a negligible effect on recorded crime rates. In fact, it might improve it. Prisons are very haphazard, selective and limited ways of reducing crime.'

Toni was getting visible exhausted at the onslaught on authority, and decided to put some of the failures of the system down to individual failure: 'In your own way you tried to enforce this Rule 1, I believe?'

'I did,' my eyes must have glimmered. 'I tried to encourage men to contribute to their own rehabilitation and rouse their self-esteem by encouraging them to make things that could be displayed in an art exhibition and ultimately sold on the open market. The monies were to go towards restitution projects and the like.'

'Knowing you, you must have met with success?'

'The prisoners threw their hearts and souls into the enterprise. Official obstruction stopped it.'

'I'm sure you're overly pessimistic about that,' Toni said, fearing to side with this person who was slipping more and more out of her control.

'No I'm not. The authorities stopped me.' My mind was engulfed with maudlin reminiscences of the treatment meted out to me in the past. After a pause I added: 'You see, the prisons are full of what I call preventable failures, and I can prevent them.'

A ripple of laughter engulfed the small audience around. Toni raised a plump hand palm in a gesture of feigned defeat. 'But why are you so anti-authority?' There was power in her voice. Her eyes, her movements.

'I'm not. I'm just selective in my criticism.'

The audience murmured sympathetically again.

'Prison officers are undervalued. They become semi-humorous, semi-bitter, cynical pessimists, institutionalised like everyone else. How can you expect a man or woman, recruited from the same social class as the inmates, to be able to set an example of rectitude; to be a role model, encouraging men to change their behaviour patterns, if there's no backing from the authorities?'

The interviewer hastily looked at her watch and reluctantly gave in. 'Let's discuss a final issue. The public are thirsting after higher punishments for criminals, are they not?'

'No. The public aren't at all clear about the basic facts of imprisonment. I think you would be surprised at the lack of vindictiveness among the public, even the victims. They prefer restitution of reformation. They do know, though, that prison makes people worse, makes them lamed in speech and outlook. I'm sure most people favour a reduction in the prison population by substituting community service. They want crime prevention schemes, not the vindictiveness of prison, which doesn't protect the public or reduce crime.'

'In brief then, can you tell the viewers what is missing from the present system? Be brief now, don't overload them,' was how she uncharitably put it. She had no intention of encouraging what she thought were my wildly impracticable ideas.

'Yes. There's a moral vacuum leading to a routine brutalization of all within the service. The result is cynicism and defeatism. There's a lack of a governing piece of philosophical prose to give a general direction to the prison regime. Everyone wants to be inspired, to have a mission statement, not all the dusty platitudes about implementing the sentence of the court, good order and discipline, and the like. Personally, I believe this is enshrined in Rule 1. Its principles should be put into operation immediately. If the Prison Department says it can't do it with the personnel it has at its disposal, then it should go about recruiting the right people: because prison is a dispiriting experience which deadens intellect, paralyses initiative, and promotes bitterness and depression. We want no more control, because the more control authority imposes, the more control it will need to maintain its grip. No more secrecy please, no more lack of accountability. Since rising prison populations may well increase crime, just stop sending them there. Every year one hundred thousand people leave society to enter this world and as long as the number is so high the penal system will lurch from crisis to crisis. Beating crime is like beating divorce – make prisons and marriage harder to get into, and easier to get out of.

LIVING ON GOLD TIME

The last word was Toni Khan's. She said with twinkling
eyes and full red lips: 'Well, thank you Dr Wildman. You've
certainly set our minds racing. Now over to those silly ads.'

'Cut.' Roger yelled.

I sat placidly stunned. A round of applause echoed from
the small audience in the cordoned off section of the buffet.
There was a flash from the bulb of a photographer's camera.
I was inwardly jubilant. It had not been as bruising an
encounter as I initially feared: not for me, anyhow.

*   *   *

I took a few days' rest before getting back to the office. Jack
was brewing the tea.

'There's a letter for you. It came in the late morning post.
It's from Perspective films. That's what it says on the
envelope anyhow.' Jack smiled voluntarily and handed it to
me.

I ripped down one edge, pulled out the contents, and read
aloud.

Dear Dr, Wildman,

I am writing to tell you that we have had
to drop the interview we recorded with you from TELL ME
ANOTHER programme one.

We are very disappointed to have to do this, but we have
done so on the advice of our solicitors. They told us that
under the terms of our agreement with Victoria Coach
Station, there was a reasonable chance of them getting an
injunction preventing transmission of the entire programme.
Additionally, we needed to return to Victoria Coach Station
to shoot more footage, and clearly we could not have done
this without first agreeing to their demands.

It will be a poorer programme without your contribution.
Certainly we will keep you in mind for another time.
Hopefully we will be dealing with a broader-minded people!

THE QUEST

Our best wishes,
Yours sincerely

Roger Utley.

'The fucking bastards have pulled me from the
programme. The bastards. They've taken out a court
injunction on the film company banning my appearances on
the show. It's a conspiracy.' I yelled with fury.

'Cool it.' Jack tried to console me by pressing a warm tea
into my hands. 'Perhaps they'll put you on at a later date,'
he said encouragingly, while glancing at the letter.

'Like fuck they will. They're out to get me. This has cost
someone a lot of money. It was my chance to say something
meaningful and they sabotaged it. Don't you see they're
trying to take me out. Stop me telling the truth. Censoring
me. They'll probably say it's against the Official Secrets Act
or something like that.'

'Stop wasting time with those silly arses,' Jack was
insistent. 'We've got films to make. You've got to get back
to Amsterdam to get those contracts signed. There's a
deadline.'

He handed me the paperwork

'Hurry back with contracts signed.' As if an afterthought:
'And bring back those masters you left there.'

On the flight over I thought about the phone call I made to
Toni Khan after I received the rejection letter. She had tried
to fob me off. She said I should not take the TV ban
personally, it was a mistake on their part to hold it where
they did – a shabby excuse. I must say I was reckless too for
putting my neck on the line. But in a atmosphere of untruth
it is difficult to think straight at all times – asphyxiation of
my ideals no less. She didn't know what was behind the ban.

LIVING ON GOLD TIME

Of course she might have been telling the truth, or she was guilty of humbug. Perhaps she was a small cog in a big wheel, and has no real power over government censorship. I liked to think so. She is told what to do by the producer, like everyone else.

Although she handled my call with aplomb, an army of lawyers and layers of bureaucracy sees off all but the most assiduous. All media people behave with blithe indifference when their own reputation is at stake. Well, don't they?'

*   *

Two of us walked across the tarmac when we disembarked at Schipol. Trevor was with me; an old friend. I had brought him along as my research assistant. While I was negotiating the films, and meeting a few people, he had to do some leg work and get me more information on what was bugging me.

When I had met him again, Trevor wore a gin-sodden, puffy face. Not the more youthful and rascally one I had known all those years ago. He was even morose – a man with large pretensions but small means, a man who once nourished ambitions and had a lust for the dazzling life and success. He sounded and looked a drab failure and I carefully watched his lips move. Judging by those moments of conversation, he had become a hermit in his head – a man who had burnt himself out as fast as a sparkler. Nevertheless our continuing conversation was filled with reminiscences, some embarrassing, some warm and encouraging, resurrecting long forgotten mental landscapes.

'What'll I have to do?' he had asked before we left.

'Nothing of earth-shattering consequence.' I had said, 'just enjoy yourself. Get your cock sucked once or twice.'

A silence had lengthened until Trevor eventually said: 'I'm coming.'

THE QUEST

I had bought a copy of *Guden Gids* and a fresh edition of *De Telegraaf,* the Dutch daily newspaper, at the airport. In the hotel lounge I flicked through the pages of the newspaper.

'What do you want, Trevor, a suck or a fuck?' I said, looking at him sideways.

'Here, steady on, take it easy.'

I flicked once again through the open pages of the paper: 'Now look here, I'm serious.' Before he could get himself settled, I handed him the newspaper. 'Turn to page twenty six.'

He did as I bid, dropping a sheaf of paper in the process. He picked it up and opened it out on the coffee table while sitting relaxed on the sofa.

I marched around the room and said: 'What do you see?'

'Volvo 440, Geniet Het Vertrauwen.' He pronounced the words badly.

'Not that, idiot.'

'What then? Come on, give me a clue.'

'The sex.'

'Oh!' he said casting his eye down the columns labelled Diverse Clubs. 'Sex Top Tien, School Jongens, Orgiebox, Lesbi Tiener, Meisjes-School, Tienersex, Billy's Gay Box.'

'Precisely. Now choose one.'

'What one?'

'Any one. Use your discretion.'

'Okay. How about Sarita, mas inst!! Div massages body-to-body spiegelk. Komt biju thuis of in een hotel door binjna heel.'

Trevor was really getting into the spirit of things. Then he collapsed with laughter.

'Oh! shut up,' I said, irritated, 'choose something straightforward then.'

'No, levity aside, here, I've got one.' He tried to appease me.

'It says, Escort Girls en snel door heel het land, ook overnachtingen.'

'Escort girls, that's it. They'll be in the know.' I walked over to the telephone.

'Now ring them up and book a date for tonight. They'll all speak English. Besides, the language of love is universal.'

'Wait, won't you.' Trevor's mood changed. 'Am I getting this correct. You want me to spend a night on the town with a call girl?'

'That's about it. As many nights as you like in fact.'

'Who's paying?'

'I will. I'll give you cash. You must come back with some information, that's all.'

He objected disapprovingly. 'Hang on. I don't know whether I'm up to this.'

'Well, it still stands up doesn't it, despite the booze?'

Trevor looked purposefully down at his flies.

'Yes, I suppose it does.'

'Well then. I'm offering you the holiday of a lifetime, and the flight ticket home.'

I held out the phone for him to take.

'What information am I supposed to collect?'

'Anything about the sex scene in general: who runs it etc., etc. Don't worry, I'll script you every night for the particulars. Here.'

I dropped the phone in his lap. He picked it up and dialled the number of the escort agency. I went to the gents.
On my return I said: 'Is it done?'

'It's arranged,' Trevor said, 'eight o'clock tonight.'

'Good. Now first I want you to ask her if she's heard of a man named Nagel. That's if it is a she.'

'And what do you mean by that, for Christ's sake,' he exclaimed.

I giggled to myself. 'Oh! nothing really.'

'How do you spell Nagel?' Trevor asked.

'N ...A ...G...E...L'

He made a mental note, then decided to write it down on a piece of paper.

'Anything else?'

'No. That's all for tonight. I'll have some more instructions tomorrow. The rest is on the house. And here's your flight ticket back.'

My research assistant was well and truly settled in. But fulfilling deadlines meant I had to beat a hasty retreat and return to London. I left Trevor with a list of things to do and questions to ask, and a message to call me every night for further instructions. I told him I expected him to pursue my interests with the integrity of the true researcher. On coming back through English customs, however, everything turned pear-shaped.

It was early morning and I went down the channel bearing the sign 'Nothing to Declare.' Although I was carrying four U-matic masters in my case, I had no intention of declaring them. I was stopped. The customs officer lifted them out of my case then disappeared off to a room behind a one-way mirror. He was away for fifteen minutes, then returned and addressed me gravely with a pitying look of superiority.

'These are hard core pornographic master video cassettes, and I am arresting you for entering the country illegally with a prohibited good. You do not have to say anything unless you wish to do so, but anything you say may be taken down in evidence.'

I couldn't work out whether he had stopped me by pure accident, or whether customs had been informed by someone that I was coming through with the masters. I thought that it was more than just a fluke. I'd been grassed up.

I was despatched to a room where I was ordered to empty my pockets and remove my clothing. I obeyed and stood there in my underpants. They muttered something between them and ordered me to dress again. One of the officers picked through the small pile of personal belongings. I was directed to a back room, ordered to sit behind a table and then left on my own.

The grey coloured room, bare and windowless, was badly lit by a fluorescent light. The door opened and my luggage was placed on the floor. The arresting officer and a colleague then sat on the other side of the table.

The man spoke: 'We believe you are a courier for an international porn racket and would like to know some details. You will be held here until we have more information.'

I thought about the conditions of arrest and chose to remain silent. I said: 'You've arrested me and I've nothing more to say.'

The two officers left and after ten minutes another man returned.

'I'm the custody officer and I'm here to tell you your rights.' He pulled out an A4 printed page.

'Name and address?'

I knew that they had my passport and it would be useless withholding information that they could get from the passport office. I gave my name and address. He handed me 'a notice to detained persons' and a code of practice. I was allowed to consult a solicitor and have someone informed of my detention. I was required to sign for the information. I requested a solicitor. The request was granted.

A small, weasel-faced man in a jumper and leather jacket appeared.

'Where's the company offices that you're operating from? Where's the business address?' He asked aggressively.

'I don't know what you mean,' I answered timidly, 'I don't know what this is all about.'

'It's better you tell me the details before we start smashing down doors.'

I had visions of the company office being wrecked in some fruitless pursuit of evidence of some sort. They would find nothing there, as everything that mattered was in Amsterdam.

'There's nothing that I can tell you.'

'We'll see about that,' he shouted as he left the room.

I heard him talking to another officer outside the door of the room: 'This looks like a big operation. Could be based in a shop in Soho. We could get him on importing into the country. It'll be more difficult if it originates from here.'

The arresting officer tried to get me to sign his statement book of what transpired between them prior to my arrest. I refused without a solicitor.

'Your rights have been suspended for two hours,' he said presently, 'while enquiries are being made.'

An hour passed before a solicitor walked in. The solicitor asked me questions relating to my detainment and why I had four films in my luggage. I explained that they were business samples. We both left for another room for fresh questioning.

Another customs officer put a cassette tape on a recorder.

'I advise you at this juncture to say, no comment, to any questions asked of you,' the solicitor said.

The customs officer began his interrogation. I replied 'no comment' after each question. The questioning was over within five minutes.

My ordeal lasted another four hours while the police presumably searched for clues. My rights were restored and I signed for the confiscated tapes.

*   *

I had a meeting with the Obscene Publications Squad a fortnight later. They tried to convince me to sign a forfeiture order on my own copyrighted films under section 3 of the Obscene Publications Act 1959. I told them they had no grounds for a Section 3 forfeiture order, and I wished to exercise my right to hear the prosecution prove its case against me i.e. Section 1 'deprave and corrupt.' I wished for a jury trial under the Act, as a jury will not convict when the defence is 'artistic merit.'

Some time after that I had a date in which to appear at a magistrates' court. Unhappily, I was to have no jury trial. Now I was defending myself and 'showing cause' as to why my films should not be forfeited.

With all the activity I was becoming decidedly edgy. In the next few weeks several things happened in quick succession which suggested to me that not everything was as it should be. Was it the suspicion and mistrust again?

My extra vigilance meant that I saw much more than usual. One morning I took an underground train to the office. The carriage was crowded. I had a seat, but a stunningly beautiful girl stood in front of me next to a person I assumed to be her mother. Perhaps she was a stage school actress being taken to an audition. My eyes scanned the contours of her of her lightly-clothed body and unblemished skin. It was like porcelain or marble. And she was not young, but extremely young. I toyed with the idea that she was not more than thirteen years old. But I knew that girls with the right make-up could be made to look six years younger. I became fascinated by the perilous magic of the nymphet's spell, the tiny pubescent thing looked in submissive mood. I became conscious of her fantastic power; a combination of naïvity and deception, of charm and vulgarity. She sported a lightly fitting summer dress, sheathing the pearl-grey young body. When she danced through the carriage door and disappeared, enveloped by blackness, I caught sight of her tight little rear. I was moved to ask myself; was she real, or was I dreaming this?

It was a magic moment for me. Such unrestrained beauty is rarely seen. I felt like a theatre director at her audition. Had I been set up? Was she an actor? I couldn't be sure of anything. Ambitious mothers frequently use their daughters as bait. A well known actor of my acquaintance allowed his thirteen year old daughter to be left alone in a locked room, to play games with older men.

The London Underground featured greatly in the weeks to come. I found myself on the Northern Line at the Angel during rush hour. The platform was jam packed. I was standing right on the edge near the line. I realised how easy it would be for me to get pushed in front of an oncoming train. I had to move back as fear overwhelmed me. How many suicides on the London Underground are really murders? On average there is one death a week on the underground. Where do people choose to die; on the platform, at the point where the train comes in, in the middle of the platform, or at the far end?

Vigilance asserts itself during bouts of paranoia. I noticed that the gummed corner of one of my letters had been opened up slightly. It could have meant my mail had been intercepted. I had no way of knowing. I had read all about the split bamboo treatment, where the security services insert a piece of split bamboo into the corner of the envelope, engage the letter, twist it, then remove it through the opening. They reinsert it in the same way after reading its contents. That's why first class letters take so long to arrive no doubt.

And there were phone taps. I listened for the clicks and noises. But I had always had my phones tapped; this I knew from working in prisons. Surveillance was ubiquitous, even in the 1980s. I came to the conclusion that people they put into mental hospitals who say they hear voices in the head, and say microphones are listening to them, are not really crazy at all. I believe them.

One day the telephone rang in the office. Jack was away. Reluctant to give the number I picked up the phone and said: 'Hello.'

'It's me, Roger Utley from Perspective Films,' the voice came back.'

I remembered the man in the white trousers and baseball boots.

'Listen.'

I listened.

'I want to do an article about you for an evening newspaper.'

'What on earth for?' I asked.

'Because I've been talking to the editor and he thinks you're an interesting enough character to deserve some copy in his paper.'

'And what makes you think it'll ever get published?'

'Publication is never certain but I'm going ahead.'

'You'll find there's probably a List D notice out on the story,' I was guessing, but everything's possible.

'What's that?'

'Don't you know? It means the government won't allow publication.'

'Phooey ...' he exclaimed, 'I'm going ahead anyhow. When can we meet?'

We met that evening. The mercurial Roger Utley noted down the salient points of the story in his filofax. I was careful to avoid the disclosure of sensitive names, keeping the topic mainly on myself and how I felt about my job and what I had tried to do. Who was Roger Utley anyway, and was he just trying to glean some information? After the interview, and after rounding off with a number of impertinent questions that I did not much care to answer, he stumbled away, re-assuring me that all was going to be well under his authority. My doubts and guesses about List D notices was probably correct, for I never heard from him again.

List D notice or no List D notice, an Irishman came to my house one day interested in buying my old car that had been parked outside my house for some time. This was the time when IRA car bombs were exploding on London streets.

From then on I had to check under the car for potential bombs before I drove off.

The paranoia wasn't pure fantasy on my part. There were three incidents in quick succession that confirmed my worst fears that I was being targeted; no doubt to discredit me before my court appearance, by charging me with an offence, and bringing any evidence I had to offer into disrepute; or simply to put the frighteners on me.

The first involved a young girl again; in the underground as usual. I sat down on one of the long seats. A girl of about nine, with a disturbed expression on her face, sat on the seat opposite with her legs splayed wide apart and feet on the seat to reveal her knickers. She wriggled and moved around, attracting the attention, not only of myself, but someone sitting along the row. Her behaviour became more overt. I raised a newspaper in front of my face and left the carriage at the next stop.

On another occasion a woman showed signs of disturbance at my presence in the British Library. In those days all pornographic material from the Private Case could be read at a special table in the North Library. I had been there for a few days checking up on nineteenth century erotica. A woman directly opposite me, no doubt a police woman, started to make loud comments to everyone about my presence and what she said I must be doing inside my trousers. I left in a hurry. Since I'd been to the library on numerous occasions, this was not fortuitous, a purely accidental or random meeting. The lengths they would go to, to discredit my case!

Finally, our office had a request for child porn to be delivered by hand. I knew the address; it was the address of police accommodation in the area where I lived.

*

LIVING ON GOLD TIME

The high tension was relieved at the magistrates' court. Of
the two magistrates present, one was a woman of about
thirty to thirty five. I couldn't believe it when she walked in
I was flabbergasted. She wore a jacket and short skirt, both
made of crinkly black patent leather, and high heeled, black,
patent leather shoes. She looked as if she'd just left
Michelle's torture chamber. Was this to be my rubber teaser
moment? I reached for my imaginary whip for *Le vice
anglais*.

*　　　*

Jack Goodman stood, propping up the bar at the Soho club.
He turned to me as I approached.

'Here comes the reluctant pornographer,' he said, with a
frankness that was disarming, 'you've come to the farewell
party then? But you're early. The guests aren't here yet. So
tell me, what did you learn from going native, as they say?'

Jack's face was bathed in a rascally smile. The dynamo of
a man looked at me, the savage piercing eyes twinkled.

'As you told me at the very beginning, the girls don't do it
purely for the money. They do it because they like it. I came
into this believing the rightwing, feminist propaganda, that
all the girls were coerced or victims of pimps.'

'Correct,' he replied, his face smothered in satisfaction.
'Me, I believe the ideal society is an unrepressed one,
sexually free. Sexual orientation is the choice of the
individual in a polymorphous sexual world. Only
authoritarian societies are repressed ones.'

'That may be so,' I said with a smidgen of irony, but
without a challenge, 'but most important for me in doing
what we did, was gaining some technical competence. At
first I was cack-handed, way behind, by not having the
technical know-how.'

'That, you couldn't help, because you were new to the
game. You learnt on the job. Anything else?'

THE QUEST

'Yes. Create your own reality, as you said. If you need a round of applause, hire some actors to do it for you.'

'That's what I said, now you see. Create your own publicity like Hollywood does.'

'But the biggest learning experience was that, as time went by, I had trouble deciding when we were off camera and when we were on it, especially during the making of those two feature films. Without formal scripts, fact and fiction merged. It's what upset the censor about our films I suppose. For him when did the real, the reality, start, and the representation, the fiction, end? Or simply, when, if ever, was the sex act simulated in our films? Life becomes counter-intuitive at that level – it seems to be one thing, but it's really another, a paradox, the opposite of what you think. It's like a quantum world.'

Jack looked at me puzzled, but replied with: 'Correct again …' leaving the sentence hanging, but I saw the answer in his face.

'Another thing. You can't carry the censor round on your shoulder all the time. Censorship is an obstruction to creativity and places a constraint on the imagination.'

'So you've realised that at last. At first you thought it was possible to compromise with him.'

'Of course, because in the beginning I knew nothing about the business at all. When we started to make so little headway, under the rules that existed, and had to outsource to Amsterdam, I knew the game was up. One last thing. I learned, that in life, you always have to challenge yourself to do things you wouldn't normally do, in order to learn something. Live beyond your psychological means, so to speak, extend your experiences of life: not take information second-hand, in other words.'

Just then the party guests came through the club door. In front, was, of all people, Julius Hoogstraten.

'What the hell's he doing here?' I burst out.'

'I arranged for a few of your encounters in Amsterdam,' Jack said ominously, and with weight.

I couldn't take it in. Whatever did he mean by arrange? I was both gratified and extremely annoyed. I jerked my head in his direction and gave him a look in which contempt was clearly a component.

'You bastard. What do you mean?'

'I mean, some of it was my doing. Everything in life is not quite what you think it is, as you've just told me. Take it as part of your adventure. Think of it as a quest, a test and proof of moral virtue, if you like; to keep a promise and be faithful.'

'What about the business people we've made contractual relationships with?'

'Oh! they're real alright.'

'And Danny Daniels?'

Jack mischievously swallowed a laugh.

'He's an actor. See.'

He pointed to another part of the room.

'Look, he's over there.' Jack could feel a smothered laugh escaping through his eyes. 'You don't know who's an actor and who's been put into you.'

I cautiously looked round, disbelieving everything.

'This is not one of your jokes, is it?' I said, just before my gaze fell upon a pair of Chinese slippers at a table by the door.

The occupant of the slippers waved.

'Christ. I don't believe any of this.'

Little by little my outburst of bad temper began to abate and I shook my head in disbelief.

Jack was genuine: 'My little game. Sorry.'

'I don't think it's a bloody game.' I stared at the far table once more. Again he waved.

'He's a non-entity. An out-of-work actor.'

'And Walter Nagel? Surely not another unemployed thespian, just resting?' I said in exasperation.

At that moment a man appeared at the door with Walter Nagel written across the front of the tee shirt he was wearing.

'I thought he was dead.'

'Apparently not. Do you want me to bring him here for you to pinch him?'

I declined and Nagel sauntered off.

'That leaves the man at the Hotel Mercury, and the two on the landing of the house in the Geldersekade, who took me to the window.'

Suddenly, Jack adjusted his sympathy level.

'Nothing to do with me,' he grudgingly admitted. 'The real McCoy p'haps. Your MI5 and all that. The information gatherers. Every pub has one. They collect info from anyone; businessmen, spies, small time civil servants. Anyone who's got something to say, they'll log it. Stick it in the old computer and use it later. It's the great information gathering society. Knowledge really is power, with electronics.'

'Come off it.' I said in a heavy voice.

'You see, they get them to merge in. Become part of the furniture. What do you think spies are like? Do the Soviet ones have a Russian hat, or sport an Order of Lenin badge on their lapel?'

'No.'

'Well then. Who really understands the web of intrigue? It's a wall of mirrors, you can never really fathom out the truth. All you'll find when you arrive at a destination is a distorted image of yourself, because, when you scream, no one's listening … it's the world turned upside down. You found that out with me before we went to Amsterdam. All questions, the paranoia of unanswered questions. The black propaganda and disinformation keeps you on the wrong trail. It saps your energy. Psychological warfare disorientates the enemy, you see. It's as good as administering hallucinatory drugs. The people in British Intelligence are at it constantly.

Even they have difficulty separating truth from fiction.
Compare it to the prison life you and I know. Out there is a
grapevine of unreliable sources of information, un-
attributable and un-footnoted. Research is a difficult and
often risky endeavour. There are few explanations where
there are any. So there is only the web made of a few badly
stated facts, rumours and bits of disinformation. What's said
is often double meant, backwards, upside-down talk; serious
matters are expressed as a joke. The code is the
underworld's. The apparatus for self-deception are as ever,
many. Listen.'

'I'm listening.'

'On one occasion I was in this club and a couple of so-
called businessmen came in with their minders. They came
right out with it: 'How would you fancy a quarter of a
million quid?' I told them I wasn't interested. The guy just
said: 'I'll bring it here first thing in the morning, in a carrier
bag, and don't be clever saying that you don't want it.' So I
said: 'Look, I don't want it,' and he said: 'You're not trying
to be clever are you, and that's not too clever is it?''

'Who were they. The Mafia?'

'Who knows. You can understand though, why everyone
sits with their backs to the wall.'

I changed tack a bit: 'Apart from my escapade trying to
make sense of this Rule 1, where do I fit into the pattern of
things?'

'It wasn't pre-ordained, believe me. It was a dance with
destiny if you like. You put your neck out. You went beyond
the boundaries of the everyday and the predictable, and had
the courage to grapple with the unknown. For you, fiction
truly merged into reality. You'd read about these things in
your books, but that was dead knowledge. Real knowledge is
living, talking, deciding and gambling with the present.
Certainties are only for the masses, like getting up and going
out to work. Life is as precarious as throwing the dice.
There's no past, no future, just the present. All events are a

surrealist painting. The redeeming feature is that they have something good to say about the new. In retrospect you can say it was a way of getting out of the prison you had created for yourself. Leaving the prison showed that you wanted to retain the integrity of this Rule 1 that you keep mentioning. But your freedom was the most important thing. Me, I live in the present. My philosophy is one of challenging the world. It's all the art of the possible. It's as awe inspiring as Michelle's torture chamber. No formal logic will satisfactorily explain it. Being out here is like being inside a prison, you never know truth for sure, and rarely come to the bottom of anything. You might have sussed out something in your researches yourself, but you're doing life too. In the rumour factory anything can be worked up into a story. As little information as possible is given out. There are official and unofficial versions, then there is the silence and the indifference. Your Rule 1 is their benchmark for the descent downwards, but they make it a downward movement, not up, not you. You, Bob, you're a meritocrat. Someone with the bad luck, like me, of being born into the wrong class, and who wants to climb out of it. The meritocrat believes that people achieve positions in society by merit alone. The old fucking 'the more you know the further you go' principle. It's patently untrue. Universities suck the intellectual marrow from people like you, and turn their abilities to good use. But the gifted few have certain gifts, but only for the ruling class. It doesn't include patience, hard work, generosity, concern for others, reluctance to betray fellow human beings, or solidarity with people in distress. What they require is intellectual ability mingled with contempt and hatred of those conditions from which the socially mobile come. A merciless ambition in other words. A virtue is made out of greed, consequently the successful become dehumanised, robbed of humanity, pure tools. And they imprison your ideas so they have no power of flight.'

Just as Jack finished his monologue, Governor Ralph Brown from Wadham Prison came into the Club, dressed as a woman. He escorted a young girl of about twelve or thirteen, with make-up, a short, black skirt, and visible red knickers. I turned to Jack.

'For God's sake! What's he doing in here? Is that his daughter?'

Jack gave me a knowing and affectionate look.

'No ... wrong again. She's his girlfriend.'

*

That meeting was the last time I saw Jack Goodman, before he melted into oblivion. Apparently, he went off to make more films. However, we had parted on the most amicable of terms.

The parting may mark the closing of a chapter, but the story doesn't end here. In more ways than one it was just the beginning. A practical understanding of filming human sexual creativity was only half the narrative. I needed to do some theoretical spadework.

Pornography is one of the few popular genres in which women are not portrayed as being punished for knowing, pursuing, and finding their pleasure.

3

With time on my hands, and rather than escape to the country, to hide in a haze of sedge, sorrel and cow parsley, I set about a search for the source of the river of human sexual and social life, and the place of sex in history.

In this chapter I'll give you a rough, formless, sketch of a few of the tributaries along which my search took place. An exhaustive and startling account of my results, and a chilling combination of my ideas, will appear in a separate volume of its own.

There's no academic pre-occupation with source material, and carefully interwoven threads of argument in this short chapter, since that breeds a kind of despair. I'll sidestep vexed theoretical questions in favour of a pot-pourri.

*

First, this censorship phenomenon that I've been occasionally banging on about. What is it, where did it come from? Almost always it connotes the exercise of state power over texts and their authors, theatrical productions, prints, pictures depicting sexual intercourse, cinema and visual imagery. For someone, somewhere needs to control; to impose authority not just on how the past is recorded, but how it is preserved, and hence manipulated. How quickly people do the job of censorship, too, by spitting on their own history. More tellingly, censorship amounts to a control of the understanding of our sexual natures; control over the very fundamentals of the production and reproduction of life, and how they should be reported in words and pictures. Just imagine, a million people were imprisoned between the end of the Spanish Civil War in 1939 and the latter days of the Franco regime in 1973. Half a million reports were issued by the censors, who went line by line through every book, play and poem ever published. Remember what Hitler said in *Mein Kampf*:

> This cleansing of our culture must be extended to nearly all fields. Theatre, art, literature, cinema, press, posters, and window displays must be cleansed of all manifestations of our rotting world and placed in the service of a moral, political and cultural idea. Public life must be freed from the stifling perfume of our modern eroticism.

Similar moves were afoot in Fascist Italy, which banned the translation of works from enemy countries and clamped down on writing by women authors – perhaps an effect of the masculine character of public life as the state machinery became militarized. The French had morally lost the Second World War before the actual military collapse. Censorship by others is one thing, self-censorship quite another. Note the ease with which most French people accommodated themselves to life under occupation; going fascist without noticing it, in other words; for the inner censor of the mind completed the work of the public censor by terrorizing their own consciences into submission.

Modern censorship has many historical precedents. Before the invention of the printing press, vellum was too valuable a commodity to consign indiscriminately to the fire. It was hard enough in the Middle Ages for authors to control the accuracy of their texts, let alone for ecclesiastical or political authorities to censor them effectively. So censorship and tolerance of revelatory writing suggested that constraint rather than censorship may be the appropriate term to describe controls over the transmission and reception of medieval writings. Let's not forget, writing itself was at that time allegorical. Functional ambiguity became self-protection. Real meaning was concealed by allegory, metaphor, and symbol; making false attributions, or the lack of consensus about the provenance of various written works, a satisfactory ruse. Writers wrote in code, or secret writing, clear to the intended audience, but opaque to everyone else. Later on with printed books, unlike hand-produced manuscripts, it was not easy to unwrite inconvenient information, since there were inevitably multiple copies of the identical offending material. Large-scale public burning was inevitable.

The English Civil Wars 1640-1660, the trial and execution of Charles 1, the 1649 Commonwealth under Cromwell, and the Glorious Revolution of 1688, were really the events that formed the fulcrum of British history – the midwife of modernity and the beginnings of our modern age. The first age of journalism began with the collapse of royal authority after 1640, which brought an end to old censorship rules. During the Civil War newsbooks were issued by the opposing sides in plain, earthy, accessible prose, containing scurrilous rumour and sexual libel. Obscenity became a weapon of war; representing Cromwell as a lecher and cuckold for instance. Not only did England become a country under surveillance, with a culture of informing, but the Civil War revealed a radical underground in English history; none too warming for the powers that be.

What was to follow these seventeenth century upheavals? Why, censorship restored in a new form of course. For a start, the hidden levers of government operations aimed at ensuring a docile stage. The Stage Licensing Act of 1737 established stringent controls over the performance of plays by granting a virtual monopoly over the stage in Britain to two royal patent theatres in London, and by requiring managers to submit new plays to the Lord Chamberlain for licensing before performance; in other words, assigning the absolute power of censorship to a member of the royal household who was not answerable to parliament. It was a move having a stifling effect on political expression, creativity and innovation in stage repertory. That means for the next two hundred and thirty years with regard to serious thought on religious, moral and political issues. Not for nothing, then, the Puritan Revolution of the mid seventeenth century was central to Victorian self-understanding.

By far the most impacting event on our lives, even up to this very day, was the French Revolution of 1789-1801. With the English Civil War still on their minds, the turmoil in France, where many heads rolled into the basket, spread a loathing that stabbed deep into the heart of the British bourgeoisie. They responded at all times in a decisive way. The consequence was fear and hatred of the British masses, and their potential for revolution and social mayhem. It was an image admirably and imaginatively exploited by the French artist Eugène Delacroix in his painting *Liberty Leading the People* (1830). Liberty is foregrounded as a female figure with right breast fully uncovered. She leads a band of Parisians, who have taken up arms and march under the banner of the tricolour which represents, liberty, equality and fraternity.

Censorship was to be even more thorough now; Puritan prudery of an extreme that would have made Cromwell proud. Make no mistake, censorship after the Revolution, and ever since, was for the lower orders only. A different priority existed for the rich. Queen Victoria's and Prince Albert's private rooms were awash with 'porn,' dressed up as the erotic art of the period. Such behaviour proved that the ruling classes could do what they jolly well liked. As long as they were in charge, the rest of humanity could not do as they jolly well liked and get away with it. Sexually explicit material was far too good for the likes of them.

The nineteenth and twentieth centuries were a time for battening down the hatches on the despised majority. If the lower orders couldn't see images of the sexual act, they certainly indulged their own sexual pleasures at all times in an unrestrained way, whatever the prudish middle classes might have thought about it. Since the masses were not afraid of themselves, they couldn't be so easily gulled into censoring their own behaviour, once they had come to see through the mirages presented to them.

As technology gradually improved, and sexual imagery moved from the engraving to the photograph, and to the visual image of cinema and TV screen, control was delegated to the safety of 'clean' hands. Canons of taste were formed and re-formed by a new generation of artists and thinkers for literature, painting, sculpture, architecture, music and film; all art forms in other words. Aesthetic responses were shaped by dynastic families who became gatekeepers of bourgeois taste; a sort of army of literary celebrities and literary hygienists. Once the middle class declared art and literature to be 'theirs,' they had to vet commentary on it, in case anyone exposed inconvenient truths that protected the canon and its stolen heritage. Having the ear of the establishment, they were the torch-bearers of propriety and good sense; sanitary inspectors of the mind; protecting us all from the cloacal regions.

The abiding fear among them, I discovered, was fear of the erect phallus – armed nature, prepared for combat. I found that the British censor in the 1980s searched intensely for evidence of erect penises in our films. Through oversight, no doubt, we had one film with an erect penis in it. What did an erect penis signify? Masturbation of course. After the French Revolution the authorities thought the querulous masses needed castration, befitting the ranks of slaves, not stimulation to excite the libido, as in William Blake's poem:

Nor shall my Sword (penis) sleep in my hand:
Till we have built Jerusalem,
In England's green and pleasant land.

LIGHT

Remember, William Blake was a man for whom 'love for the holy' was best expressed in the 'projection of semen,' thus combining religious and sexual ecstasy.

Not that reverence for the phallus was anything new. In the Classical world of Greece and Rome they loved it; so too did the nature religions of India and Japan. Large wooden phalluses can be found in the doorways of many a Tokyo restaurant.

Worship of the generative power of nature as the source of all things, goes back to the Bronze Age and beyond, through to prehistoric times. The world over, it forms the embroidery between some of the most ancient of superstitions of the human race. The phallus was the ancient emblem of creation, the power of nature sexualised, a fructifying principle and worship of a general principle of man and nature – male and female. The reproductive organs represented the fertilizing, protecting and saving powers of nature, in a world where the principle of fecundity mattered, and agricultural plenty was important. Sacrifices to the generative deities were embodied in Indian lingham/yoni rites, pagan rituals and serpent imagery.

Among the remains of Roman civilization for instance, statues of Priapus, altars dedicated to him, gardens and fields entrusted to his care, and phalli, figured in a variety of shapes as a protecting power against evil influences of various kinds. Phalli were sculptured into walls of public buildings, placed in conspicuous places in the interior of the house, worn as an ornament by women, and suspended as an amulet on the necks of children. Erotic scenes covered vessels of metal, earthenware and glass, intended for festivals as votive offerings. The bearded goat was dedicated to Priapus as half man, half goat; a priapic Pan. Later on the maypole took the place of the phallus. Imagine, little girls in summer dresses dancing innocently around the maypole in the summer sun.

LIVING ON GOLD TIME

Christianity in the middle ages was not immune from priapic influences. Note the rude gestures and postures of sexual carvings on English medieval churches. They are not directly interpretable as fertility symbols, or pagan idols, but Christianized as pedagogical works. Such works dealt with sexual customs and the salvation of medieval culture, and lent support to the Church's moral teaching. Christianity in the Middle Ages presented pleasures of the flesh as part of the chaos of the Fall ultimately leading to damnation.

As I've tried to explain, placing dread on places, and sexual practices, are inventions of a later time, a by-product of rules, and not part of the evolutionary record.

*

Around the year 1715, a pamphlet entitled *Onania*, purportedly written by a reformed Puritan physician named Balthazar Bekkers, made its first appearance in London. Masturbation, or the sin of Onan, it said, led to a flood of curses. The trinity of ideas that would dominate in particular the nineteenth century, sin, vice and self-destruction, is seen here for the first time. The Christian sexual ethic outlawed this practice and classed it as one of the most unnatural, i.e. heinous sins in the sexual domain. Any emission of semen for non-generative purposes was an offence against nature. Masturbation, in the view of Thomas Aquinas, was a vice more damnable than intercourse between mother and son. But his views were the extreme case. Masturbation's unpardonable nature stemmed from its interference with procreation, directly through the loss of sperm, and indirectly through impotence, and the devastating consequences for the body that weakened intellect, led to the loss of bodily strength, pains and pimples, acute chronic illness and suicide. *Onania* intertwined the medical, moral and the religious, and attacked sin. It had phenomenal sales success. The remedy for masturbation was chastity, followed by early marriage.

The eighteenth century, at the beginning of the modern age, had therefore discovered and initiated a new scourge, a great terror. And so began the censorship of the body. Although based upon a tissue of lies, it lasted for some two and a half centuries. It was a moral panic on a monumental scale. The solitary act of pleasure had been substituted by insanity as the end product for those addicted to self-pollution and self-abuse.

Before the eighteenth century nothing in the published medical works placed masturbation in a particularly worrisome light. The Church taught that everyone was born sinful as a result of the original sin of Adam and Eve. Sexual practices were associated with guilt or shame, but there was nothing to suggest they caused any fear, and not the slightest denunciation of potential health risks. Condemnation of them was not based solely on the notion that it was an unnatural act. Condemnation was supported by divine word; by biblical texts in other words, and essentially two passages. First, the Crime of Onan in Genesis (38, 6-10), when Onan, rather than take his brother's wife and produce a child for the dead brother, spilt his seed, or sperm, through masturbation. Onan's crime, punished by death, was neither masturbation, nor coitus interruptus, but his refusal, contrary to his duty, to furnish descendants for his brother.

The second text was a passage from St Paul in the first Epistle to the Corinthians (6, 9-10), where no one guilty of mollities could inherit the Kingdom of God. Masturbation was part only of a theological dispute; the physical aspects never came into play.

When Samuel-August Tissot, the Swiss Calvinist and Vatican adviser, produced his work *L'Onanism* in 1760, everything changed for the worse, as he succeeded in turning the fear of masturbation into a form of mass hysteria. His portrait of danger said all illnesses could be put at the door of masturbation. Its novelty as a force lay in the fact that it seemed to be a strictly scientific work. To say anything in favour of masturbation became an outrage against society. Morality followed medicine. Masturbation was now a form of suicide. Since the theory of bodily 'humor,' influenced medical treatises, these 'humors' were placed in a hierarchy. Pride of place at the summit was sperm. Since sperm was seen as an essential oil, seminal loss was a true catastrophe for the overall functioning of the human body.

Why then, wasn't seminal loss through intercourse of serious consequence? Because coition was solicited by nature, but solitary pleasures were solicited by the imagination, so the reasoning went. As Tissot was a physician he therefore needed to produce remedies for the illnesses he described. For the young girls and boys from the bourgeoisie, who were his favoured clients, there was to be an arsenal of measures to combat the evil. There was prevention, restraint, imprisoning the genitals, supervision and the cure of marriage. The principal weapon in the battle for prevention was gymnastics and physical exercise, good diet, hard bed, censorship of books, newspapers and paintings – even the Bible! Privileged children were to be kept away from the 'dangerous classes.' Tissot's influence radiated in multiple directions – among physicians, educators and the general public, seemingly spontaneously. Isaac Baker-Brown, a prominent London Surgeon, who later became the highly respected president of the London Medical Society, even recommended female circumcision; an operation which he performed enthusiastically on children and adults.

The philosophers Immanuel Kant and Voltaire were against it, Jean-Jacques Rousseau in his *Confessions* admitted he masturbated all the time, for years, But in the text of his work *Emile*, it was to be denied to the young. Rousseau's confession was nothing if not forthright, as masturbation allowed young men at will to dispose of the female sex and to make a tempting beauty serve their pleasures without needing to obtain their consent (meeting a better class of bird in the modern vernacular).

Reaction to Tissot could be seen as essentially a bourgeois reaction, as its moral code was based upon savings, self-control and forethought. But Tissot's demonstration of the harmful effects of masturbation also seemed to provide answers to many questions, for which he was applauded. These ideas were successful for their receptivity. Many things that were obscure became clear. Masturbation furnished the explanation and easy key. Furthermore, since the amorous escapades of the sons of the rich were regarded with an indulgent eye, it formed the medical backing for their preying on working-girls, as coition was far less harmful than masturbation. On the question of the relationship between masturbation and illness, no medical school offered any new and valid scientific explanation, only a host of new cases. Tissot's influence continued because medicine was unable to come up with any better diagnosis to replace those derived from his works. Physicians also found themselves relieved of their obligations to heal, since masturbation was an act of suicide. There was a certain degree of kinship between witchcraft and the anti-masturbatory obsession in the nineteenth century, producing in its wake all the mental suffering experienced by the young.

It was, however, all a sham based upon a lie. One of the two big anti-sexual shams I'll outline in this chapter. The other was the opposition to primitive promiscuity conducted by the academy. In all the texts mentioned by Tissot in his work there was never a question of masturbation in the originals. The theme of both ancient and modern authors is that of disorders produced by venereal excesses in general. More tellingly, the real causal relation between masturbation and illness had been inverted by him. Masturbation, far from being a cause, was in truth an effect. Insanity, hysteria and other neuroses and physical problems were most often a cause rather than an effect of masturbation. Old men were seen to masturbate in hospitals because that was an effect of senility, not the other way round. Masturbation had not made them insane, but insanity had made them masturbate. Simple. Moreover, Tissot exaggerated the effects by presenting the most serious disorders, only observed in the smallest minority of cases, as its ordinary effects.

Who should be indicted for two hundred and fifty years of lies? Why, religion of course. Most physicians were prisoners of tradition until the last quarter of the nineteenth century. The notion of masturbation as a destroyer, reigned practically unchallenged. The best challenge would have been to try and show that mental illness among the rich and famous was the result of excessive masturbation. But no such luck.

The publication in the late 1890s of Havelock Ellis's *Studies in the Psychology of Sex* produced a sea change, although in the UK the courts declared it was obscene. Volume II published in the US in 1899 on auto-eroticism declared that masturbation and sexual intercourse should be classed as typical sedatives. The only risks according to Havelock Ellis lay in excess.

But despite these gains, for the bulk of the troops traditional notions remained strongly entrenched and they were faithful to tradition. Ellis was incapable of clearing the decks. Sigmund Freud was in the camp of the conservative racists when he declared that the stultification of Arab youths was due to excessive and totally uninhibited masturbation. Freud believed it could lead to neurotic disorders, reduction in potency, and the preservation of the infantile condition. The bogey was still around at the end of the Second World War, particularly in the boy scout movement, and its persistence was the fault of physicians, educators and parents. Threats from parents came in the form of having a child's penis cut off, stunting his growth, blindness, or having abnormal children in later life. Freud considered such threats of amputation as the classic origins of the castration complex; a theory overly developed by him in his own work. Alfred Kinsey's study in 1948 of the *Sexual Behaviour of the Human Male* made the startling revelation that masturbation was extremely common, widespread, and a banal phenomenon. Thus there was a natural transition to the notion that it was normal. Only Catholic authorities persisted in speaking of it as a sin, while others said that in its relief of sexual tension it was a gift of God and was positively good and healthy.

How many young people in the two hundred and fifty year history of the scourge, masturbated without fear of harm to themselves is difficult to tell. I have my suspicions that threats were confined largely to the middle and upper classes because they had something to lose, real or imaginary, while the mass of the population couldn't have cared less about the physician's dilemma. And yet, if anything, as science evolved and abandoned its old notions in the twentieth century, it was generally the upper classes who managed to readjust to the changes in ideas. It was apparent that sections of the lower classes continued to believe the teachings of the earlier generations for far longer. Such ideas became embedded through propaganda, recapitulation, censorship and the hold of religious faith. As it spread, the belief that masturbation was harmful tended to produce its own proof. Each time it was found that masturbation offered an explanation for a condition otherwise difficult to explain, this explanation reinforced the notion that it was a scourge. It could still have a snowball effect, but largely in the mind of the poor, ignorant or uninitiated only.

The masturbation moral panic of the eighteenth and nineteenth centuries was the consequence of medical practitioners and Christian mentality being inextricably intertwined, in terms of personnel and outlook, combined with a lack of professional separation in an emerging medical science. Religion poisoned understanding, and as a result the science of observation, experiment and proof suffered. Disease was a weapon in the battle to enforce social order. It was thought that if medical knowledge was uncontrolled and diffused outside the ranks of the privileged, the independent-minded might have no respect for secular authority. The long-standing medical obsession with masturbation came as a bonanza for Catholic moral theologians, because it furnished them, as transmitters of God's authority, with additional evidence and legitimacy. Ironically in the twentieth century, now that physicians and pedagogues have gradually bidden the subject farewell, masturbation is safely back in theological hands.

The reasons for panic go deeper than the issue of professional misconduct alone. The wayward phallus was a challenge and a threat to the good order of the Victorian bourgeois family, sexual bondage within marriage, and hence private property. At all costs, anything that threatened to bring about revolutionary disorder, whether it was within the realm of ideas or not, had to be squashed.

The evolutionary priority of monogamous marriage had to be prioritized at all costs. By the time Havelock Ellis wrote his work, in society at large views were changing regarding evolutionary priority. There was an interest in sexuality, domesticity and the origins of the family. Some felt that Victorian marriage was a dehumanising distorting and hypocritical tyranny exercised over the well-being of men and women. They argued that sex should not be held in connubial captivity with the wife as a household nun. However, the majority of the informed drew the line at allowing sexuality to escape the control of domestic institutions. Don't forget that for the middle and upper classes an authorised set of sexual taboos was essentially in place as early as the 1830s: the renunciation of all sexual activity, save the procreative intercourse of Christian marriage; the education of both sexes in chastity and continence (the masturbation fear); secrecy and cultivated ignorance surrounding sex; the bowdlerization of literature (later, all visual images); general suppression of all mention of bodily functions – in short, the whole repressive pattern of purity, prudery and propriety. While classical evolutionists may have debated the details of social evolution, none doubted that marriage was essential to securing the social order. Deep down they couldn't understand a society without bourgeois rules, for nineteenth century British society was defined by the territorial state, the monogamous family, and private property. It follows that primitive society, therefore, must have been nomadic, ordered by blood ties, and promiscuous, with a democratic equality of sexual access. A paranoia regarding revolution helped obliterate this from the enquiring mind. In the last resort, taboos were a bulwark against the presumed violence and moral chaos of something even worse than masturbation and the wayward phallus, something called 'primitive promiscuity,' that was presumed to exist in the early evolution of the human family. And the worship of the monogamous family comes as no surprise. The Victorian family men had access to huge numbers of captive servant women in the form of household domestic slaves. Unthinkingly, such men gave the freedom of sexual access to themselves alone.

The beginning of the second of my anti-sexual shams of the post French Revolutionary period, came about in the discovery by the counter-cultural movement of the *fin de siècle*. Sex became an object of study, although later it was buried, especially in anthropology. But not before both shams had become potent weapons of the class war in ideas.

Primitive promiscuity, the incest taboo, the evolutionary priority of matriarchy versus patriarchy, kinship pattern and the like were hot topics at first when the laws that governed sexual identity and behaviour seemed to be breaking down, and there was breakdown of the mid-Victorian sublimation of sexuality. However, by the mid twentieth century they had all but disappeared, or been sanitised, by those chorusing the need to return to civilised conduct, social stability and sanity. Once again sexuality went into hiding, under an anthropology of normative social systems. Sexuality was easy to forget. Only for the psychoanalysts were sex and sexuality non-negotiable. Its practitioners claimed sex as their own, and in the process were most doctrinaire on questions concerning it.

*

The second anti-sexual sham initiated by the Victorians, gripped primatology well into the late twentieth century. Our concept of primate society for many years during the Cold War was a generalisation about specific baboon society. The duty of research was to censor and suppress all information that questioned, or did not conform to accepted views on human parenting and propriety That meant neutralizing sexual promiscuity. Even the birds became monogamous. Researchers could interpret their protected information in any way they wished, as long as it did not contravene the unwritten contract between politics and science. The authorities preferred to offer contracts only to those deemed a 'safe pair of hands.' The discovery of the species *pan paniscus*, or bonobos, at first known as pygmy chimps, is a case in point. A deafening silence took hold around them. They were first discovered in Zaire in the 1920s, but their outrageous sexual behaviour consigned them to oblivion for over a generation. When it came to baboons, the favoured ones, a most important factor was ignored. Dominance and aggression among them depended upon which troop we were looking at, and under what conditions. The major contrast between humans and pongids (pan, gorilla, pongo) is that humans are highly environmentally adaptable. Pongid species, by contrast, are mostly isolated, tied to narrow ecological niches by diet and lifestyle, and vulnerable to sensitive disturbance. They have the ability to learn a behaviour like humans, but it is questionable as to whether they have the ability to generate it.

As we focus in on *pan paniscus* as a blueprint for social evolution, the reader should be made fully aware that their ecological niche is in an equatorial rainforest with plentiful supplies of food.

To understand them let's look way back in deep time, in the pre-history of civilisation. Let's create a model of prehistoric or unrecorded historical relationships. The model should enable us fully to understand the implications of the coming of civilisation upon social and sexual life, and a formula for understanding the flexible and free social formations through the five million years or so of human evolution. Bear in mind that we are in search of a mode of production, and its contingent sexual relations, that has survival potential. I must emphasise flexible and free here because I don't believe we could have evolved without it. What is derogated as promiscuous by the anti-sexual shams of the academy, will be proven to be the natural sexual state for the successful evolution of the human species. Polymorphous sexual behaviour is built into our psychological make-up, as a result of this evolutionary experience.

Let's invent our own evolutionary chronology; think the unthinkable and be the dutiful disciples of no one but ourselves. We'll choose Africa as the starting place, principally because the African ape, our simian friend, looks to be a worthy kissing cousin of ours. Humans are more similar in the structure, DNA, protein chemistry and facial expression and the social behaviour to the tropical apes of Africa than any other living species of animal.

We use the term *Homo* for the first bipedal ape, or those walking upright on their hind legs. The origin of a bipedal form of locomotion was so fundamental a change, or so replete with profound evolutionary potential, that the roots of humanity are certainly there. The bipedal event occurred through speciation, or rapid change in a small population in reproductive isolation in a separate gene pool. What caused it? – a network of different solutions to different problems, contrasting solutions to the same problems, as well as the same solution to the same basic conditions. Bipedalism provides the possibility of improved efficiency of travel. The primary adaptation of a hominid is an ape's way of living where an ape cannot live. High mobility, flexibility of social formation, and rapid intellectual advance, is the key to progress. Two other factors aid advances; tools for brain and hand development, and climate change for the tempo of evolutionary change. All allow for the large-brained *Homo sapiens sapiens* (anatomically modern humans) to see the light of day. Whatever sceptics might say, nothing will alter the fact that for humans to sustain and rapidly perpetuate themselves over space and time, they require a highly flexible and adaptable set of social and sexual arrangements to facilitate change. Therefore, we must search for a behavioural repertoire for society and sex, unfettered by the preconceptions and rigidity of civilisation's processes. It has to confer an evolutionary advantage upon the participants involved in it, and, as a consequence, is favoured by natural selection.

Small groups with high mobility aid the speciation that is responsible for almost all evolutionary change. Pioneers always point the way, not the stay-at-homes. Evolution is replete with developments at the periphery, by pioneering hominid groups who retain their evolutionary successful features and variations. They tend to mate with others possessing equally peripheral and valuable evolutionary variations.

Where is our model? Primatology is a good starting point, as always, but to its more neglected aspects we must turn.

Some of its qualitatively important aspects must be brought to the forefront, to act as pointers to possible prehistoric human experience. I will give emphasis to hitherto neglected social behaviour among primates, like co-operation rather than conflict, sexual and social equality rather than dominance, group cohesion rather than alpha male charisma, conflict resolution rather than war, and most of all, promiscuity rather than monogamy. Of course the simple biology of somatic-self maintenance, or basic economics, governs all social configurations.

The genetics of the chimpanzee-human continuum says that we share 99% of genes in common, and a near identity of proteins. The human-ape branch grew out of the primate tree about thirty million years ago. In other words we share with chimps at least twenty million years of evolution that we do not share with monkeys. Small wonder that in respect of anatomy, mentality and sociability, apes differ more from old world monkeys than they differ from us. Not that primatology necessarily renders flexible conclusions, but the study of monkeys and baboons with their characteristic territoriality, only provides a companion snapshot with present society, not a study of evolution over time. And what's more baboon models of male dominance and aggression have had a disproportionate impact upon our ideas about primates.

*

In our model of development, I postulate that the characteristics of open, rather than close group organisation, has typified the pongid-hominid line. So it is responsible for the sexual and social forms taken by human society

What do I mean by open organisation? Open groups are nomadic, with nothing approaching the territorial ownership of large apes. The same is true in property owning civilisations for that matter. Nomadism makes for little in the way of routine movements. Chimps do not live in permanent groups at all. Whereas with monkeys, hierarchies of dominance structure the behaviour of group members, and control the limits of sexual relations between individuals; in large apes there appears to be much free personal choice. Adult chimp males have an innate urge to roam and explore. They tend to form small, active mobile bands of two to five individuals, which travel fast over long distances through the forests. Bands may be exclusively male, but may carry young females.

Certain remarkable habits of behavioural inheritance are found only in large apes and man, and are evidence of great behavioural plasticity and inventiveness at a very early stage of pongid evolution. Such behaviour includes the use of tools, weapons, drumming and repetitive rhythmatic body movements akin to dancing. In addition pongids make beds.

I believe human hunter-gatherer society evolved out of ape-like nomadism, free choice in sexual selection, and wide recognition of relationships, which pre-adapted proto-hominids to evolve in certain directions. Only permanent, settled agriculture for humans allied to civilisation-imposed territoriality. Human society begs comparison with the pongids. At its simplest level, it can confidently be predicted, that the most natural groupings to develop were those of a number of friendly or related females and their offspring, accompanied by ageing or domestic-minded males.

Two typical hominid social institutions were clearly in operation – the extensive mobility of groups, and the absence of a family as we now recognise it. In its place a sense of community and common purpose evolved. The prototypical hominid grouping, at the core, was the matrifocal group of mother and offspring, often in association with other friendly or related mothers. Elaborate kinship networks I postulate as being of an extremely late invention. Benefits from status hierarchies had absolutely no relevance prior to the impact of civilisation. Paternity, likewise, was disregarded, as it had little contribution to make to survival. Bands were not territorial units, with territorial policy-making objectives. They were capable of large migrations, having polymorphous and multiple sexual relations over wide areas. Hominids were co-operative with little organised leadership at any level, and an absence of inter-group aggression. The requirements of living together, under permanent settlement, imposed great strains on this ape-like inheritance of behaviour and temperament adapted to nomadism and fluctuating groups. Permanent settlements, above all, are situations of social captivity.

To understand how open-group social organisation pre-adapted and pre-determined the direction of change, we will look for a moment at pongid social formations. I have singled out *pan troglodyte* chimps and *pan paniscus* bonobos – the two sibling species to be recognised as sentient. With the genus *pan* we share the same range of emotions and similar mental processes, though they are technically greatly inferior to us. Self-awareness is their hallmark. Bonobos have unique enough behaviour to cast greater light upon human sexual characteristics. Their features can be considered as one, except of course for the extreme sexual lasciviousness of the bonobo.

The two characteristics of chimps are their stationary and mobile social groupings; fission and fusion in fact. There is a free and constant flow of individuals of both sexes back and forth from group to group. Fission is the ability to leave a group at a whim. Fusion enables them to maintain regular and multiple social ties within and between local groups.

Stationary and mobile unit groupings are another major characteristic of chimps. Sex among them is relaxed, non-competitive and amiable, with no exclusive rights or sexual monopolies. Permanent partners are non-existent. Free choice allows freedom of either sex to request, accept or decline sexual advances. Usually female choice is paramount. Chimps are sexually obliging but not non-discriminatory. The social function of mating is greeting and tension release. Their egalitarianism is a property of the social system, and necessary for survival.

Primate sexuality, particularly that of bonobos, can serve as a hominid prototype of sexuality relevant to homo sapiens. The general body characteristics of bonobos show similarities to early hominids, especially their overall build, which is more gracile and less muscular. They are bipedal for quite long distances. They differ from chimps by their relatively long legs, narrow shoulders, small head, red lips and long, fine hair on the head, neatly parted in the middle. They excel at sociability. They prove that individuals can co-exist without relying on competition or dominant-subordinate rank. Thus they have plenty of time for sexual procreation.

The number of copulations per day from adolescents upwards is great. Their day is divided between resting, travelling and feeding. Fission and fusion, and group division are more or less the same as the common chimp.

When we turn to the bonobo's socio-sexual behaviour we observe unique primate peculiarities, akin only to humans in the variety of positions adopted. What then are the bonobo's sexual peculiarities that rank it as so important for human evolutionary comparisons?

The bonobo exhibits several of the traits considered critical for bonobo/human comparisons: face to face copulation; extended female receptivity; and a connection between food and sex. The female has a dramatically extended swelling phase, causing her to be sexually attractive and responsive to males through three quarters of her menstrual cycle. Significantly, bonobos become sexually aroused remarkably easily, even during solitary play, and express this in a variety of sexual positions and genital contacts. The bonobo male's genitals in relation to body size, surpass in size those of the average human male.

Whereas common chimps mate almost exclusively from the rear, bonobos regularly mate face-to-face, thus allowing for eye contact. This is an important component for both the initiation and maintenance of sexual activity. It is the first unique factor in the sexual repertoire of these animals. Face-to-face mating in humans shows that they had next to no significant predators from very early on. The entire female genital area of the female bonobo is rotated, and the clitoris is fully extended and well defined. During arousal it may elongate to twice its normal length. Hand signals represent a qualitatively different type of information exchange from that reported for any other non-human primate. The gestures are always made from a bipedal, upright position.

A very important facet of bonobo sex, is that ejaculation during copulation is not a part of sexual activity, as many penises remain erect after intercourse. This points the way to sex having a different meaning for these creatures. Also, other members of the unit groups appear to be drawn to the mating activity. Infants being frequently involved. Mothers may mate while holding an infant . Young and old move towards copulatory pairs to sit in close proximity, watching the activity. Among immature bonobos, interference during mating appears to be motivated by desire to participate rather than disrupt. Not that sexual mating lasts very long; perhaps half a minute of fifty pelvic thrusts.

Another sexual peculiarity is the female-female copulatory bouts of rubbing. Face-to-face positions means clitoral insertions and rhythmic muscular spasms also occur. The function of such rubbing is the easing of tension during group excitement. It is possible that multiple, female sexual orgasm evolved for such rubbing, rather than face-to-face copulation.

The third sexual practice of special interest involves adolescents in erotic contact. Bonobos may put an adolescent penis in their mouths. Masturbation, genital massage or penis fencing, almost always male-male, is associated with tension release among males. A victim of aggression might invite an aggressor to masturbate him as a form of reconciliation. Mouth kissing with tongues among juveniles is common as a form of reconciliation or compensation for loss of privileges.

Sexual variation between age groups is the fourth aspect of the psycho-sexual social behaviour of note. All pairings and combinations are possible, except full mating between mother and adult son. This seems to prove that incest is a function of the availability and accessibility of females in humans as well. Adult sexual contacts with the young are uncommonly intensive. Females will often insert the penis of the juvenile male into themselves. Females may accommodate other juvenile male partners. Thus juniors get their sexual coaching from the experts – the adults. After copulation, males mount and thrust at juveniles of either sex. All this is made possible by the fact that males have penile erections from six months after birth.

In the domain of social skills bonobos excel at individual compatibility and sociability. Surplus energy that under harsher conditions would have been spent on merely surviving, has been directed at affiliative behaviour, feeding and food sharing elicit copulatory activity on virtually every occasion. A high degree of food sharing is interwoven with copulation. The mere sight of food causes penile erections in male bonobos. Socio-sexual behaviour occurs when a potential for aggression exists. Bonobos use sex for pacification. Food being exchanged for copulation is a sexual negotiation. The aggressive impulse of males towards females is suppressed by copulation. The sex contract hypothesis cannot account for all sex that goes on at feeding time. Sex occurs at every age and sex combination, whether food is shared or not, and is initiated by dominants as well as subordinates. Besides, a sex contract to enforce monogamy is a phantom of the deluded human mind. Self production and reproduction of the species go together. Food and sex are one; a united phenomena in human history as well.

The art of sexual reconciliation may well have reached its evolutionary climax in the bonobo. Social life gives the impression of being ruled by compassion, with bonobos having their emotions under control. There is a virtual absence of complex tactical manoeuvring during antagonistic encounters. They are mild and simple. Sexual conflict resolution and reassurance is the key to bonobo social organisation. Individuals learn its strategic function at an early age. The common chimpanzee virtually lacks this function of sexual behaviour. Sex as a reassurance aid accounts for the fact that three quarters of sexual behaviour serves no reproductive function whatsoever, as males never achieve intromission or ejaculation during contact with partners, other than mature females.

The primary role of such behaviour is to enable co-existence of the sexes not to conceive offspring. Copulation is social behaviour, reproduction only secondary.

Bonobos are promiscuous, no doubt resulting from lack of sexual competition between males. They have found that the more sexual competition, the less time there is for actual copulation, and the more exclusivity of partner results. Clever bonobo! In consequence, they have a greater vocal repertoire, greater socio-sexual repertoire, and relative absence of aggression. Dominance hierarchies pall into insignificance, even in mounting behaviour. They have larger temporary associations that are almost exclusively bisexual.

In similar fashion, humans developed because they were sexual, and not in spite of their sexuality. Competition among themselves, the bonobos have decided, is for suckers, just as it is for humans. Certainly for humans, competitive aggression can only possibly arise if one male corners the market in females. There can be no aggression where sex is free. Human males who believe human females should be consigned to the role of second class citizens are the stupidest of humans. Let females be free and males will have more sex, not less.

Amazingly, among bonobos, alliances are not along kin lines. Even with adult sons there is no evidence of mutual support. This finding bolsters the contention that the family under human civilisation underpins an artificial form of support arrangements, in opposition to the naturalness of collective agreement and sexual repose. It also means that where children are treated as social property, as opposed to private property, it is fundamental to wider social harmony. Human society under this regime would be relieved of the association of sex with family bonding .When human civilization eventually took control, however, and society was controlled by men, families were held responsible for children, paternity became important and dominant men wished to control sexual relations to prevent their property being inherited by anybody but their own children. Private property existed for the first time, and so did sexual repression. Male parental investment in recognising offspring – a paternity guarantee – is a phenomenon of human civilisation alone, and not a condition of evolution.

Bonobo females rank the same as males, with strong female associations. To understand fully the radical implications of male-female equality among them, we must understand the long period of dependency of the son on its mother; perhaps three to four years. If anything, males lead a life following their mothers. To adult females then, all males appear childish. All researchers should pay closer attention to future mother-son relationships as the fulcrum of social stability among animals. Such relationships are an obstacle to strong alliances of adult males united by a male bond. Females have an all round cohesive effect on socio-sexual life among the bonobos. The high social status of females is related to the cohesive grouping tendency. The consistency of mixed parties and prominent mother-offspring sub-units is a social structure which provides a feasible model of the basic society from which human society evolved.

The key to unlocking the social structure of prehistoric humans is the life history of females.

What do we learn from chimp lifestyle? Nomadic existence with open group organisation; community and common purpose; co-existence rather than competition, fission and fusion, mobile and stationary groupings of childless and childbearing adults, a carnival of copulation; sexual selection with free personal choice.

When it comes to bonobos? Sex and copulation is everything: equality of sexual access; much female bonding; females who rank the same as males; little aggression and few kin alliances.

From my model we cannot say that primate comparisons spread to all humans, in all places, at all times, under all circumstances. But frankly, no other flexible arrangement is so pregnant with innovative potential, fluid enough to guarantee selective advantage, and flexible enough to guarantee physical mobility. We cannot prove that early humans were like bonobos for instance, but we certainly cannot assume their behaviour was anything like the restrictions elaborated upon by every writer on the subject I have read, and the academics who gnaw away at long, clean-gnawed bones.

As prehistoric society developed for humans, and civilisation took hold, divergences occurred. By civilisation I mean agriculture, immobility, sedentary occupations, class distinctions, inequalities and population pressures. It took hold sometime around 10,000 BCE, and went through stages of social development depending on climate, location etc. The characteristics of advanced civilisation that we understand as well developed during the phase of written history, and existing today, include the following new developments:

- Territoriality and population pressure.
- Monogamous pair bonding, the family, and sex only with a licence.
- Inferior position assumed by women after the world historic defeat of the female sex, in favour of private property and paternalism.
- Gradual belief in innate gender inequality and the desirability of unequal sexual access.
- Sexual competition between males as a consequence.
- As with economic and social inequality, there was to be inequality of sexual access and sexual rationing. Hence, only sex within marriage.
- Lack of free choice in sexual relations due to exclusive rights, sexual monopolies and coercive male pressure.
- More aggression – competitive aggress can only possible arise if one male or a group of males corner the market in females, and therefore sexual accessibility is by coercion, bondage slavery or other artificial means. There can be no aggression where sex is free, and males don't control sexual or social life.
- Social conditioning – sexual control – who controls the body controls the mind. Elite social groups control women in order to control men. Women are withdrawn by various means from free range among men (sexual rationing and cultural practices and distinctions), so the demand for sex is greater than the available supply. By this means men are brought into line, whenever it is deemed necessary.

*

Some of this can be brought to the forefront if we look briefly at the invention of organised religion. Female sexual repression, and their denigration and disparagement, was consequent upon the growth of religion and civilisation. For religions are male-dominated, or appeal to the interests of men in power. The strong gods are all males, and the stories, psalms or sutras are written by men to control other men by controlling their women. Homosexual men also organise religious communities. I would even go so far as to say that active or passive homosexuals invented Catholic Christianity, and promoted it as bachelor theology. All the repressive teachings of the church stem from this, as do their teachings in relation to women. Catholic Christianity, and male homosexuality of the ancient world, had in common a low regard for women. In particular, they took over the Aristotelian idea that women were incapable of friendship – that friendship, the most exalted relationship open to adults, was possible only between men. Aristotle opened monastic eyes to the most fundamental cause of women's inferiority – woman, in fact was an 'imperfect' or 'incomplete' man.

Since men love each other, not women, they love living together. Little wonder, therefore, that what they say is misogynistic. When men punish themselves by separating themselves from women, or women punish themselves by voluntarily accepting the theology of men, they develop an overweening desire to punish others, primarily the innocent.

Whence came the joyless Jesus, where we have marriage, with the sexual enjoyment excluded from it, bound with sexual pessimism? How could a regime, imposed by an unmarried oligarchy, hold sway over a subordinate and largely married majority?

The Gnostic-Stoic legacy of the ancient world, which Christianity has preserved to this day, presented the sex act as dangerous and difficult to control, detrimental to health, and a squandering of energy. Nothing was to be for pleasure's sake.

Gnosticism had a contempt for life, espoused celibacy and the superiority of the unmarried over the married state, and saw marriage as a generative partnership alone. Mix this with fear of female blood, and intercourse with a menstruating woman, and we have the fear of blood corrupting men's semen. Blood of a woman in childbirth was even regarded as more noxious than female menstrual blood. Later on in Church history, the dogma of the Virgin birth, and the historicising of an ancient metaphor produced a concrete history of chastity complete with sequels. The idea of virginity spread through Christendom.

The two great pillars of Catholic sexual morality were St Augustine of Hippo and Thomas Aquinas. Augustine, the greatest of all Fathers of the Church, was the man responsible for welding Christianity and hostility to sexual pleasure into a systematic whole. The history of the Christian sexual ethic was shaped by him, and like many neurotics, enveloped by anti-sexual flights of fancy; he divorced love from sex, alloying it with a new factor – sexual angst both personal and theological. According to Augustine, it is sexual intercourse or rather sexual pleasure, that has transmitted original sin from generation to generation. He identified pleasure with lust, to such an extent that any attempt to follow his train of thought induces a sense of nightmare.

Catholic theology attained its zenith in Thomas Aquinas paving the way for the demonisation of marriage itself. He made it fashionable for theologians to dissect sexual intercourse into numerous sexual acts, in order to weed out those that were sinful. This set theologians to argue among themselves over which was more sinful, lust felt for a beautiful woman, or an ugly one. Intercourse with a beautiful woman was more sinful as it was more delectable. Where it was thought that there was no sexual intercourse between Adam and Eve in Paradise, virginity went hand in hand with immortality. Marriage, on the other hand, was associated with death. Woman was the eternal temptress all along, and was expected to 'keep silence' in Church. Women as second class men were consigned to a cloak of invisibility. Little wonder, therefore, when the witchcraft scare took hold in the Middle Ages, the baneful *The Malleus*

Maleficarum an its coital positions with the devil, quoted more liberally from Thomas Aquinas than from any other authority.

The Catholic Church, in particular, is loath to abandon the dictatorship it has presumed to enforce on the matrimonial bedroom for almost two thousand years. It is amazing what an abundance of men has spiritually reproduced throughout history Such men are quite unqualified to pronounce on their pet subject. They have consistently laid claim to supreme competence, enveloping themselves in a divine aura, while devoting much of their lives to the pursuit of utter nonsense. The pseudo-theological specimen cabinet would be a rich source of amusement, had it not on display figures who have been responsible for countless marital tragedies and heartaches.

*

Phew! Where do we go from here? Back to the present day, I suppose. As if we haven't left it! Perhaps we can see still or moving images of what we do all the time. I'm not so sure.

There is nothing so dangerous to the moralistic mind as a woman who enjoys, and is seen to enjoy, sexual intercourse. And there is nothing so dangerous for humanity than the moralist mind in full flood. Plebeian sexuality in particular causes maximum alarm: eroticism is as unsuitable for servant girls as atheism, and likely to lead to unforeseen disorder. Modern day agitators for social purity loathe the sexual precocity of working-class girls, as they did in the nineteenth century, often regarding them as passive victims of male sexual abuse and the beastliness of male sexual veracity. The presumed connection between sexual self-control and social restraint, or love of God and respect for secular authorities, is still with us.

LIVING ON GOLD TIME

The hostility to working-class eroticism and the refusal to trust the less educated with the images of sexuality never died. The first precept of all moralists since St Paul that one has to be unkind in order to make people good is highly favoured, but cunningly not mentioned now. The boundaries between high and low culture for them are clearly unequivocally defined. Belief in the traditional Christian precepts of obedience, and in the social and political dangers that will ensue if people do not submit to authority, is alive and kicking, though. Officialdom is empowered by Christian teaching and conformity to authority. Politicians and administrators, with crude opportunism and hypocrisy, confronted by issues of sexuality have invoked Christian values, while not themselves professing Christianity. They are the 'Mrs Grundys' of this world, followers of the famous fictional character in English literature named Mrs Grundy. Her name is synonymous with prudery, regulation of sexual pleasure, and tropes of speech, hatred of sex, and for the guarding of children from unnatural masturbatory harm. She was a regular purveyor of good taste. At the first sign of moral laxness one could remark: 'And what will Mrs Grundy say?'

Meanwhile, back on the farm, belly-aching anti-porn campaigners: those with a screw loose - the mentally ill whose reason has been destroyed by religion - the sanctimonious - those best suited to prayer, rescue work and the scourge - the mad, the bad, and downright crazy – are allowed advance publicity in a non-competing jurisdiction, to declare that sex is violence. On their moral agenda acts legal in themselves are transmuted, by slight of hand, into acts not legal in themselves. They encourage women to think of themselves as victims, while making women envious of men having their sexuality catered for. Even male masturbation aggravates them, because the few heterosexuals in their midst feel sidelined and disposable.

They forget that to the free, sane and untainted mind, everything is pure; filth is only in the eyes of the beholder.

Let's not forget moral superiority in general, the, 'my art is your porn syndrome.' Pornography's sole purpose, it is assumed, is to excite the sexual appetite with little concern for the ascetic response. Since soft-focus eroticism depends upon the social class of the originator, the middle classes, who share literary and artistic pretensions have made this theirs, and theirs alone. No longer keeping faith with the 'deprave and corrupt' definition of obscenity, and wanting a place in the sexual sunlight, these groups occupy themselves with the craft of the film-making, writing, etc. Eroticism is not pornography, they cry in horror. For them eroticism has a genuine plotline, with character development, that helps to emphasise the erotic elements. Erotica, they say, is about more than sexual acts and arousal, in that it involves the inner lives of characters, in character development, complexity and non explicit elements. They see pornography as formulaic, repetitive, making use of stock characters, and generally lacking in stylistic experimentation. Devoid of the complex nature of desire, they gush over their own sexual feelings.

I think they take themselves far too seriously. There's a big dollop of class snobbery here, and an unacknowledged belief that porn and masturbation are for the non-celebrities, the poor and ugly, and worst of all, by Christ, the feared masses.

However, any division of sexual imagery into high and low culture paves the way for the dismissal of popular genres. Even anti-pornography feminists have embraced the erotic, largely, I suspect, because the label, 'erotica,' enables it to be sold in 'respectable' locations.

A division between erotica and pornography has produced cultural hierarchies, and the strategic drawing of boundaries between the more or less acceptable. Pornography need not be interested in character development or motivation, or the building up of sexual tension; it is not necessary to ask didactically why the characters want to perform the given acts, or compare them on a scale of narrative dynamics, emotional and sensual realism, or literary and visual value. Moreover, don't the self-obsessed middle classes, females in particular, masturbate to their erotic heroes?

Maybe the erotic is pornography that dare not speak its name.

Sexually explicit imagery allows women to be desiring subjects in a subculture that accords their sexualities with value. Here, the pleasure-seeking female sexual agent, is celebrated, rather than condemned as an immoral prostitute, as she is by the moralists.

Quite frankly, I'll stick with my quote that opens this chapter.

Update 1: The Video Recordings Act 2010 (Legislate in Haste Repent at Leisure)

In 1993 the Video Recordings Act 1984 was amended but underwent no significant changes. It was amended again in the Criminal Justice and Public Order Act 1994 when the Press tried to pin the murder of a child on a video. Additionally, the amendment extended the definition of a video recording to any device capable of storing electronic data, which of course includes works available on DVD, CD and CD-ROM.

In August 2009 it was discovered that the Video Recordings Act 1984 was unenforceable, as the European Commission was not notified about it under directive 83/189 which had to be implemented by 31st March 1984, twelve months after its notification to the Member States.

The reason why the Act should have been referred to the European Commission is because it constitutes a restraint on intra-EU trade, in that it entails that videos/DVDs which have not been certified by the BBFC cannot legally be imported from another EU country and then sold or rented in the UK. Margaret Thatcher, the then prime minister, had signed the Single European Act in 1986.

The mistake was not spotted on two subsequent occasions in 1993 and 1994. It was finally discovered during plans to update the law and introduce a new video-games classification system.

In 1998 a procedure was laid down for the provision of information in the field of technical standards and regulations, Directive 98/34/EC., so the provisions of the Act which related to video classification and distribution in the UK were unenforceable until the EC had been correctly notified of the technical standards.

In 2009, the 1984 Video Recordings Act's classification and labelling requirements could not be enforced against individuals in UK courts because the Act was never officially enacted, and until the situation was rectified, it was legal to sell and supply unclassified videos and computer games, although many retailers agreed to observe the regulations voluntarily. The Police and Her Majesty's Revenue and Customs were told to stop bringing prosecutions until the Government brought in emergency legislation to re-enact the 1984 Video Recordings Act.

Pending prosecutions under the Act were abandoned, but the Government claimed that past convictions could not be challenged. All the suffering, prison sentences for crimes which never existed, and expenses imposed were to no avail. You cannot prosecute someone and convict them on the basis of legislation that has never been in force. **The Government had been behaving unlawfully for twenty five years. People who had previously been prosecuted were unable to overturn their convictions or seek and receive compensation.**

The Government had made it clear that they intended to re-enact the legislation. Rather than let the Government rubber stamp this non-Act, and proceed as if nothing had happened, it was a perfect opportunity to engage, finally, in a sensible debate about video regulation, which had been quite impossible in the over-heated atmosphere of 1984. Did such a debate occur? No! The press got away scot free without taking its fair share of blame for mounting an assault on reason. They had played an absolutely key role in panicking the Act and its later amendments onto the statute book in the first place.

In December 2009 the Government introduced new legislation, the Video Recordings Act 2010 which repealed and then brought back into force parts of the Video Recordings Act 1984 which related to the regulation of video recordings, after the required notification was provided to the European Commission in October 2009. This made the legislation enforceable once again, as well as allowing it to be amended by the Digital Economy Act 2010.

The Video Recordings Act which gained the Royal Assent on 21st January 2010 and commenced the very same day was debated in the House of Commons in just one day on 6th January 2010. It was first presented (first reading) on 15th December 2009 and the second reading, committee stage and the third reading all took place, one after the other, on 6th January 2010.

Update 2: Sex on the Net

Sex and technology are more thoroughly mixed together
than ever before. Ever since I had contact with film-making
in the 1980s, there have been considerable technological
developments within all digital media. These advances have
been accompanied by the expansion of a younger, and
previously neglected, media-savvy audience. The 1980s was
the era of the VHS; the two decades since, are decades of the
internet, where technologies used for sexual purposes, have
aided the emerging development of the internet for
commercial use. Indeed, it is often claimed that porn drives
technology, and that sex has shaped the internet as it
currently exists.

The internet offers new forms of communication, data
transmission, and community building through social
networking sites and Web 2.0. Advocates claim that we are
witnessing a new era of user-generated content and devolved
distribution. Therefore, there is greater access to porn in the
context of media proliferation and deregulation. Porn has
been integrated into the business plans and revenue streams
of mainstream corporations. It has pioneered models of
online commerce, and for much of the 1990s, was the only
sector of online media that was making money by charging
for online content on a pay-per-view basis. US Porn
companies made significant investments in research and
development for security and payment software, which they
marketed to the rest of the industry. Porn has also been a
significant factor in driving the expansion of broadband.
Transitions have been made from VHS and DVD rental to
online distribution. Consumer demand for sex has driven the
development of servers, streaming software, chat forums and
e-commerce payment systems. As early users, porn
consumers accelerated the diffusion of new technologies and

increased sales, thereby reducing costs for subsequent buyers. New business and delivery models have helped to demonstrate the potential of the internet for retail. Porn has been important in sustaining new media forms, until significant revenue streams can be generated from non-porn content. Furthermore, it has sustained media hardware production, and a range of online businesses such as hosting, router, server and bandwidth companies.

As bandwidth has become cheaper, and the tools of online publication and sales have become more accessible and easier to use, the nature of the industry has changed to favour peer-to-peer networks and user-generated content. Amateur, or DIY porn, with its rawer and rougher styles, cheaply produced and easily accessible, has become the staple of a plurality of websites. Usually based upon a subscription model, it has been accompanied by a culture supporting discussion and fan sites that cater for a full range of sexual tastes. The appeal of using the internet for sexual purposes has been attributed to accessibility, affordability and assumed anonymity. Users can access a wide variety of media without a high level of technical expertise or income, and the illusion of anonymity encourages them to indulge desires they feel unable to express elsewhere. Porn has been repositioned closer to popular culture, like any other, and has moved from marginal locations in shabby, backstreet adult bookstores and sex shops, into global mainstream entertainment, viewable from the home. Thus, there has been a removal of many of the obstacles related to discreetly obtaining and viewing sexual imagery.

The rise of amateur and user-generated content was spawned by the development of the digital camera and camera phones that have made it easier to produce and share images. Whether user-generated content with its low quality production values is really film-making, is another matter. Web 2.0 has surfaced as a platform for hosting and streaming material. Just as video replaced film, and subscription sites challenged DVD consumption, so, too, does streaming and file-sharing challenge the subscription model. File-sharing technologies pose many challenges. If content generation and distribution become further democratised, they will be increasingly difficult to control. Moreover, user-generated content threatens to reduce the life cycle of porn products, and make it possible for users to develop their tastes much more quickly, thereby becoming more discerning and demanding consumers in the process. The future market will demand more content, greater variety, better quality and reduced costs.

Web 2.0 is a term used as a euphemism for applications and services considered trendy or cutting edge, fashionable, or edgy, and contemporary. A new economy has emerged within the online community made up of practitioners who are, often for the first time, making money out of their own sexually explicit material. The economic infrastructure of mass communication, and the values and attitudes of the consumer culture, are affecting how the sex industry is organised, and sex as a product is marketed. For some, it is a democratising process, a participatory culture, more egalitarian than the otherwise static landscape of adult entertainment, and more in tune with participation through social networking. Pornography is reframed as recreational fun and educational leisure. Amateurs can upload their own sexual material to a site to control their own data for personal profit. It builds and extends a shift in production methods established by the advent of camcorder technologies.

The mobility of sexually explicit material is evident via wi-fi, mobile phones and laptops. One's bedroom can be turned into a live amateur porn studio with increasing ease, thereby smudging the boundaries between producer, performer and consumer, albeit with, at present, low resolution material. Amateurs can also address their potential audiences directly in cyberspace. The potential for 'subversive' imagery in the digital age is obvious. The appeal to the customer is that the performer will do what you want in this mix of media, lifestyle and sexual practice. This certainly disturbs the boundaries between reality and representation, where sex is not simulated by fictional cinematic representation. Since reality shows and celebrity shows dominate contemporary mainstream media of all kinds, the mixing up of the ordinary and the spectacular, the real person and the performers, is inevitable, as is widening the visibility of sexual subcultures. Unavoidably, the axis of heterosexual normality will shift, allowing taboos to be more easily broken and the hidden spaces of obscenity increasingly more visible.

One online variant of user-generated, self-authored content, are sites dedicated to amateur erotic writing, where an online readership creates porn for their own pleasure and shares it for no profit, voting and commenting on the productions they like best. Internet sex, therefore, displays a diversity that has eluded the pornography industry. Gays, lesbians, bisexuals and transsexuals, can gain access to support networks specifically designed for them. The voices, interests and desires of women also prove to play a significant role in internet sex. Pornography has become an interactive and creative collective of critical audience members, well outside the stereotypical audience of isolated and shamed masturbatory loners, although masturbation continues to be its raison d'être.

Other developments are backed by digital cameras, the rise of the confessional culture, and reality television. With the internet as host and stage, one novel form of self-display is the, rate-my-erotic-picture website, of the 'do my titties look good in this?' variety; or 'do you like my arse?' People post erotic digital pictures of themselves for viewers to rate. Participants thus maintain creative control over their own productions and expand the content for online and offline sexual encounters.

All this is on the credit side, but on the debit side, as porn mutates and proliferates, myths, panics and old anxieties resurface in a new form of 'stranger danger.' Policing taste, and criminalising people on grounds of taste, has become an issue again. Like the old Purity Movements, new moral guardians fret about the normalising of sexually explicit material, and the internet as a conduit for perverse imagery and sexual deviation. Sex and the media now appear to be everywhere and nowhere. Images seem to invade reality and warp it. Some people long for the imagined age of innocence once again. Now we are all supposed to look at pictures as a paedophile would, and judge whether images will be viewed by the 'wrong' kind of person, with the 'wrong' kind of feelings, and use this as the rationale for prohibition.

Legislation returns; in the UK the government endorsed Internet Watch Foundation, provides internet service providers with a list of banned sites which they are required by law to prevent customers from accessing. As a consequence, freedom offered by the internet is characterised in terms of unfettered access to porn. This is becoming a means of extending the power of the state to intervene in the private, and especially the sexual affairs, of its citizens. Once again everyone, that means you and me, needs 'protection.' In 2007 a proposed amendment to the UK Criminal Justice and Immigration Bill, included a clause to criminalise the possession and consumption of 'extreme pornographic images.' This became known as the Dangerous Images Act.

However, the shift from criminalising producers and distributors, to criminalising consumers, accords with a wider trend; a trend that abdicates State responsibility for the regulation of obscenity. The cornerstone of porn legislation still remains the 1959 Obscene Publications Act, an Act that is now practically unenforceable, but one that every government since its introduction has failed to substantially revise. The Dangerous Images Act does not clarify the status

257

of obscenity, but, rather, continues to obfuscate the legality of porn. The Act emphasises the actions of individual consumers. Is this the government's 'hands off' protection of online commerce? We shall see.

If you Loved This Volume You Might Like

Vol 1: Growing Up Working Class

Vol 2: High Hopes and Low Company

Vol 4: Take It From Me

All **Come Press** books are available online.

E-mail: sales@comepress.com for details

Come Press
27 Old Gloucester Street
London WC1N 3AX

Lightning Source UK Ltd.
Milton Keynes UK
UKOW04f1959240214

227072UK00016B/1096/P